AWAY TO SEA

A recent photograph of the Author.

AWAY TO SEA
Life in Blue Star and Golden Line

by
Capt. A.W. Kinghorn

With Best Wishes,

AW Kinghorn

P.M. Heaton Publishing,
Abergavenny, Gwent
Great Britain
1996

ISBN 1 872006 12 4

© First Edition November, 1996: Capt. A. W. Kinghorn

Printed in Great Britain

Published by P.M. Heaton Publishing, Abergavenny, Gwent, NP7 9UH
Printed by The Amadeus Press Ltd., Huddersfield, West Yorkshire, HD2 1YJ
Typesetting by Highlight Type Bureau Ltd., Bradford, West Yorkshire, BD8 7BY

THE AUTHOR

Sandy Kinghorn, now in his sixties, has been at sea since 1951 after two years pre-sea training at the Cadetship H.M.S. *Conway*. Throughout his career he has served with only two companies, namely the Blue Star Line of London and Singapore's Golden Line.

Married for forty years, he and his wife Brenda have three grown up children and to date four grand children.

He is a regular contributor to the magazine *Ships Monthly* and has had two previous books published. His well known auto-biographical *Before the Box Boats* outlines his earlier years at sea with Blue Star, while his *Captain Martha MN* is a fictitious account of the 'first woman captain in the British Merchant Navy'.

ACKNOWLEDGEMENTS

The author wishes to express his thanks to all those who have assisted in the compilation of this book, particularly to Robert Shopland of the magazine *Ships Monthly*, the many people who have kindly supplied photographs, and to his many friends in Blue Star and Golden Line.

CONTENTS

Author and Acknowledgements 5

Foreword 7

1.   As We Were 8

2.   Some Australian Recollections 17

3.   The Heavy Lifters 28

4.   Eastern Ladies 48

5.   Box Boat Voyage 55

6.   The Beacon Hill 65

7.   Rolling Down to Rio 73

8.   The Falklands 81

9.   The Sailor's Wife 96

10. Five Days Late! 111

11. Christmas at Sea 120

12. Fresh Horizons 129

13. Christmas in Port 1989 147

14. Kaohsiung Revisited 156

15. A Cargo for Xiamen 163

16. The Perfumed Seas 174

17. Shanghai Christmas 181

18. Carry it Bulk 194

19. Sugar From Siam 206

20. Golden Harvest Home 218

21. Captain and Son 228

22. China Clipper 237

23. I Sailed with a Man 247

Gratitudes 255

FOREWORD:

When I was a young man on Tyneside, back in the early 'fifties, mothers would ask their friends, "Where's your lad now?" The reply very often was, "He's away to sea!" – for in those days Britain was supported by a large seafaring population, as she had been for countless generations. This book is dedicated to all those ladies – mothers, wives and sweethearts – whose lads still go – AWAY TO SEA!

1.   AS WE WERE

When I first went to sea in 1951 as a cadet in the Blue Star Line of London, the British Merchant Navy ruled the waves and continued to rule them for another twenty years.

Now, the British Seaman is so endangered a species as to be almost extinct. But it is not my purpose here to attempt explanations or offer excuses, merely to try and place on record something of what was, in many ways, the last of a glorious era.

I can only speak with personal experience of the fine cargo liners of the Blue Star Line but many other British companies had equally large crews and equally high standards. Refrigerated ships carried larger crews than most because of the extra machinery and work required to carry general cargo in one direction and refrigerated food produce in another. Some British companies traditionally had non-British crews such as Indians (in those days called Lascars) while others carried West Africans, West Indians, Chinese or Arabs. South Shields has long been the home of a nucleus of Arab seamen – so long in fact that legend has it they were first brought from the Levant to stevedore the Roman ships which came regularly to the Tyne supporting the legions manning The Wall . . . our own blue-painted ancestors being at that time considered unemployable savages.

Although it is still called the 'Merchant Navy' our mercantile marine has never been a centrally organised service in the sense that the Royal Navy is, although during both world wars and certain minor conflicts government control was exercised to a certain extent, especially when ships sailed under convoy. With the coming of peace, however, merchant shipping reverted to private enterprise. True, much of our life was ordered, still, by the British Shipping Federation, whose doctors gave us our 'medicals' and the National Maritime Board's little red book was tightly packed with minimal working conditions, interpretation of which often provoked lively discussion:– at sea between Master and Men and in port, between Union Official and Company Personnel Officer.

The Merchant Shipping Act of 1896 (with subsequent amendments) held sway and we 'signed on' for each voyage at the Shipping Office under the eagle eye of a Superintendent who carried all the weight and dignity of the Board of Trade. A magnificently worded document called the Articles of Agreement was 'opened' by the Master, then signed by each member of his Crew. Rules governing ship's discipline included in the Articles were read over to the Crew by the Shipping Master before they signed. Although the Articles would lead one to believe that we were actually employed by the said Master, he and we were, in fact, employed by the Shipowner who paid us all.

By so signing we promised to conduct ourselves in an orderly, faithful, honest and sober manner, to be at all times diligent in our respective duties, and to be obedient to the lawful commands of the said Master. The ship's trading limits were to include only places 'between Latitude 70 degrees North and Latitude 60 degrees South' and the voyage must not exceed the stipulated time (up to two years) without a new Agreement being drawn up and signed. Regulations for maintaining discipline listed offences for which, if found guilty, the culprit could be fined one day's pay for the first offence and two days' pay for second and subsequent offences. All fines and forfeitures (No work, no pay) could be remitted by the Master at the end of the voyage 'for subsequent good behaviour' and often were. It was difficult for the lads to get into mischief on the long haul home from New Zealand and the 'Old Man', like the rest of us, was usually in a more cheerful frame of mind homeward bound anyway. Offences included 'taking on board and keeping possession of any firearm, knuckleduster, loaded cane, sling-shot, bowie knife or dagger, or any other offensive weapon . . . without (delightful insert) 'the concurrence of the Master'. Drunkenness and the use of Insolent or Contemptuous Language to the Master were crimes most heinous and allegedly guilty parties would be summoned to the Master's Dayroom next morning for 'Logging' (so called because all had to be entered into the Official Logbook). The Master was prosecution, jury, and judge, although the culprit was allowed to bring along one of his shipmates as witness for the defence if he so wished. He rarely so wished as, returning alone to the messroom after a logging session he could tell his mates "What I told the Old Man to go and do . . ." whereas a witness might spoil this account with the truth. A delightful and true story is told of a Master of my acquaintance concerning the logging of a certain Donkeyman the morning after his day's Absence Without Leave (another offence) When asked, as required by the Act, if he had anything to say, the Donkeyman replied, "You're a silly old chump, Captain" (or words to that effect) To which the Master replied, "That contemptuous language will cost you another day's pay – anything more to say?" Red of face the Donkeyman repeated his accusation more colourfully; and so the fines mounted until, perhaps tiring of this exercise in Maintaining Discipline, the Donkeyman burst out, "You're a *hard* old chump, Captain!" to which the Master generously replied, "Have that one on me!".

The same Articles stipulated minimum rations the Shipowner must feed us (via the Second Steward) down to the last lentil, and these regulations were sometimes discussed with a Second Steward who was suspected of cutting his issues of pound and pint rather fine. Everyone who went to sea professionally in the Merchant Service was a 'Seaman' – even the Stewardess – except the Master and Apprentices and – relic of the War – was registered as an Established Seaman 'on the Pool'. But by the 1950s many companies

9

had their own Pool, albeit unofficially; and within the general framework of the Merchant Shipping Act each Shipowner ran his own ships independently at his own cost and to his own profit; for profit was and is the only reason for owning and operating any merchant vessel. Subsidies may be provided by a government which wishes the shipowner to continue operating ships in order to maintain a nation's maritime self-sufficiency in time of war – viz the USA – while other nations subsidised their fleets in order to attract foreign hard currency. But commercial considerations now, more than ever before, dictate that a merchant ship must operate as profitably (ie: as cheaply) as possible, employing all modern technology to save fuel and manpower: and if she falls below the required standard of profitability she is flagged-out, sold, or otherwise disposed of. Governments are less than eager, these days, to subsidise, especially British governments. But during the 'fifties and 'sixties British ships were run extremely profitably and the national exchequer prospered on the 'invisible earnings' so engendered. Dozens of companies owned between them hundreds of ships, all under the British flag, employing many thousands of British seamen – with some of whom it was my privilege to sail. The ships were registered in London, Liverpool, Belfast, Southampton, Plymouth, Newport, Swansea, Cardiff, Glasgow, Leith, Hull, Newcastle-upon-Tyne . . . Stag Line even carried North Shields upon their sterns, last of a long line to do so. The men who manned these ships came from all those ports and from inland also. Not all engineers were Scottish, for the sea was, then, a worthwhile – even an honourable, calling, while in those days of Conscription it offered an alternative to National Service in the armed forces, to which all young men of 18 were called. The catch in joining the merchant navy as an alternative was, one must remain at sea until 26th birthday whereas the NS conscript was released after two years or eighteen months.

To train these aspiring seamen were many institutions, some very old established. Each port had its sea school with the result that even galley boys and stewards could pull an oar in a lifeboat and use a portable fire extinguisher. Real training, of course, came when the lad finally got away to sea, from his first ship onwards. For those with eyes to see and ears to hear, every ship is a schoolship.

Promotion to upper ranks came slowly but not too slowly to kill ambition. In some companies promotion seemed to come more quickly; laws of supply and demand applied and there were many ships on divers trades from which to choose. A healthy turnover rate usually enabled those who were keen and could stand the pace to rise as high as they wished. Engineer officers had served a four-year apprenticeship – if not always in an engineering shipyard, then at least with heavy machinery, and the system of engineer qualification was similar to that for deck officers in which examinations had to be passed after the prescribed seatime had been acquired. Most deck officers had served a three or four year cadet or apprenticeship whilst some determined stalwarts worked their way up 'through the hawsepipe' without benefit or privilege. A lad with anything about him soon learned the basics of his trade before the first step up the promotion ladders, his second's 'ticket'. With this first hurdle behind him, the aspiring deck officer might get a fourth mate's: only being promoted to second mate when he had a first mate's certificate, which he took at least a year after second mate's. The first mate (chief officer's) job only came with a master's certificate and then a period of ten or eleven years would elapse before promotion to command. Most companies had a nucleus of their own men – called in the Articles 'Company Servants', who were able to maintain what were, on the whole, very high standards in all departments. Ships were labour intensive because much of the work had to be carried our manually and few ships were designed for easy running. Since, for several generations, a seafarer's work had changed little, continuity – almost from father to son – helped preserve standards. Owners took pride in their ships which had to be maintained clean and smart, a good advertisement wherever they sailed. Those who manned them were in no small way ambassadors for Britain at grass-roots level. Of course, not all seamen – or masters either – were paragons of virtue, but generally a wholesome, healthy attitude prevailed. There were enough men to cover the work of any who fell sick and the depth and breadth of experience of the seniors enabled them to infuse their juniors with a sensible outlook.

Today's electronic gadgetry is taken for granted but was, then, something we only read about in technical journals – about as real to us as science fiction. My first two ships boasted magnetic compass, echo sounder which occasionally worked, and dubious direction finder (DF). Communication was by the dots and dashes of the radio officer's wireless telegraphy for long range, aldis lamps and flags for short range. No VHF, walkie-talkie, radar, not even a gyro compass and certainly no auto-pilot! For this reason, to steer the ship, maintain lookout and keep standby, three sailors were required for each four-hour watch, a minimum of nine. To cope with the constant work of cleaning and overhaul several dayworkers were also carried and a deck 'crowd' could number fifteen, led by the Bosun, who was the Chief Officer's right hand man and who supervised the deck crew. A highly experienced sailor, he was able not only to splice rope and wire and organise his men efficiently, but keep accurately that increasingly complex piece of paperwork, the sailors' overtime book. In Blue Star the bosun's mate was called the Lamptrimmer, though trimming lamps was, postwar, rarely on his job list. 'Lampy' was the deck storekeeper who issued the sailors with paint, brushes and cotton waste for cleaning . . . the *Columbia Star's* lamptrimmer was Charlie Soderblom, an ancient Finn who was very economical. "Cotton vaste? You want vaste? Vot did you do with the vaste I gave you last veek?"

11

He also spliced ropes and wire, making cargo gear and beautifully stitched canvas covers for ventilators and wooden lifeboats, for his boyhood had been spent in sail. At the end of the day he cleaned the paintbrushes . . . "Put ze pots over zaire, brushes in ze brussery" as the turpentine pot where brushes were cleaned was called.

Senior deck petty officer was the Carpenter whose tasks were many. Daily he sounded bilges and water tanks noting their contents, looked after the hatch covers, repairing all manner of equipment around the decks and in the wood insulation with which the holds and numerous tweendecks was sheathed. Outward cargo from the UK/Europe was general, often including long steel girders which, when being swung in and out, often caused damage. He was the plumber who cleared blocked scuppers and mended broken taps, and he battened out the holds with wooden dunnage ready to load the next refrigerated cargo. Occasionally, Carpenters took upon themselves airs and graces, seeming to believe theirs was a Holy Calling, as practised by the Man in the Bible.

Able-bodied seamen (ABs) were the senior deck ratings, holders of AB's certificates, able to steer, splice, overhaul derricks and cargo gear, often working unsupervised aloft maintaining blocks, shackles – all the complex rigging of a ship's cargo derricks which could number 26 on a large vessel. All this gear had to be kept in perfect order, each item clearly marked to match its individual certificate of worthiness, not only for safety and efficiency's sake but to satisfy the increasingly stringent requirements of port authorities, especially in the USA, Canada, Australia and New Zealand. The deck crew also scrubbed and dried holds in between cargoes for stipulations where the carriage of food was concerned were, rightly, strict. They also cleaned, chipped off rust, and painted the ship. A ship which looked smart had a distinct advantage over one looking tatty and neglected on the premise that:– If They Care For Their Ship They Will Care For Our Cargo . . . Efficient Deck Hands came next after ABs, then Senior and Junior Ordinary Seamen (SOS and JOS). The Deckboy was a lad with less than one year's seatime, often a first tripper.

Engineroom ratings were similarly organised and almost as numerous. The Chief Engineer headed the Engineroom department, responsible for all things onboard mechanical. Under him came the Second Engineer whose 'bosun' was the Donkeyman or Engineroom Storekeeper who ran his squad of mains Greasers – the men who kept the main engines well oiled and the engineroom clean, smartly polished and painted. Refrigeration Greasers looked after the refrigeration machinery which, in those days, consisted of large and complex engines, while donkey Greasers looked after the auxiliary machinery. Cleaners and Wipers also worked below, for an engineroom cannot be safe if it is dirty. Fires can start so easily. Too much oil in the engineroom bilges, a leaking valve, a jammed gauge or an overflowing oil tank have been the causes of many a fatal fire afloat, so cleanliness was (and still is) next to godliness.

The Catering Department was led by the Chief Steward or Purser, who had probably served for years through the ranks from Galleyboy to Chief Cook, and it helped if he had a Cook's certificate so that he could organise galley and plan menus effectively. The Second Steward saw to and organised the cleaning of the accommodation, public rooms and alleyways in passenger and officers' accommodation, issued stores and clean linen once per week. The Chief Steward himself was responsible for the issue of tobacco, beer and other dutiable goods. In those days ships did not have officers' or crew bars. Beer was issued at the Master's discretion; which ranged from no-limit-provided-no abuse, to none at all. It may be said here that the former ships were much happier and generally more efficient than the latter, dry, ships; for if liquor were totally banned, ingenious ways were found of obtaining it, sometimes at the expense of the cargo (which often included best export quality). If no liquor was available to the crew, after perhaps thirty days at sea, they were liable to take off in the first port. Returning bleary eyed and broke several days later they stood, naturally, to be logged as AWOL. It had to be finely balanced system to work. A well-fed crew, well-led, sympathetically treated and cared for were usually no trouble at all and a real pleasure to sail with. I have sailed with many such crews, often in those ships where the work was hardest and most demanding.

Desertion? Well, it was not uncommon for a few hopefuls to chance their luck in Australia or New Zealand, besotted by the charms of some Wild Colonial Girl – though same lady would usually drop said lover boy as soon as he became a Deserter on the Run. Some lads who made it by jumping ship (or 'skinning out' as the expression was) settled into respectable middle age in their newly adopted country, but always the fear of discovery lingered. I know of a Company Manager, pillar of the society which he had climbed since jumping ship years before – whose car came into an accident through no fault of his own. The subsequent police inquiry revealed that he was, still, an illegal immigrant, and he was deported in ignominy. Legal entry in those days to Australia and New Zealand was not difficult and, forever, easier on the mind. But it was no uncommon thing for the mate to send the second and third mate to scour the local pubs at sailing time. When found, it was a good humoured case of "Have one with us for the long road home, gentlemen, then we'll accompany you back onboard . . ."

In many ways the most important man on any ship is the Cook, who toils day in and day out to feed his shipmates. Anyone else onboard can have a sub-standard day and nobody notices – or at least no serious harm results. But if your poor old Cook has an off day he stands to find a string of

13

indignant men at his galley door telling him they "wouldn't feed this to the wife's cat!". On a cargo ship carrying twelve passengers – the maximum which can be carried without becoming a Passenger Ship – there was a large team of stewards. Senior Assistant Steward (alias SAS) and Bedroom Steward, Pantry Steward and Saloon Steward and Assistant Stewards ad infinitum – awhile the kitchen staff included a Second Cook as well as the Chef or Chief Cook, Butcher, Baker and Galley Boy, who, with the Pantry Boy, peeled mountains of spuds daily and cleaned up after the others. During the sixties it became customary for the ratings to have a Messman also, to serve crew meals and ensure their hot meals were indeed served hot.

The Chief Officer – the Mate – was responsible under the Master for the stowage and carriage of cargo and the cleanliness and maintenance of everywhere outside the engineroom and steering flat which were the domains of the Second Engineer. On a four-mate ship he was a dayworker but when only three mates were carried he kept the 4-8 watches at sea, taking star sights when not only the stars were visible but – at dawn and dusk – a clear horizon also. The Second Mate was the navigator who kept the 12-4s, fixed the ship's position at noon daily and laid out courses to steer on the charts under the Master's direction. He also looked after the bridge and its equipment, understudied the mate and calculated the vessel's stability based on the centre of gravities of all cargo and the contents of fuel, water and ballast tanks. The Third Mate kept the 8-12 watches at sea and (in Blue Star, not always in other companies) assisted the master with crew wages accounts – especially towards the end of the voyage when the Portage Bill, listing all earnings and deductions had to be balanced – when the Master was busy conning his ship through fog and bad weather in the Western Approaches to the British Isles. He was also the unofficial medicine man, dispensing aspirins, black draught, sticking plaster and penicillin injections as prescribed in that hallowed tome, The Ships Captain's Medical Guide. Only a ship carrying more than one hundred persons need carry a doctor, though in those days a doctor might wish to travel by sea to or from taking extra qualifications such as at the Liverpool School of Tropical Medicine. Thus carried, the doctor signed on for one shilling (5p) per month and if his wife and children accompanied him as paying passengers, at least it made for a cheap family ride. On any ship a qualified doctor is a tremendous asset when injury resulting from accident occurs. Even an appendectomy is usually a relatively simple operation to a doctor, though not for the Ship's Master operating probably for the first time on radioed advice from the nearest medical centre.

Cadets and Apprentices were young men learning their trade in time-honoured fashion. On some ships they were without doubt seen by shipowner and officers alike simply as cheap labour, but the better companies gave their cadets a study room and encouraged them to use it. The Merchant Navy Training Board set exams annually which all cadets and apprentices must take. A question sometimes asked – What is the difference between an apprentice and a cadet? can be answered by stating that in reality there was, latterly at any rate, little difference. Technically an apprentice was bound to his employer by finely worded indentures while a cadet was not. Some young gentlemen who were, in fact, apprentice, preferred to call themselves cadet– and vice versa. In Blue Funnel Line they were called Midshipmen. How they were worked and taught their trade onboard ship depended largely on company policy, implemented by the Master and officers as they deemed correct. Applied intelligently even such menial tasks as chipping rust and cleaning bilges – in moderation – ensured a future mate knew what was required to keep his vessel ship-shape. Often Study Afternoons were granted on days when the weather was too bad to do any work of a more physical nature. Some companies put all their cadets into one or two Cadet Ships where properly qualified instructors and extra officers ensured the ship was run almost entirely by her large crew of cadets, who did all necessary work coupled with ample schoolwork. These ships, run almost on Royal Navy lines, were indubitably superb vessels – but it is debatable whether they adequately prepared a young man for his future career in 'ordinary' ships manned by 'ordinary' seafarers.

In the large twin-screw motorships of that era, the engineer officers led by the Chief Engineer, comprised Senior and Junior Second Engineers, likewise two Thirds and two Fourths, a couple of Electricians and at least two Refrigeration Engineers. Also several Junior Engineers. When she was new the *Fremantle Star* even boasted a Hydraulics Engineer, such was the novelty of her hydraulically opened and closed hatches. Engineer Cadets came along in the sixties, often – alas – looked down upon by those who had been brought up The Hard Way.

And what of this man who led them all, this fellow whose lawful commands they must all obey? Like his Crew, the Master may have come from anywhere in the British Isles or Commonwealth and I have sailed with captains from Australia, New Zealand and South Africa. Most were very good at their job and appreciated that Merchant Shipping Acts notwithstanding, a merchant ship is run largely by example. With the finest accommodation in his ship, given afloat and ashore the best attention of anyone onboard – while having to carry out what some saw as the least arduous work, it may be wondered if the Master did, in fact, justify his fantastically high salary? The one weight which maintained the balance, however, was – in a word – responsibility. Responsibility for the ship, her people and her cargo, total and well-nigh absolute – at sea at any rate. As his vessel's owners' representative he had to be alert to chicanery which may be attempted against him anywhere in the world – often very cunningly. He must ensure that his ship was always afloat (unless in drydock), the right way up, going in the right direction with adequate fuel, water and provisions on board to reach the next source of supply on her voyage, and she must at all times be well maintained and as safely run as any ship can be. Onboard ship he carried out his work in the full glare of his shipmates' gaze, to their approbation or otherwise. If able and willing to accept this responsibility, to occasionally endure long periods of perhaps several days and nights continually on the bridge without sleep in fog or bad weather, making vital decisions under stress, accepting all the perils of the sea, the Master had indeed the best job afloat. After over forty years at sea, half of them in command, I still think he has.

2. SOME AUSTRALIAN RECOLLECTIONS

My first voyage took me to South America and the next two to the west coast of North America via Panama, all in the *Columbia Star* of 1939 vintage. So it was with considerable pleasure that I viewed my next appointment as cadet in the *Saxon Star* for a voyage to South and East Africa, Australia and New Zealand . . . Loading a large general cargo in Middlesbrough and London we had called at Capetown, Port Elizabeth, East London, Durban, Lourenço Marques (As Maputo was then called) and Beira, sailing from Portuguese East Africa – Mozambique – on the last day in June, 1952. In Beira we had loaded three thousand tons of copper 'cigars' each about a metre long, square cross section of perhaps twelve centimetres – produce of Rhodesia for Port Kembla, New South Wales. Also onboard were cartons of South African canned fruit and fish from Durban, several large cases of ostrich feathers, plus one hundred tons of bagged asbestos (not recognised then for the lethal stuff it is!).

Disembarking our Portuguese pilot into a smartly manned rowing boat which took him to his anchored steam cutter in the broad estuary, we set off on the twenty-three day passage across a wild and wintry Great Southern Ocean, to Melbourne, my first Australian landfall. On our small Phillips' radio we listened awe-struck to a race meeting, commentated in what I soon came to recognise as the Australian racing dialect, before our pilot boarded off the entrance to Port Phillip – the Rip – from the steam pilot cutter, *Akuna* had once been the German Governor of New Guinea's official yacht. Built around 1912, her bowspritted clipper bow, graceful counter stern, tall yellow funnel and lofty masts made her more picturesque – if no more useful – than the Port Phillip Pilots' second cutter, the straight stemmed *Victoria*. The duty cutter of this pair cruised off the entrance to Port Phillip in all weathers, providing pilots for ships bound up to Williamstown and Geelong as well as for Melbourne and Port Melbourne?

Well – it was explained to this 'green' lad fresh out from the 'Old Country', – Port Phillip is the bay, twenty five miles long, somewhat more wide, which extends from Point Lonsdale at the heads to Hobson's Bay in the north, from Frankston in the east to Geelong on Corio Bay in the west. Port Melbourne consisted of two wooden piers on the north side of Hobson's Bay with Williamstown west across the mouth of the River Yarra, up which and near the city lay Melbourne's docks and river berths. Pilot safely aboard, deep-draft ships like ours took the South Channel, skirting the shallows and Mud Islands before turning north round the Hovell Beacon. Shallow draft ships – coasters and fishing craft etc – used the more direct West Channel. Many wrecks have occurred in these waters and a gloomy reminder of the entrance's dangers was the wreck of the Australian vessel *Time* which, we

17

By 1954 the *Saxon Star* had three cadets, pictured here with their gangway lifebuoy, featuring Saxons dexter and sinister.

learned, was eventually used for target practice by the Royal Australian Airforce, but our pilot cheered us up by handing the captain a green canvas bag containing – MAIL! I was learning how precious mail from home is to the seafarer, and Port Phillip pilots are the only ones I know world-wide who provide this kindly and thoughtful service. Usually you have to wait until the ship gets alongside her berth, hours later.

From our anchorage in Hobson's Bay, where we awaited clearance, we pondered the middle years of last century when these very waters were crammed with anchored sailing ships, deserted by their crews and often their captains too – all gone off to the gold rush 'diggins'.

After clearing through Port Health and Customs we headed up the muddy river, eventually getting assistance from an ancient two-funnelled tug and the even older *Eagle*, single funnel. The river wound through open marshland rich in bird life and for the first time I saw black swans in their native haunts. We went on, slowly so as not to wash away the river banks, past old broken wooden wharves where lay the hulks of sailing ships used to bunker the still numerous coal-burning coastal steamers. *Shandon, Agnes Muir, Marjorie, Rathlin Island* and *Rona* were still identifiable under their various stages of decrepitude, rigged down to lower masts, each with the conspicuous upper part of a vertical donkey boiler protruding above the upper deck for supplying steam to the winches. Derricks were the spars which had originally carried sails. It didn't take much imagination to visualise these now battered, grimy little vessels in their heyday, carrying a press of gleaming canvas, driving out from Britain with general cargo, helping to build and supply the new nation, racing home round the Horn with bales of wool screwed tight into their holds. None of these hulks survives as such, though *Rona* has been restored by a dedicated band of enthusiasts to her original 1885 condition – a pretty little three-masted barque under her original Belfast name – *Polly Woodside*.

We berthed in Victoria Dock where were many similar ships to our little *Saxon Star.* It was Saturday morning and no work would begin until Monday so we had the weekend to relax and see the sights. The Australian Coast at that time provided employment for many ships, from the elegant passenger mini-liners of the Adelaide Steamship Company, Huddart Parker, McIlwraith and McEachern and the Melbourne Steamship company, to the heavily-built general cargo vessels of the Australia Coastal Shipping Commission – which eventually grew into the Australian National Line. A class of these River Boats was built 1944-7 in Australia, with reciprocating steam engines and LP turbines driving single screws. Sturdy, bridge-and-engines-amidships vessels, their colours then were a yellow lined black hull, stone-brown upperworks surmounted by a black cowl-topped funnel with two narrow yellow bands.

To the sternly conservative nineteen year old minds of 'me and my mate', the River Boats presented a refreshing return to tradition – when ships looked like ships – for even in the 'fifties there were signs of change – that henceforth ships would not always look like the ships we so admired . . . There were, however, numerous other vessels of considerable antiquity to cheer us, many of them painted, under the distinctive owners' funnels, reddish brown all over – to colour-match the iron ore so many of them carried as their staple cargo. Broken Hill had black funnels with two narrow blue bands reminiscent of the Norwegian Wilhelmsen' Tonsberg ships. Howard Smith had white funnels with black tops and named his ships *Age, Aeon, Time*, while British tramps too, found coastal employment. Ropner's had many carrying coal and iron ore coastwide in mostly wartime-built vessels of around 8,000 tons.

The docks were busy with British cargo liners – often – though we little thought it, the best and last of their type, before the container revolution changed it all. At one time I saw lying alongside the same quay in Victoria Dock the *Wellington Star* and *Tasmania Star*, handsome twins almost identical except for their engines; the 'Welly Boot' had twin-screw Doxfords while the 'Tazzy' was a single screw steam turbine vessel. For at that time motor ships had to use the expensive diesel oil as fuel while steamers burned the much cheaper heavy oil in their boilers, and many companies would build a class of ships, some with diesel power, others with steam turbine, comparing running costs one against the other. At that time the diesel was cheaper but less reliable, burned expensive fuel and needed much in the way of frequent machinery repair, while Pametrada steam turbines cost more initially but then ran for years, reliably and on cheaper fuel. It was no fluke that many of the big companies were returning to steam turbine propulsion – until the sudden steep hike in fuel oil prices of the early seventies combined with steady strides in the economic running and reliability of the motor ship dealt steam turbine propulsion a fatal blow. But at the time of which I write the arguments pro and con still raged, not only among our engineers – most of whom were either committed totally to either steam or diesel and saw no point in arguing!

The *Trojan Star* came in, to swell our Blue Star numbers to four, and here *was* a ship to admire! Built in France as *La Perouse* as long ago as 1916, she came to Blue Star in 1925, retaining her four masts and quaint funnel with gallery at half height. Then the *Rhodesia Star* arrived at Port Melbourne to load wool at Princes Pier. Unlike nearly all her Blue Star sisters she was not refrigerated and was one of a pair of US-built former aircraft carriers of the escort type – the famous 'Woolworth' carriers whose sister, *South Africa Star* was to have me as her chief officer ten years later. The now long-gone Australasian branch of Cunard, Port Line, was represented next by the *Port Vindex* after conversion from her wartime role as the British-built escort carrier *HMS Vindex* in which she helped defend convoys to North Russia. In tribute to this service she was renamed *Port Vindex* post war, thus becoming the only Port Liner not actually named after a port. There were Shaw Savill liners and Clan liners, Blue Funnel and Bank Line, Federal Line – descended from sailing ships and named after English counties. The Scots tramps of the Baron Line and Lyle's of Glasgow contrasted with the cool clean colours of the Scandinavians. Jardine's and China Nav traded to the East, as did P & O's subsidiary E & A. All were represented in Melbourne in 1952.

All these ships had large crews and Australia provided for them lavishly. A dear lady in Melbourne, Mrs. Daines, would put on parties for cadets, apprentices and junior engineers in her gracious home. The padre at the Missions to Seamen organised bus outings and intership football matches, families took us home and made us feel like honoured guests. Going to sea, to Australia, was indeed a great life!

Meanwhile, back in the docks, cargo work proceeded at a leisurely pace. Eventually the asbestos was out, and the ostrich feathers: time to go to Sydney to unload our cargo of canned goods, a three day passage at our speed of what usually amounted to just under eleven knots. Off the famous Sydney Heads we embarked our pilot from yet another elegant cutter – this time the *Captain Cook* which not only boasted a bowsprit over her clipper bow, but a figurehead also. Sydney Harbour – Port Jackson – was thronged with commercial traffic with ships lying at all the numerous wharves. The opera house had yet to be built but The Bridge towered overall – seeming higher then than it does today as Sydney, we found, was, like Melbourne, a city of mainly low-rise buildings round which trundled cream and green single-deck trams. We berthed well up the harbour, above the bridge, at Glebe Island which in those days was a peninsular of old wooden wharves backed by quaint wooden office and warehouse buildings.

'Me and my Mate' – as cadets had long described themselves – made the most of Sydney, seeing 'Kiss Me Kate' and 'Call Me Madam' at the Theatre Royal. Today's youngsters would consider us terribly old fashioned in that we always went ashore dressed in sports jacket and flannel trousers, with neat shirt and tie and highly polished shoes. In those days jeans were strictly workwear – never considered fit for anything else. But it wasn't just us who dressed up to go ashore – everyone did – and some of the best dressed to step down the gangway were our elderly greasers – motormen as they later became known – who rarely went ashore in anything less than a three piece navy blue suit, collar and tie, polished black boots. The Australian dockers (called Wharfies) seemed at first to be a desperately militant lot but most – when one got to know them better – were kindly, good-hearted men who laughed a lot and pulled each other's legs mercilessly. Most, in those early 'fifties, had been in the war – latter-day Anzacs – who spoke familiarly of the Libyan Desert, the great battles across Europe, and New Guinea where they fought desperately to prevent the Japanese invading their homeland. It all helped pass the time on cargo watch when we cadets would be stationed down a hold checking the unloading.

There was talk, even in the fifties, of moving Sydney's commercial port south down the coast to Botany Bay, mainly because traffic congestion on the roads around numerous coves and bays in the harbour did not make for distributional efficiency. Also – and many hinted that this was the real reason – the harbour is ideal for yachting and watersports – which sordid commerce was inclined to disrupt! The last time I sailed out of Sydney Harbour, in the *Auckland Star,* September 1976, yacht races were in progress and the water was thronged with craft of all kinds – not just the participants of course but thousands of spectators – through whom we had to pick a very slow and careful course, frequently blowing warnings on our siren, seeing boats full of people disappear under our bow, to fend themselves off, waving and cheering. It seemed as though we of the commercial world were now very much out of place!

From Sydney (back in 1952) we made a swift, short dash down to Port Kembla where we anchored for several days awaiting a berth to unload our copper. The sprawling town of Woolongong was the epitome of heavy industry, and would stretch our copper cigars into miles and miles of telephone wire cables spanning the continent. My mate Ted and I became friendly here with a Church Youth Club (of all things, said our shipmates!). The good

21

The Saxon Star entering Sydney which at that time was not the high-rise city it is today.

young people had never met English lads before, never visited a ship, and went out of their ways to make us feel at home and welcome. It was even arranged for us to go camping with them at the weekend but once again commercial considerations took over – and we sailed instead for New Zealand.

Next voyage we again loaded in Middlesbrough and London's Royal Albert Dock for South and East Africa, where Captain MacDonald received orders to proceed to Melbourne and Queensland, to load frozen beef and butter for the UK.

Crossing the Great Southern Ocean this time took us close to Amsterdam Island – a tiny outpost peopled by a few French radio operators working the meteorological station, with whom our Sparks dotted and dashed. We had no copper this trip and the ship was almost empty – six cases of ostrich feathers and a few hogsheads of Rhodesian tobacco do not require much stowage space – so the mate had an ideal opportunity to prepare for our forthcoming frozen cargo. Our five cavernous holds, each 27 feet deep, only had one seven-feet tweendeck above, so the work of preparation was not unduly laborious, but took time and required care as we rolled our way east. The ship – built 1942 – had what was then quite modern refrigeration in that cold air was forced around the cargo space by powerful electric fans situated over nests of mechanically-cooled brine pipes in special fanrooms at the ends of the holds and tween decks. But it was a pretty basic system in that all cargo had to be carried at the same temperature – frozen for meat and butter – chilled for fruit – so only one or the other could be loaded. A modern reefer ship can carry various cargoes simultaneously through a range of temperatures in different cargo spaces, from deep freeze to lightly chilled. Cadets played an active part in cleaning and dunnaging fanrooms and holds with the sailors. Though the special jobs like cleaning bilges were reserved for 'me-and-my-mate'.

Most of our cargo was to be loaded at Gladstone, a little town then, barely more than a village, on the shores of Port Curtis; an almost-tropical, near-landlocked, island-studded natural harbour of great beauty in which, it had been proclaimed by Victorian politicians, the whole Royal Navy could safely ride at anchor. Fortunately for us the Meat Works Wharf – miles out of town – had been unapproachable since the Great Cyclone of 1949 pushed up sandbanks, so we went to the Town Wharf instead, only ten minutes walk from the 'metropolis'. Today I understand Gladstone is indeed a roaring metropolis but in 1953 it was a delightful sleepy hollow where we made many friends who remained friends. The Port Curtis Sailing Club made us hon. members and were having a regatta to which we were invited, including the post-sailing socializing, lubricated with foaming great glass jugs of iced beer . . . The *Saxon Star,* suitably dressed overall in her best show of flags, became the winning post for the annual Brisbane to Gladstone Yacht Race.

People who had never visited a deep-sea ship before came aboard with wide-eyed interest – amazing how many persons can cram into a tiny cabin party! Later they took us home to evenings round the piano where concertina, ukelele and tin whistle provided accompaniment. There was no television, no tape cassettes in 1950s Queensland. The Ford Model 'T' and its contemporaries were common transport, but our rustic idyll here was rudely interrupted when we were called round to Port Alma to load a consignment of frozen beef from the Lakes Creek abattoir at Rockhampton, whence it came along a single track railway over the marshlands. Port Alma, then, consisted of a tumbledown wooden wharf and a few tin sheds but the predominant memory is of mosquitoes and sandflies. The sharks in the muddy Fitzroy River seemed to sneer at our attempts to catch them. Nine days of this and we were glad to return to Gladstone.

Members of the Port Curtis Sailing Club were carpenters to trade and built their own boats, finding the correctly shaped knees grown to size and near-shape in the swamps. They were not short of planking timber, either – only of good straight lengths of pine for masts. Our dunnage timber – new, special 'food-clean-quality' came in six by one inch planks which were laid over *three by three inch* bearers, and it was these latter long into the night, while rain beat down on the iron roof and flies clustered round the lamps that our new friends found so interesting, as we discussed boatbuilding. Generously Ted and I offered them as much as they'd like – "Well, a few sticks would be very much appreciated, lads! How about half a dozen pieces?" (each piece was about ten feet long) No problem! We'd go down to the ship for it now, where piles and piles of it lay around the decks ready for use down below. A rainy dark night – we needn't call the mate at this hour, and he was sure not to mind anyway – found us quietly walking down the gangway with a few lengths over our shoulders while the ubiquitous utility truck (Oldsmobile 1926) parked alongside. Cries out the night caused us to halt in our steps. "Stop thief, come back, come back!" It was the mate. We HAD disturbed his slumbers, and when he realised the culprits were his own cadets his wrath knew no bounds. Confined to Ship for the next few days, we felt he was over-reacting somewhat, and our friends were upset, even going to see him to make the peace. Peace made all round our social whirl resumed . . .

We sailed from Gladstone with heavy hearts – we had almost become residents – but cheered up during our passage inside the Great Barrier Reef to Cairns, crossing the Tropic of Capricorn just north of Gladstone. Cairns was, and still is, a major sugar port, but we loaded frozen beef there. Not the modern cartons of boneless beef, but burlap-wrapped 'ox' fores and hinds, heavy to handle but cheerfully loaded by our Melbourne wharfies' Queensland cousins. While the lower hold was being loaded the burning sunshine was kept out of the 'tweendecks by canvas screens draped around by the cadets (who else!).

All this time ship's maintenance continued and 'me-and-my-mate' spent most of our waking hours when not on cargo watch, chipping rust off the ship's side rails – miles of them! Applying several coats of red lead, then white undercoat and gloss, we had to admit our efforts contributed to our little ship's smartness. The 'Crowd' were painting masts and funnel, also round overside gleaming black and by the time we left, our *Saxon Star* was a credit to all, much admired by our friends ashore. Rollers were not yet in vogue and all paint was applied with either brush – often 'bent-on' to a bamboo pole 'manhelp' – or by cotton waste wads. Occasionally Chippy the carpenter and 'we' would be called down below when the wharfies were at their meal break to repair some broken insulation wood – and as the cold air was always 'on' to preserve temperatures when loading was suspended – it was jolly cold below. But Chippy would revive us when we climbed out and up to his cabin with a drop of rum he kept especially for 'the preservation of life'.

Cargo was rarely worked at night and as cadets' overtime at one shilling and sixpence an hour (7.5 pence) was considered by the mate to be prohibitively exorbitant, we had most nights off to go ashore. . .

In Cairns we met a family living in the lovely little sloop *Wind-Call*. We had been told to look them up by the folks in Gladstone, and were able to help scrub the sloop down, paint and varnish her when she was hauled up on the slip, for which our reward was always a splendid supper. Ship's food was good and plentiful, but cadets are always hungry and never miss out on offered extras. Of course, by this time our Go Ashore rig was a little less formal; – sunhat, shorts and shirt usually sufficing – even shoes seemed superfluous in North Queensland. Leaving Cairns, we were pressed to take some superb fish – caught by the *Wind-Call* family's little daughter, which called for a big fry-up in the galley as we headed back south to our final loading port of Townsville. The *Saxon Star's* cook was a kind hearted old boy, prematurely white haired which may have been caused by his being torpedoed and sunk five times during the war. One night in the North Atlantic his ship was torpedoed, but survivors were all taken off by a destroyer coming alongside – only to be herself torpedoed before dawn broke. We liked him, but this did not prevent our yearning for the large apple pie he had baked and left to cool on his bench just under the barred porthole, open for ventilation in those pre-air conditioned days. Devising a means of opening the galley door that night, we crept in, stole the pie, gorged ourselves upon its entirety, and turned-in feeling sinfully replete. Next morning the cook spoke to us, pretending not to notice our probably guilt-ridden features. "You know lads, I had a bit of pastry left last night, and I know you two gannets are always hungry so I baked a pie for you. And would you believe, some lousy thieving blighter's stolen it during the night!".

In the *Saxon Star* only the topmost hatchcovers of each cargo space were insulated: box-shaped cork-filled wooden hatch covers called plugs, fitting wedgelike between the portable athwartships beams, were tamped down when loading had completed. Any gaps remaining were caulked with oakum and payed with hot molten pitch. The pitch boiler, normally stowed away at sea, was brought out and erected on deck, its little furnace fed with sawn dunnage-wood, tended by 'M.A.M.M.' who would improve the shining hour by dipping Woodbines in the liquid pitch as far as possible, then leaving them to dry hard on the boiler's rim. The undipped end could be lit after the sealed end was pierced, cigar-like. These Pitchblend Specials, as we called them (low tar?) went down well at parties. Miraculously we survived these nicotine novelties, and when all the holds were full of frozen beef and butter we sailed from Townsville, up north around Cape York, through Torres Strait – for Liverpool via Aden and the Suez Canal.

Next voyage was to New Zealand but after that we returned to Australia via South and East Africa, to Tasmania for apples which were, then, carried in the colourful wooden crates seen in every British greengrocer's shop. We loaded at the tiny hamlet of Beauty Point before completing at Hobart. Our weather eye noticed several little sailing ships still trading around Tasmania then – the pretty little ketches *Lenna* and *May Queen* brought in sawn timber from the outports, the three masted schooner *Claire Crouch* also sailed in, while the hulked *Alma Doepel* humped carbide from the Risdon factory. At that time she looked on her last legs so it was pleasing to see her recently refitted and sailing our of Melbourne as a 3-masted training ship. Tasmania too was delightful – twelve days in Hobart had most of the lads almost engaged to be married.

This was how trade between Britain and Australia had been carried since steam took over from sail a century before. A ship took around thirty days out, spent a couple of months 'on the coast', then took a month to get home. The first time I went out in a box-boat, twenty years later in *ACT 5*, we took just twenty-two days at twenty-two knots to reach Fremantle from Liverpool round the Cape. Containerisation not only cut down time at sea on passage, it reduced time spent loading and unloading to such an extent that – in a container ship – a whole night in port is now a luxury. But the Port Phillip pilot still brings out the mail!

Hobart, with Mount Wellington in the background. A lovely place!

3. THE HEAVY LIFTERS

Blue Star were not into heavy lifting until 1962. True, most of their ships included a fifty or sixty tonner in their working rig of up to twenty six cargo-lifting derricks – called 'booms' by the Americans – and, technically, any sling of cargo weighing over three tons is a 'heavy lift'. But big items – locomotives, boilers, power station equipment and factory installations such as steel and paper mills were special, requiring ships with large holds fitted with ample securing points, large hatches, and heavy derricks.

Blue Star were (and are) basically a reefer company, famous for the carriage of meat, butter, fruit etc world-wide . . . and the relatively small hatches of a reefer ship do not lend themselves to heavy lifting. Outward bound, however, the regular liner trades on which they engaged – to South and North America, South Africa, New Zealand and Australia, comprised non-refrigerated general cargo from Britain and the Continent (long before the EEC was born or thought of). It was common to load steel in Middlesbrough, glassware in Antwerp, all manner of industrial and domestic equipment in London, cars from Dagenham, general cargo in all shapes and sizes in the Bristol Channel, Liverpool, Glasgow and Continental ports from Hamburg round to Genoa. This trade with the Southern Dominions – general cargo outward, refrigerated and other primary produce home, was shared with the Port Line, Shaw Savill, New Zealand Shipping Company and Federal Line – all British – with others participating to a lesser extent.

The established 'heavy lift' companies were Bell Ships, Clan Line and the German Hansa Line which traded to the Persian Gulf and India and occasionally had to be chartered for heavy items to Australasia. Of course, because they carried the heavy lifts they got the rest of the power station, sugar mill or whatever was being shipped also. Boilers weighing 250 tons would be accompanied by lesser items right down to the nuts, bolts and fuse wire. With a booming demand for heavy machinery in the 'sixties the shipping lines established on the Australasian service realised that much valuable freight was being lost to them, and, characteristically, Blue Star Line alone decided to have a heavy lifter themselves.

Fortunately, not all their thirty-six ship fleet were, at that time, reefers. There were two general cargo liners acquired soon after the war to satisfy the need for non-refrigerated produce such as hides, tallow, grains (including the highly-profitable birdseed from Brisbane), milk powder and casein, cartons of canned meat and fruit – and wool, which at that time was enjoying unprecedented prosperity. These were the *Rhodesia Star* and *South Africa Star* built in Tacoma, Washington in 1943/4 as the escort carriers *Estero* and *Winjah*, for the US Navy.

Planned as standard US cargo liners each ship measured 492 feet x 69.5 feet and must have presented a frighteningly short flight deck to aircrews having to land upon them in bad weather. However, they helped satisfy a dire need as convoy escorts and both passed to the Royal Navy becoming His Majesty's Ships *Premier* and *Reaper*, serving with modest distinction until the war's end when they exchanged the White Ensign for the Stars and Stripes once more. There was little demand for the 'Woolworth Carriers' post-war however and many were converted to cargo ships. Blue Star bought the pair and had them converted to their own requirements at Mobile, Alabama, in 1948, retaining their Allis Chalmers double-reduction steam turbines geared to a single shaft and Foster Wheeler oil-fired boilers. High, boxy superstructure, typical American-of-that-era, belied sweet underwater lines and they were capable of a sustained 17 knots, only disadvantage being occasional clouds of belching black smoke erupting from the funnel without warning. The *South Africa's* maiden voyage took her to Hamilton, Bermuda, where elegantly dressed guests at a waterside hotel, watching this brave new cargo liner arrive at their port, were suddenly enveloped in a dense pall of oily soot . . . After the immediate post-war boom both ships spent time laid up and it seemed as though their days were numbered, at least with Blue Star who were developing the carriage of reefer produce with increasing sophistication.

The sudden need for a heavy lift ship, however, made either of this pair the ideal choice for conversion. Because she happened to be in the right place at the right time, the *South Africa Star* was chosen. It had been post-war company practice to name ships after nations and places rather than the tribal appellations 'Saxon', Trojan' and Celtic' popular prewar, and since Australia and all the other regular places visited already had ships named after them, it was time to 'bring in' the African market, as it were:– though both ships did, in fact, spend most of their lives in the Australian and New Zealand trades. In 1962 the *South Africa* was sent to Hamburg for conversion at the Howaldtswerke shipyard, where I joined her as chief officer. One of the German managers and I found ourselves on the harbour ferry together one day and fell to discussing, of course, the many ships around us. At that time Britain was the builder of the world's largest and finest passenger liners and I asked the manager if the Germans had any plans to compete in what looked like becoming a lucrative market in the cruise industry. He replied sadly. "No, we Germans have neither the financial nor technical resources, nor the shipbuilding skills needed . . ." . That was in 1962.

Fascinated at the work being carried out, I was not a little apprehensive at the prospect of becoming responsible for slings of cargo weighing up to 180 tons, the new derrick's safe working load. The old mast had been lifted out and now lay rusting on the quay, so much scrap metal. The new mast, of special high-tensile steel, had just been shipped by floating crane. Because of

South Africa Star, with heavy derrick and Welsh hat on funnel, which was designed to take smoke away from the ship. *(FotoFlite)*

South Africa Star loading her first heavy cargo at Liverpool, January 1963
– after the guys had been correctly rigged!

its construction material it needed no supporting shrouds or stays and was, at the time, the largest unsupported mast afloat. The blocks were enormous, taking up to six sheaves of heavy wire rope but whilst the rigging was intricate it was well thought out and worked well when properly set up before work commenced. I had, of course, some experience of heavy derricks, but only handling lifts up to thirty tons or so. Formerly, any really heavy item had been loaded and unloaded by either a floating crane or similar lifting apparatus mounted on the quay – it was only when undivided loads weighing more than the ports' lifting capacities began to be carried that the need for a ship's own very heavy derrick arose.

Under my supervision the bosun and sailors had rigged our new derrick for its first lift, in Liverpool – a large stator for the Hazelwood power station near Melbourne. We were waiting for the low-loader vehicle carrying it to manoeuvre alongside on the quay when a red-faced stentorian bellow assaulted my ears from the bridge.

"Mr. Kinghorn, you've got that forward guy rigged in the wrong blasted place – you'll never get the stator aboard that way!".

The captain had intervened – rightly, too, as I saw at once when I thought about it. – I had not yet got the habit of envisaging the derrick in its swung-out-and-in positions . . . Amused at my discomfort naturally, the bosun and sailors soon put matters right. Thereafter we worked as a practised team and became proficient. Different from frozen meat!

It is customary for dock labour to work cargo in and out using the ship's winches and derricks or quayside cranes, but it was soon realised – even by the wharfies – that perhaps Heavy Lifts were safer in our hands – after we had made the first one look particularly difficult! The wharfies soon settled to do the hooking and unhooking while our crew, under my direction, actually controlled and drove the winches. Rigging the gear and unrigging it again for the long voyage home was hard physical work – real seamanship – and we took delight in proving wrong the local stevedore and his men who would bet us cases of beer (!) that we could never get the derrick ready for work by 7a.m.

Heavy items were usually put ashore during meal breaks when the wharf was otherwise quiet so the officers' saloon rarely saw us in uniform. Meals were taken as convenient, boiler-suited in the duty messroom. Happy days! One of the *South Africa Star's* most notable cargoes when I was there was a whole new steel-making process from the Tees, near Middlesbrough, out to Whyalla in South Australia's Spencer Gulf. Huge 95 ton 'eggs' accompanied by 75 ton 'rings' in which they would be mounted, sat upon and around No. 3 hatch, immediately forward of the bridge. Mounted on 12 x 12 inch baulk timber laid across the coamings and ship's side bulwarks, they were secured with ship's anchor chain and made an impressive deck cargo. The rest of the new plant, heavy lifts included, was stowed below decks accompanied by

South Africa Star, unloading at Pyrmont, Sydney. The wharfies hooked on and unhooked the heavy lifts.

much of the equipment for a new ship being built in Australia for which we brought the propeller, anchors, anchor windlass and chain, much of her machinery and two fibreglass lifeboats secured athwartships on our No.5, aftermost hatch. Our old ship must certainly have earned her keep that trip!

Unloading in Whyalla had barely begun the morning we arrived, when, during the lunchbreak, smoke was seen coming from deckcargo stowed near the stern. Perhaps a spark from the tall funnel of the coastal coal-burning steamer astern of us had caused ignition – we would never know.

Our after deck-cargo included glass jars of acid in wire crates packed round with straw, and these were already burning. Most of us were at lunch, only an observant sailor, one Brian Bucksey, spotted the smoke and gave the alarm. As one man we poured out of the saloon, dressed of course in best uniform, just as the blaze erupted. Hoses were brought into action at once, which was just as well as the deck cargo was now well and truly alight and flames were spreading via canvas hatch tarpaulins to the tweendecks below, in which was stowed explosives for a local quarry. Drums of oil were rising like miniature domes of St Paul's with the heat and as our lads tipped a furiously blaxing case of what turned out to be toe-puff over the rail into the water it exploded with a brilliant firework crescendo. Warm work, but we had attacked it just in time and when the hastily-summoned Whyalla Fire Brigade arrived – all the firemen had to do then was help us drink the beer laid on by a grateful consignee – who just happened to be aboard for lunch! The big items we swung out that afternoon, feeling well pleased with our day's work.

We must have become quite adept at this work however as the company decided heavy lifting was sufficiently profitable to justify a brand new ship with 300 ton derrick, so getting us for a while (1966) into the Guiness Book of Records.

The new ship was to be called *Australia Star*, second Blue Star liner to bear that name – the first being one of an illustrious class built during the 'thirties and recently arrived in shipbreakers hands'. Ours was the first Blue Star ship to have a bulbous bow – albeit a modest one by later standards – and came from the Southwick yard of Austin and Pickersgill, Sunderland. I stood by her building as chief officer.

The *Australia Star* was a graceful ship – unusual in a purpose-built heavy-lift vessel – with elegantly curved stem and short raised forecastle. Bridge, accommodation and funnel were placed abaft amidships on a long, raised poop which ended in a nicely rounded stern. Cargo hatches one, two and three were forward, five and six aft, with three and four paired athwartships to give wide access below. The only reefer space, 112,000 cubic feet, was in No.5, well clear of heavy lifting, while No.6 was a 'tweendeck over cargo tanks used for carrying liquid chemicals. All hatch covers were hydraulic which – after initial teething problems – worked well.

South Africa Star unloading heavy cargo at Whyalla, 1963.

35

South Africa Star at Pyrmont, Sydney, unloading a 139 ton Ferranti transformer.

Watching a ship take shape on the stocks is fascinating. She was erected in the open, section by section – each part being built under cover, then cut down to 30-ton sections – the limit of the slipway cranes – trundled out to the building berth on trailers and hoisted into position, there to be secured by bottle-screw-tensioned wires and spot welding, until welded permanently. Grit blasters came nightly to clean rust and mill-scale off the erected sections after they had been permanently welded in place and part of my job was to examine this blasting work each morning and pass it for painting – or indicate which areas must be reblasted. Grit blasting raises tremendous clouds of dust so that until the air clears it is impossible to inspect – which was why the work was done at night, when no other people were about.

The shipyard was just eleven miles south of home – across the Tyne, and whereas at first I would take a bus to North Shields ferry, then a train from South Shields to Sunderland, then another bus to near the yard, (which took about an hour altogether) this civilised and quite shore-abiding mode of travel was soon disrupted by Dr Beeching closing the passenger line between South Shields and Sunderland. In support of the now-redundant railwaymen the bus drivers went on a go-slow – and getting to work could now take half the morning which was ridiculous and I began to share some of the frustrations of shore employment. My wife, however, since her eighteenth birthday, had owned a fine Raleigh drop-handlebars semi-racing bicycle; – gleaming with chrome spokes and wheelrims, white mudguards and blue paint. I would go to work in style (she decided). The first day went well – ten minutes to the ferry, time for a cigarette onboard across the river to South Shields – a steady forty minutes pedalling and there I was – the only master mariner on two unpowered wheels in captivity! Speed averaged almost twelve knots, depending on wind and tide. After the first week I felt as though I had been run over by a steam roller. A busy day at the shipyard crawling over an unfinished ship, sandwiched between a daily total of 22 miles cycling caused muscles to screech where I did not know muscles existed! My first puncture was a nightmare; – not so much the repair of it – that, after all, was kid's stuff – but the terrifying roar of lorries and other traffic hurtling past, along the road as I worked . . . However, as my wife soothingly prophesied, I would soon get used to it and of course I did. And it was wonderful to arrive home in the evening and decorate the dining room after tea.. But the growing ship was beautiful to behold, as my wife realised when I took her to the launch, where we stood with all the dignitaries on the launching platform and watched the newly blessed *Australia Star* dip gracefully into the Wear.

After a period of recession shipbuilding was booming in the mid-sixties. The Wearside yards of Doxford, Thompson, Bartram, Laing and Austin & Pickersgill built between them a greater tonnage in 1964 than did the mighty River Tyne. Whereas Austin's old Wear Dockyard had built its last coastwise collier and Short's Pallion Yard had also recently closed, the latter's river berth had been taken over by Bartram's and our *New York Star* was fitting out there.

My ship's propeller and rudder were fitted before launching and the ship was towed under Thompson's big crane at Palmer's Hill for three weeks while the main engine was installed under the eagle eye of our Chief Engineer, Mr. Edgar. An 8RD Vickers' Sulzer, the engine was built at Barrow-in-Furness and shipped round to the Wear in a coaster. An indulgent shipyard lent me a single-oared boat in which I would scull around, inspecting parts of my vessel which otherwise could not be reached. Occasionally I sculled over to see how the *New York Star* was getting on, when her stand-by mate took some leave. Aboard my own ship a huge masthouse was built on the foredeck abaft No. 2 hatch ready to take the giant Stulcken masts and derrick.

She was the first Blue Star to be air-conditioned, the first to have pneumatic bridge control of the engines – and of course, the first purpose-built heavy lifter. We who would eventually take her to sea even composed a song, to the tune of that old commercial jingle The Ovaltinies. We called it The Heavy Lifters. Like to hear it? No? You can't be serious! It went like this, with derrick-swinging actions, of course.

THE HEAVY LIFTERS
WE are the HEAVY LIFTERS, playing with our toy.
The *Australia Star*, has got by far
The BIGGEST GEAR
NEVER FEAR (a doleful note crept in here)
We are the CARGO SHIFTERS
Shifting lifts with joy.
And when we SWING, that MIGHTY THING
We're happy, little, boys. . .

Original intentions were to complete the ship, then sign on a crew to take her over to Hamburg under own power for the big stick to be installed. But, due to unforseen circumstances, completion in Sunderland was delayed. The Germans were ready to ship the derrick, so it was decided to tow the *Australia Star* across the North Sea, then back to the Wear for completion.

We sailed from the Wear on 22nd August – a beautifully calm, clear Sunday morning, in tow of the Dutch tug *Schelde* owned by Smit's of Rotterdam. Still shipyard property, we were officially in charge of the Foreman Fitter, his crew consisting of two other fitters, five Dutch sailors from the tug, a contract electrician and – guest artist – me. I had asked to go – my first deep-sea tow – and it seemed my master's certificate helped with the insurance so I was allowed. By this time the ship neared completion – we had electricity, fresh, sanitary and fire water, a galley stove and almost-completed cabins. Victualled for the trip by a Sunderland catering firm we discovered, as soon as we got to sea, that we had seven cases of toilet rolls (for a three-day run) plenty of food and tea, but no teapot. . . In the pre-teabags era this was an essential item, but a search eventually discovered a large enamel pot left below by the cleaners. All was well!

Our speed under tow averaged 5.7 knots, course almost due east, and we kept in touch with the *Schelde* by radio telephone, maintaining a watchful eye on where the towing bridle wires passed out of the forward fairleads – frapped with well-greased canvas against chafe. Embarking our first pilot off the *Elbe 1* lightship, we made fast two river tugs to help with the steering as ours was not working. At 2 am on the 25th we were off Cuxhaven where we changed tugs. As my Sunderland shipmates had little experience of such work – the heaving in and making fast of heavy towlines – this job fell to the Dutch sailors and lucky old self. All the way up the Elbe special light signals warned other ships of this 'hulk in tow'. At 0440 we changed tugs and pilots off Brunsbuttell (near the entrance to the Kiel Canal). By now it was daylight, the river banks green and lush in the morning sun, warm on the mellow brick walls of high-peaked thatched farmhouses and the occasional old windmill. At the Deutsches Werft Finkelwerder yard lay the *Barcelona Star*, a beautiful little white-hulled reefer recently bought from Ferdinand Laiesz's 'Flying P' Line where she had been the *Piraeus*. Her captain and I dipped ensigns to each other as we passed. Although I held no official rank, I found I was 'the mate' up forward and the 'second mate' aft when we made fast and let go tugs, the 'third mate' when I met the pilot at the pilot ladder (which in my AB's hat I had rigged a short while previously) and 'the captain' when I was with the pilot on the bridge. At 11 am we changed pilots and tugs for the last time. Our new pilot – a gentleman of the old school – was so concerned at our lack of numbers that he came and helped make fast the tugs himself! This off Blankenese, where music greeted us, welcoming us to the City of Hamburg – a nice touch – and at noon we tied up to St Pauli Landungsbrucken. We were to shift over the river to Stulcken's own yard at 3 pm but a gale sprang up – too strong to attempt to shift an empty ship with no engines I decided, with which the pilot wholeheartedly concurred. Amazingly deep sleeps followed. Over twelve hours.

Next morning was calm as we shifted over to our berth in the Fahr Canal where Stulcken posts and derrick awaited us on the quay – massive tubes of high-tensile steel which had to be pre-heated before welding. Since the first 'jumbo' derrick of this type had been fitted over ten years ago in Hansa Line's *Lichtenfels* more than sixty had been built and over forty were presently under construction under licence all over the world. The derrick – able to serve two holds, forward of and abaft the masts – was always ready for use and needed

39

no rigging or unrigging, practically no maintenance, and only three men to operate. There were no guys to rig wrongly! It was the brainchild of a delightful old gentleman, Willie Sprengel, who – I was disarmingly told – "did good work during the war on the design of our submarines".

On Sunday 17th October we shifted down to the Greisenwerderhafen, then a wild and lonely place surrounded by marshes – a wilderness of trees and numerous canals – where to buoys fore and aft and with both anchors down, the derrick was tested, gradually putting it through its paces with water-filled barges weighing – eventually – 330 tons, the required ten percent overload. A crowd of Shipping People arrived in the green and white ferry *Burgomeister Monkeburg* to watch, while at our Marine Superintendent's suggestion I had laid in a modest stock of hospitality to help the occasion along. The following Saturday, 23rd October, we departed in tow of our old friend the *Schelde*. We had another calm crossing in which, in late October, we were fortunate, but back in Sunderland the weather deteriorated and completion in North Dock was a miserable business. An old no-longer-used coaling dock, it was open to the South East – out of which a gale blew steadily for a week. The ship parted her lines and broke adrift. Without benefit of tugs or engines, with dozens of shipyard workers and one fourth mate aboard, she made her first voyage. Careering up the river after having bounced off a (fortunately) vacant oil jetty, she eventually fetched up alongside the bulker *Kirriemoor* fitting out for Runciman's at Palmer's Hill. Extensive repairs were necessary but we finally commissioned on 8th December, on passage from Sunderland to the Tyne where we were to load our first cargo next day – a 147 ton stator from Parsons for our old customer, the Hazelwood power station near Melbourne. That night I was, of course, keen to get home. But Captain MacPhail quite rightly stated that first we must put this new derrick through its paces, making sure no hitches would occur on the morrow when, again, a large party of interested spectators had been invited by Blue Star Line. All went well until we tried to trip the lifting block through the huge derrick-head catapult 'Y' – to shift it from No.2 to No.3 hatch. Nothing happened. Dead. Call the electrician. He fiddled around, getting nowhere – not surprisingly under the newness of our situation. In mounting concern Captain MacPhail told me to call Herr Sprengel who was staying the night at the Station Hotel before next day's big demonstration. Dear old Willie came hot foot in a taxi, still in his pyjamas under a raincoat. "Have you a match, Herr Kinghorn?" was his opening gambit. Well, we all smoked in those days and he probably needed one as much as I did. But taking it, he entered the masthouse which was now filled with a long bank of switches and automatic cut-outs. Studying this immense array carefully, he poked in my Swan Vesta and said, "Now try". The derrick worked and we marvelled – a 300 ton derrick worked by a single matchstick.

Testing the *Australia Star*'s derrick to 330 tons at Hamburg, October 1965.

The tip occasionally came in useful later on!

This 147 ton stator had scarcely tightened the derrick's wires, a fact which became significant later, when we finally sailed out of London into a howling Southwester off Ushant.

Few situations are more awesome than a really severe storm at sea, but seamen are trained from the beginning of their career to deal with the elements, to master storms and survive. And given a well-found ship they can usually manage . . . but it can be quite frightening at the time. A Southwester carries the whole of the North Atlantic before it, piling up in majestic grandeur tremendous waves which shatter on the Brittany coast to rebound in wild, seething confusion. Before dawn, my watch on the last day of the year, we were pitching into it at reduced speed, still scooping up the occasional sea but comfortable. Then, out of the blackness ahead a fearsome gleaming white crest towered above the bow, luminous in the masthead light's reflection. Inexorably it thundered aboard, burying the whole foredeck in a roaring torrent.

By the time I'd pulled back speed on the bridge – control a second monster took us . . . then she shook herself like a dog. Something was amiss. Using the beam of the aldis signalling lamp as a searchlight –

> The Jumbo saw I at a glance
> Tossing its head in sprightly dance!

By this time, of course, Captain MacPhail was on the bridge, he hove the ship to and I climbed forward to inspect the damage. The derrick's wire forestay, leading from the huge catapult 'Y' had parted and the wire ropes, falls and topping lifts, had fallen slack due to the derrick having been used far below capacity for its first cargo lifts. As the ship pitched into the swell the derrick jerked, each jerk tightening its wire ropes around the winch drums but leaving more and more slack aloft. Came the dawn – a racing confused white-capped grey sea with sky to match. Deck cargo had suffered damage, the forecastle deck had been strained. We sorted out the mess, licked our wounds, and carried on to Australia.

Yes, heavy lifting was interesting work!

Loading Australia Star's first heavy cargo at Newcastle, December 1965
– with the help of a matchstick!

Australia Star loading in London's Royal Victoria Dock prior to maiden voyage, December 1965.

Arriving at Sydney, maiden voyage, February 1966.

She had remarkably fine lines – seen here loading wool at Hobart, maiden voyage 1966.

Transferring a heavy boiler from *M.V. Afric* at Darling Harbour, Sydney, 1966. The *Afric* had just left when this picture was taken.

4.   EASTERN LADIES

'THE LINER, SHE'S A LADY', WROTE KIPLING.
In January 1969 I was enjoying home leave after an interesting four months in the Suez Canal's Great Bitter Lake aboard the *Scottish Star* which had been trapped there in the Arab-Israeli War of 1967 – when I was seconded to Austasia Line as relieving chief officer and flew to Singapore to join the *Malaysia*, ex *Hubert*. Austasia Line of Singapore was Mr Vestey's Far Eastern Fleet, operating mainly ex-Booth Line vessels on the run between Singapore and Australia.

A beautiful ship, smaller version of the immediate post-war *Argentina Star* class, her Pametrada turbines driving a single screw achieved a steady, silent 15 knots.

Whereas the Blue Star ships carried around 75 passengers each, in first class, *Malaysia* retained her Booth Line accommodation and carried 140 in first and second classes, the former in cabins amidships and below decks forward, the latter aft. Senior officers were British and Australian – these included the purser, chief steward and chef – juniors were Singaporean, Malaysian or Indian. Ratings were all Singapore Chinese, the first time I had sailed with 'Men from the East'.

This was also my first voyage as mate of a Passenger Vessel and whereas the purser and his crew looked after the passengers, I found I had to get my deck crew to work round them, so to speak, for passengers were encouraged to use the ship as their hotel in port and only deserted us entirely at the annual Singapore drydocking. Thus, deck scrubbing was carried out long before the day began and painting had to be done to ensure minimal inconvenience to the customers. The roar of the chipping hammer, music in the mate's ears aboard a purely cargo ship, was strictly *verboten* and when I pointed out that a certain bulkhead did indeed need chipping the captain owlishly told me to use the rubber hammers. Overhauling cargo gear would involve sending down blocks and festooning the decks with black oily wire ropes – not entirely compatible with children playing or parents sunning themselves in deck chairs. These noisy, dirty, *cargo-ship* jobs, I was loftily told, would be done "at the next drydocking".

My initiation to Chinese New Year came at sea and I nearly caused a mutiny by strictly forbidding the setting off of fire crackers. "But we ALWAYS set off fire clackers!" wailed the deputation sent up by the crew. All I had been trying to prevent was the ship going on fire! But they were a good crew who worked well and every time we approached Singapore, even after only a short trip up the coast, their euphoria (called The Channels in British ships) swept away any preconceived ideas I may have entertained about Inscrutable Orientals.

From Singapore we proceeded up Malacca Strait to Penang, then Port Swettenham which is now called Port Kelang, loading and discharging cargo at each port – frozen beef and lamb in our reefer holds and manufactured equipment – domestic, industrial, medical and agricultural in our non-reefer spaces. In Malaysia we loaded mainly timber – strapped bundles of sawn hardwood planks and rubber in smooth fifty-eight pound bales, dusted with french chalk to prevent them sticking together in the heat.

At Port Swettenham we moored to a buoy, first unshackling the port anchor and using its chain, an interesting seamanship exercise with which I *was*, fortunately, familiar. Cargo was then worked from and to lighters using the ship's derricks. In Port Swettenham a team of girls came aboard and, stark naked, cleaned out the tallow tanks – washing themselves and each other out on deck afterwards, to the agonised excitement of our younger members, raising blood pressures, causing the elders to splutter into their gin. Back in Singapore we loaded more cargo until we were full, then took on more passengers. It was impossible to keep to a precise schedule – rain in port often delayed cargo work – but this did not seem to worry our passengers who were content to enjoy the ride and arrive when the ship did. We were the last 'regular' passenger liner on this service and they were making the most of it.

Some of our passengers were service personnel travelling to and from Singapore which, then, was supported by a powerful Australian military presence. Others came from Britain, America, Africa and Asia, making as cosmopolitan a mixture as could be found anywhere afloat.

Four lifeboats were carried on the boatdeck amidships but only two aft and every voyage without fail a deputation would approach me from the second class and ask why *they* only had two lifeboats when there were more of them than the first class passengers who had *four.* Integrated boat drills never seemed to dispel this illusion, or perhaps someone was having his leg pulled? Church service was held each Sunday at sea in the first class lounge and was usually well attended by those passengers and crew who wished to come. I suppose they were a captive congregation and the one hymn we did *not* sing was 'For Those in Peril on the Sea' – might give the wrong idea!

Southbound the *Malaysia* would call at Moreseby, New Guinea, usually spending one night there, with many of the local expatriate Australians making the ship their club. The lounge was a large, pleasant room at the after end of the midships accommodation, dark-wood panelled with white ceiling (called the deckhead in a ship) with small tables and potted palms opening onto a wide teak-decked verandah overlooking the afterdeck, with more potted palms and cane furniture around which glided immaculate stewards dispensing hospitality in frosty glasses tinkling with ice.

We would often meet old friends here in the Burns Philip and Butterfield and Swire's 'China Nav' ships, while our regular Torres Strait pilot would board to guide us down inside the Great Barrier Reef to Port Alma in Queensland, somewhat larger now than the isolated wooden quayside in the marshes it had been during my cadet days. We loaded 200 ton of hot liquid tallow here in the now-clean cargo deeptanks for Sydney, only two days down the coast.

Whilst alongside in Walsh Bay, one of Sydney's older suburbs, we lay loading and unloading our ten-tons-per-gang-per-hour, average rate for assorted break-bulk cargo, when the huge new box boat *ACT 1* of London arrived at the container terminal nearby. I strolled across to meet old shipmates, for she was one of Associated Container Transportation's Blue Star managed vessels. They were distraught. The huge shoreside portainer crane which should have handled their cargo at a rate exceeding ten tonnes per *minute* was broken down and all cargo work at a standstill!

With the crane repaired within the hour (to sighs of relief) container exchange (as they called it) proceeded at an impressive rate. *ACT1* sailed that evening and was home and outward bound again before the *Malaysia* had left the Australian coast. As they say, time is money!

From Sydney we proceeded to Port Kembla for steel, then to Melbourne where the last of our southbound cargo was unloaded. Next port was Hobart, Tasmania, for apples. Number 2 was already cleaned and cooled but No. 3 hold and 'tweendecks were filthy, shabby and strewn with rubbish. A thorough clean up was required and a coat of varnish on the hold's plywood side and end bulkheads (the walls) would add that final touch of class for which Blue Star ships were justifiably famous.

The captain said we would never do it in time – only a day and a night at sea – which presented an irresistible challenge. Pitching in with the crowd to show'em how it was done, I found myself fully committed. But by the time we steamed up Storm Bay all spaces were clean and cool, gleaming with fresh varnish. Lloyd's surveyor in Hobart, who had to pass the spaces as fit to load before we commenced, was impressed. Fortunately he failed to notice the varnish was still wet – still tacky four weeks later when we unloaded the apples in Singapore . . . fortunately the apples remained untainted!

Northbound we loaded in Sydney and Brisbane taking, among other items, one hundred new Holden cars for Indonesia, unloading them at Tanjung Priok, the port for Jakarta. From here it was an interesting passage up the Banka and Rhio Straits, with lushly green islands and fishing craft in sight all the time, back to Singapore where I transferred to the other passenger ship, the *Australasia* of 1950.

Launched at John Cockerill's Hoboken yard in Belgium as the *Baudouinville* for Compagnie Maritime Belge's West African service, she became the *Thyseville* in deference to the newly built *Baudouinville*, which, in 1957, was named after Belgium's new king. The West African colonies won independence and the need for a large passenger liner fleet evaporated. This happily coincided with Booth Line's need for another ship on their Liverpool – Amazon – West Indies service, so *Thyseville* was bought and renamed *Anselm* following the company's long tradition of naming their Liverpool ships after English saints. Her hull topsides came in Belgian grey, a shade which clearly appealed as it gradually replaced black and a short-lived lavender in all but the Lamport and Holt vessels of the Vestey fleet. In 1963 she became the *Iberia Star* – magnificent in Blue Star funnel – serving for a couple of years as the fifth ship on the South American run, with *Argentina, Brasil, Paraguay* and *Uruguay Stars.*

Whereas the *Malaysia* was a smaller replica of the type of ship I had grown up with, the big Belgian was a liner in the grand manner, seeming much larger than her size and tonnage suggested. By this time all her passengers were one class, paying different fares according to cabin occupied but allowed full use of all public rooms and facilities. In the *Malaysia* we rigged the wood-and-canvas swimming pool which was the norm but here there was a superb built-in pool with changing rooms and showers!

There were spacious bars and lounges and my own palatial cabin even had its own teak 'front door' onto the boat deck as well as the usual inside entrance. In my previous life only captains were allowed such luxury! There was even a chapel. Passenger cabins ranged from a truly superb suite with all mod cons through single and doubles with own bathroom and toilet to four-berth family rooms with facilities around the corner.

As mate of course I was responsible for keeping all this accommodation properly painted and discovered to my amazement that the paint store contained 24 different shades of red, all for cabin doors, going right back to Belgian days. The Chinese bosun and I spent happy hours deciding the names for each shade so he could paint it on the tins in Chinese for his crew's benefit. Eventually, as more shades materialised out of the dim recesses, we had to settle for numbers – Number One Red, etc. Clearing blocked cabin drains was another job our Chinese carpenter and I tackled with gusto. Some amazing objects eventually came to light in the scupper pipes' sharp angle bends, usually in the depths of the engineroom . . . a lady's hairbrush, a coffee cup, a toy lorry. . .

Both ships carried four mates so I enjoyed the luxury of being a dayworker most of the time: cleaning hatches and clearing scuppers, checking paint and other deck stores, matching cargo gear items against their certificates, supervising the deck crew at their work. But in the evening a whole new world opened up when I became the Executive Chief Officer, mess-kitted and cummerbunded, listening to passengers tell their fascinating travellers' tales. . .

Originally on the same run as the *Malaysia,* the *Australasia* was now on the Fremantle – Singapore service. Compared with *Malaysia's* round voyage of twelve or thirteen weeks with land in sight most of the time, *Australasia* made a three-week round voyage, seven days at sea in each direction with open ocean between Australia's south-west corner and Sunda Strait guarded by the still-smouldering remains of Krakatoa. More exciting for our younger passengers was Christmas Island which we made a point of passing closely. The harbour master would kindly oblige per VHF radio telephone in a suitably deep voice and ask them if they were all being good, for – as they all knew– Christmas Island was where Santa Claus spent his summer holidays.

Australasia's machinery was less glamorous than the ship and taxed to the utmost the skill, experience and sheer hard work of Chief Engineer 'Teapot' Harry Fairclough and his team. Teapot had been with the ship since here Booth Line days and was credited with being the only chief who could make her go.

The air-conditioning plant, however, seemed to have beaten even Harry's ingenuity and occasionally caused him to smart under passengers' comparisons with that other ship on the run, Blue Funnel Line's superb *Centaur.*

The hour before dinner was a pleasant time when elegantly dressed passengers congregating in the various attractive bars worked up the appetite for a six-course dinner with an aperitif or two. One evening as the ship glided into the tropics this happy interlude was interrupted by a sound, as of a mighty rushing wind: there was a 'WHOOSH!' and years of soot and grime from long-disused air-con trunking descended thickly over all. Harry had got it working!

On another occasion the passengers had just joined in Singapore, we had moved out into the roads to complete loading from lighters, when, as dinner was being served, a generator failure plunged the ship into total darkness. Quick as a flash our well-trained waiters produced candle-in-orange table lanterns, to Harry's unflappable "Bet you don't get candle-lit dinner first night out on the *Centaur!*".

In Singapore I swapped back to the *Malaysia* while her regular chief officer went on leave and it was in some haste that we moved off our berth at Keppel Quay to make way for the *Centaur* with disembarking passengers. At anchor in the Eastern Roads we loaded a vast assortment of second-hand building site equipment for outback New Guinea. This included a large cement mixer and several pieces heavy enough to need our 50-ton jumbo derrick. As it had not been used for years its rigging plan was, unsurpisingly, missing, but the bosun and I put our heads together and soon the sailors had it broken-out with blocks, shackles and wire ropes strong enough to do the job.

Swinging all this assorted hardware aboard from a barge was totally absorbing and it was only days later at sea that I realised, with horror, that in our haste to leave the quay I had left two insulated reefer-hatch covers on

Austasia Line's *Malaysia.* *(Airfoto, Malacca)*

Keppel Quay. They had been landed to facilitate loading, got hidden under a pile of dunnage wood, and in our hurry-up departure remained there forgotten. I confessed to the Captain who smiled, having done the same himself when he was mate once. A radio message to Singapore enlisted the help of Blue Funnel Line whose *Rhexenor* happened to be loading there for Melbourne direct. There the hatch covers awaited our arrival, demonstrating once again that, regardless of international or company rivalries, shipping people help each other.

There was no night navigation at Tanjung Priok, no lights in the harbour lighthouses and the company wanted us on our way. Fortunately the captain and Indonesian pilot were old friends and – since the moon was full on a clear night – we crept away at midnight without using tugs, the novel spectacle of a blacked-out lighthouse on the breakwater, silhouetted against the sea of beaten silver. In Singapore we entered Keppel drydock for annual refit – all those noisy, dirty *cargo ship* jobs being attended to, and it was time for me to return home after what, even in 1969, was an unusual kind of seafaring.

Containerisation was coming and the ships were getting old. Plans to convert the *Malaysia* into a box boat were dropped and when the *Australasia* went to Taiwan breakers in 1972 the *Malaysia* took over the Fremantle run for another four years before she, too, went to the scrapyard. But not for scrap!

Instead she was converted into a sheep carrier, dominated by a plethora of mushroom ventilators but still recognisable as I found in Colombo, entering that port in a new container ship three years later. Thus she ran reliably –

The *Australasia.* *(Airfoto, Malacca)*

and, I was told – highly profitably, until 1984 when aged 30, she was broken up in Port Alang, India.

The second *Baudouinville* of 1957 passed first to P&O as the *Cathay* and is now the *Shanghai* of Shanghai, owned by the People's Republic. I saw her in Shanghai recently, still looking every inch an Eastern Lady.

5. BOX BOAT VOYAGE

In the box boats, life was different.

"Twenty four hours in port – a whole night – make the most of it!" Port Taranaki, New Plymouth, New Zealand – carved, dredged and built – against opposition from nature and the powers-that-were in Wellington a century ago, it grew to become the world's leading cheese exporter in the 1950s and '60s. As the container age dawned, the little city – ever with eyes to the future — welcomed new trades – to the Caribbean, USA, India and the Persian or Arabian Gulf. No matter that funds sufficient for portainer cranes were lacking, the port would cater for ships with their own cranes. And the Box Boats came. Shaw Savill sent the new *Dunedin*, New Zealand Shipping Corporation *NZ Caribbean,* Andrew Wear sent his *Willowbank* and Blue Star their latest *Australia* and *New Zealand Stars.* I joined the latter vessel as she was completing at Brigham and Cowan's yard at South Shields late in 1978 and was her master for the next 2¹/₂years.

New Zealand Star followed the *Australia Star* from Haverton-Hill-on-Tees, the last ships to be built there:– 168.87 metres long, she had a beam of 25.2 metres and as no drydock on the Tees was wide enough to take her she was towed to the Tyne for completion. Her 6 cylinder sulzer was the last large marine engine built by Barclay Curle and Co; Whiteinch, and has a bhp of 17,400 (12,799 kw). The engineroom may be unmanned at night, in the modern manner. But as winter deepened strikes broke out in Britain and it looked as though we were in for another Winter of Discontent. Naturally neither the builders nor the shipowner wanted the new vessel delayed by a strike, so – as completion approached, I was instructed to come down next morning in my best uniform, with cap, and formally take over the ship. Then, if trouble broke out in't yard, we could sail away unhindered. Thus, with red ensign proudly flying aft, the Blue Star houseflag was hoisted with ceremony and I duly Took This Ship To Be My Lawful Vessel, as the shipyard and company managers cracked open a bottle of Newcastle Brown Ale and thanked the Lord for small mercies. Regardless of pending strikes, the winter weather was too awful for outside painting and a squad of shipyard painters sailed with us as far as the Panama Canal, going a long way to bringing us up to what would be expected of Blue Star's latest liner on her maiden voyage.

At Panama, as usual, I anchored just inside the breakwater waiting a pilot to take us alongside Cristobal for bunkers. When he came the pilot said the tugs were away undocking a passenger ship, we'd have to wait. "Unless", he said hopefully, "you could manage without tugs, Captain?".

Well, we had a powerful bow thruster – the first I had seen – so I agreed, and in we went, berthing alongside the pier with never a hitch. As is

Mr Edmund Vestey, the Owner, welcoming Mrs Thea Muldoon, who launched the vessel at Haverton Hill, and her husband, New Zealand's Prime Minister, aboard the *New Zealand Star* on her maiden voyage at New Plymouth, 2nd March 1979.

customary then, I invited the pilot in for a farewell drink. "Well thanks Cap, but no, I'd best get along home . . ." "Well, congratulations, anyway!" I said. "Congratulations? – " "Congratulations – this is the first time this ship has berthed anywhere – it's her maiden voyage – and you've done it without tugs!". "Gee Cap, I guess I'll take that drink after all. Thanks!"

I was now, I realised, in the new technological age. Thanks to our weather fax-machine I had received up to date positions of an Atlantic hurricane north of the Azores and had consequently taken a southerly course – longer in miles but shorter in time, so avoiding putting my new ship through the ordeals of hurricane weather.

Twenty four hours is a long time in port in a box boat, a measure of the cargo discharged and loaded – more in one day than a conventional ship could work in ten. That maiden arrival in New Plymouth we were greeted by Mr and Mrs Edmund Vestey, the owners, and New Zealand's Prime Minister and his Lady, Mr and Mrs Muldoon, who had launched the vessel into the Tees.

Because the container operation aims to keep ships at sea carrying freight-earning cargo, time in port is minimal. Cargo planning is carried out before the ship's arrival and has already been discussed with the ship by telex. In each port the cargo planner is now a key person (not always male I discovered, even in New Zealand!). Employed by the shipping company's representatives to co-ordinate the cargo working, the planner is provided with booking lists detailing cargo to load, be it general, chilled or hard frozen. He/she also has the ship's vital statistics which indicate cargo already onboard, plus the distribution of her oil fuel and water ballast. Helped by computer the planner decides on stowage in such a way that the first cargo to be discharged will be on top, and so on, so that her draft, trim and stability are at all times acceptable, within the given parameters. (Draft is the keel's depth below the waterline, trim is the difference between draft forward and aft. Stability, of course, ensures the ship remains right way up). Torque on the vessel's structure is also important and must not be allowed to strain the ship so advice is given about future use of fuel, fresh water and ballast.

Before containerisation these calculations were the work of the chief officer (the mate) but now insufficient time in port means all calculations are made before the vessel's arrival, by the planner. Unloading and loading often proceed simultaneously and the cargo plan is continuously updated. Streamlined customs documentation and modern cash-flow arrangements have lessened the paper-work formalities of cargo shipment – all part of the container revolution. A box boat's capacity is given in TEUs – twenty feet equivalent units. The standard international container is 20ft x 8ft x 8ft but there are variations – forty footers and general 20 footers are now often 8ft 6inches deep, but the TEU remains the standard norm, a measure of capacity following in the tradition of the tun, a barrel which became a 'ton' measurement of 100 cubic feet – still the way a ship's gross and nett 'tonnages' are calculated. Lloyd's Register gave out TEU capacity as 721.

When cargo work is in progress the ship's mates (as her deck officers are still internationally known) must be ever alert to see that containers almost identical in appearance showing no indication of contents, are moving in and out according to The Plan. The engineer officer in charge of refrigeration keeps pace with reefer cargo work, connecting and disconnecting cooling as required. The other engineer officers and motormen press on with the endless work of machinery maintenance, the deck crew takes advantage of a fine day to get overside, painting, and stewards load stores. Cargo work proceeds apace.

In this ship refrigerated containers in the holds are kept at the required temperatures by connecting each box to the ship's cold-air system, and also by cooling the holds themselves. Reefer containers carried on deck have their own clip-on refrigerating unit which takes electrical power from conveniently sited deck sockets, or are provided with their own individual 'integral' cooling motor. In a conventional ship hatches tend to be smaller than those in a box boat, where there is not underdeck space and all cargo movement in and out is vertical. The container is inserted by crane into the top of the cell's guides and slides down vertical steel rails into place. Hatches are wide as possible and space between the vertical and the ship's side is occupied with ballast water tanks and the internal underdeck walkway which runs right around the ship, often called the Burma Road, from which doors and ladders provide access. Weight concentration in a box boat is greater than in a conventional ship where cargo is distributed over several 'tweendecks as well as in the hold.

A week's work by old fashioned standards is compressed into 24 hours but because this port is tidal we must wait until high water to sail, allowing us a few hours respite in which the kindly New Zealanders look after us well.

Dwarfing the 'Sugarloaf Harbour's' three peaks, snowcapped Mount Egmont forms a striking departure backdrop – as we head down through Cook Strait, south to Port Chalmers – another prosperous harbour which put itself on the container map by sheer determination. This port for Dunedin used to resemble a musical play's stage set, from dark tunnel left to grey-and-white steepled church right, along a row of quaint waterfront buildings, a scene which can have changed little since the Albion Line's clipper *Dunedin* loaded the first cargo of New Zealand frozen lamb and carried it successfully to London in 1882. A century later the container revolution has rung up the curtain on a new setting – stacked rows of multi-coloured containers dominated by Otago Port's towering green portainer cranes. We were only hours here before sailing down the lovely harbour flanked by green hills dotted vividly with gorse, out past Tairoa Head where the nesting albatross broods over coastal gun emplacements built in a war of long ago. Also from long ago on our chart, are depths of water in fathoms, in hairline – 'from soundings by Lt James Cook in *HMS Endeavour,* 1769. . .'

Pilot away, we head south again past Bluff, through Fouveaux Strait, out into a stormy Tasman Sea. As the ship pitches and rolls her twist locks are tested to the full. These small sturdy fittings do away with time-consuming lashings and secure deck containers' corners to those directly below, down to the steel hatch lids. With three containers high – 24 feet – lurching over a crazy 60 degree arc gyrating wildly, they withstand enormous stresses. To minimise these I have by now eased the vessel onto a more comfortable course and reduced speed. She is a splendid seaboat and rides well but there is no point in belting along at 19 knots if this will damage the ship and her cargo – one heavy sea coming aboard can cause untold chaos and may endanger the vessel. After several hours of riding out the storm, wind abates from force 11 to a mere near gale. Sea and swell subside and I resume course for Banks Strait, between Tasmania and the Furneaux Group of islands. In Bass Strait another gale slows us down to make me more than half a day late into Melbourne. Time is money more than ever before but safety always comes first. Care of the ship, her people and cargo is always paramount.

The Port Phillip Pilot embarks off the boiling rip, hands me the green canvas bag of mail he has so thoughtfully brought out, and takes us in

Mid-ocean horserace meeting, in fancy dress, naturally!

through the Queenscliff Heads where a sharp starboard turn takes us into South Channel along to the Hovell Beacon and up the placid waters of the Bay to Swanson Dock. We'll spend up to 48 hours here as this is our trade's main port. Portainers load the ship, rythmic and steady, in and out, in and out, pausing only to move along to the next hatch.

The through-concept of containerisation means that as soon as cargo is aboard and hatches secure for sea it is time to go. The bow thruster, a small but 1,000 hp transverse propeller in the bulbous bow has its own diesel engine – care and joy of the engineer cadets – and enables us to sail without tugs if necessary; as well as berth without, as we found at Panama.

Passage across the Great Australian Bight to Fremantle is often boisterous especially if an unforecasted front sneaks up from the south as often happens. Fremantle provides a few hours' welcome break but is an optional port. Unless cargo bookings there are heavy it is cheaper to rail containers across the continent to Melbourne, thus saving Fremantle port dues. Our northward cargo includes not only such traditional exports as meat, butter, cheese, fruit, milk powder, wool and hides, but also the new manufactures – machinery, electrical equipment, prefabricated buildings, canned beer, – even New Zealand carpets for Persia! On deck amongst the containers are a large cement mixer and a couple of large trailers for carrying live sheep overland in Iraq.

This is February and we have fine weather across the Indian Ocean. A modern ship with a relatively small crew – we are 30 all told – can develop a

The Captain (Honest King Horn) and Chief Engineer (Yassa Marrowfat)
were the Bookies (of course!)

pleasant family atmosphere especially with a few wives and children aboard and perhaps even a couple of passengers. Highlight of the social scene is often the Horse Race, in which home-made wooden horses are pushed around a homemade canvas course laid out in the smokeroom to the throw of dice. We hold this meeting in home made fancy dress, fish and chips wrapped in newspaper are served at half time and the betting on the tote is fast and furious, with a proportion deducted for charity, often the RNLI but in this ship, the Seamen's Children's Home in Hull, of which several of our crew are Old Boys. The captain and chief engineer, heavily disguised, are the Bookies . . .

After eight days we come to Bombay having kept well out to sea up the Indian coast to avoid fishermen. In tiny boats, often little more than dug out canoes with a tiny rag of sail and only a candle as dubious lighting, often difficult to see by day – never mind at night! – they fish on the banks in their hundreds. The large dhows which still ply the Indian coastal trade are magnificent sights, three-masted, rigged with every conceivable sail. It seems they carry an Indian government subsidy and are, with their complete lack of mechanical power, a far cry from our own computerised data-logged satellite-navigated ship. But, we sometimes wonder as we race past them, might not they, with their low running costs and ecology-friendly simplicity, still be operating long after we in our modern vessels have priced ourselves out of business?

India did not welcome containerisation enthusiastically. Businessmen were for it, unions against for less men are employed. Politicians tried to balance the crying need for economic expansion with already desperate unemployment. Container ports were planned, speeches made passionately for and against. Until its new container port is built wise old Bombay cautiously allows fully cellular container ships with their own cranes or derricks (like us) to take precedence over the less sophisticated vessels which crowd the anchorage awaiting berths. If we can be in and out within 48 hours we get priority. If not, we join the queue and a long wait in a modern ship is economically unacceptable.

This voyage we are planned to load a thousand ton of cargo here for the Gulf. Frozen buffalo meat, chilled eggs (enough of which came aboard to create a local egg shortage!) and single deck buses, made in India. These are not containerised but a bus fits neatly into a container space on a hatch top and as many as possible are loaded. Under such circumstances the ship has some say in what goes where, co-operating with the tall bearded Sikh who is our cargo planner-cum-stevedore – an ex Indian naval officer who organises and controls his workforce brilliantly, bringing order out of seeming chaos daily.

Bombay is fascinating. Indira Dock, built long ago as Alexandra Dock, resembles London's Royal Docks in their heyday. Walkie-talkie radios are yet to come and coal-burning tugs toot their sirens in reply to whistle signals from immaculately white-uniformed pilots. Always over 97% utilised, the port is crowded with old cargo liners, many of them ex British, old friends under new colours. They wear now the ensigns of Malta, Panama, Liberia and a host of others – flags of convenience – and were made prematurely redundant when British and North European owners containerised their fleets (or went out of business). Now these old ships eke out their remaining years on the low-freight trades, much as did the latterday sailing ships when steam took the cream.

By what seem to us superhuman efforts our local team have loaded and secured within the allotted time and we depart, past dark grey warships in the naval dock on our way out. One of these was an elderly cruiser with wide, truncated funnel and six inch guns. Why was she vaguely familiar? Of course! She was the *Delhi,* formerly *HMS Achilles* of River Plate fame, the New Zealand member of Commodore Harwood's trio which trapped the *Graf Spee* in Montevideo in 1939. Laid up, she was due for demolition when a timely conversation between Mr Muldoon and Mrs Ghandi at a Commonwealth Prime Ministers' Conference resulted in a six inch gun turret and a containerful of her memorabilia being shipped to New Zealand, in our ship – naturally! – to be unloaded with nostalgic ceremony in New Plymouth for Auckland's famous Museum of Transport and Technology.

Skirting India's oil rigs across the Arabian Sea we come to Muttrah, near the ancient port of Muscat, in Oman, where a morning temperature of 120F in the shade (49C) made Bombay seem cool by comparison. Near this place Tim Severin was building his reincarnation of Sinbad the Sailor's ship in which, when completed, he cheerfully sailed to China.

Surrounded by Oman's harsh rugged brown hills Muttrah is an efficient little port swept into the container age by an enlightened Sultan. By Royal decree the dockers are all local lads (unlike most of the Gulf ports where labour is imported). Berobed Arabs pray to Allah at appointed times then swing cheerfully into action unloading a modern container ship in a delightful combination of old and new.

Early next morning we enter the Straits of Hormuz – often busy, occasionally almost deserted, sometimes foggy (at which times, of course, busy!). Traffic routing operates here now as it does in the English Channel and other busy waterways, and the chart's purple arrows direct us north of the Quions, those famous island rocks which spoke of misery or happiness to the tankermen of old, depending on whether they were going to or from the Gulf – without air-conditioning! We berth a few hours later at Jebel Ali, new container port in the Emirate of Dubai.

Ten years before, the Gulf's ports had been dhow and steamer anchorages with old wooden jetties, but growing oil prosperity brought increased trade and ships lay anchored for weeks awaiting berths. With no unemployment problems to delay containerisation every sheikdom built at least one container port – vast concrete complexes – and now, except in the Gulf's upper reaches, ships waited no longer. So it is in Jebel Ali where a swift container operation has us on our way to Bahrein in ten hours. Here, too, turnround is rapid, especially since better light buoys were installed enabling ships to sail and arrive around the clock instead of in daylight only. Within hours we are heading for Dammam, Saudi Arabia, where bunkers are cheaper than water (but our ship makes her own fresh water, enough across the Indian Ocean to last us around the Gulf). A sandstorm hits us between Dammam and Kuwait, filling nostrils and the air-conditioning system with fine brown dust – more like talcum than sand – reducing visibility to a couple of cables (two tenths of a mile). In daylight it is like steaming along surrounded by a tall sandstone wall – unpleasant but we are soon through it. Off Kuwait, a very busy port, I am directed to a spot in the crowded anchorage into which we squeeze between ships as best we can (blessing the bow thruster which enhances manoeuverability marvellously) until we can embark our pilot next day. This venerable Arab gentleman in naval uniform and Arab headress knows his harbour inside out and takes us past the shimmering city whose most 'Arabic' buildings are not mosques but water towers designed by an Italian! An old American passenger liner (Grace Line's *Santa Paula)* set in concrete is now a hotel and conference centre, supplementing the large, modern hotels which, like all Kuwait, are 'dry'.

This first voyage the Iranian revolution is in full swing and at first our local agent warns me against attempting to enter, fearing trouble against The Decadent West. It is soon realised however that, decadent or not, we are bringing much needed food so are grudgingly allowed in, to the port of Bandar Shahpour, soon to be renamed Bandar Khomeini, on the edge of the desert. Next port is Umm Qasr, in Iraq and we are the first British ship to have visited these parts for a long time. Our progress around the Gulf is rapid and cargo bookings changeable, so once again the ship has considerable say in what cargo goes where in the ship. Each port is in a different country, often barely on speaking terms with its neighbours and the speedy, efficient exchange of cargo information between ports, so vital in the box boat world, depends more upon the ship itself here than elsewhere. You carry your information with you. Our Umm Qasr agent stepped aboard at 10.30am, and yes, he would like a beer. Twelve hours later he was still with us, still steadily accepting canned hospitality. I had switched to lemonade long ago, after lunch, but our agent had a mighty thirst for Swan Lager. When he eventually rose ponderously to his feet to go home to Basra, this immense man flung his arms around my neck, gave me a smacking kiss, vowed eternal friendship and steered a remarkably steady course off across the desert road. He assured me his wives were always delighted to see him. Port Health was an extrovert who cheerfully promised to marry both my daughters and keep them in immense luxury, if I would just send them out here . . . Meanwhile, the chief officer got on with cargo work, unhindered by officialdom! Umm Qasr is a port without a town, developed well to the west of the Iran-dominated Shatt Al Arab on which stands Basra. The name means Mother Castle and the reputed site of the Garden of Eden is close by. Herds of camel roam the desert sands and the nights were cool.

A Russian ship was unloading military hardware surrounded by barbed wire entanglements and armed guards, which did not stop two of their officers coming to arrange a football match, bringing me a bottle of vodka as a goodwill offering. Our crew played theirs on a sunbaked sandy pitch and the score was a close run thing:– 7-1 in their favour. The losers shouted the after game drinks of course, which was just as well as the Russians told us their own ship had no bar and very little beer. Naturally, the day ended with Anglo-Soviet relations at a cordial level.

With the Iranian revolution, and international feelings at the head of the Gulf discernably tense, we were not sorry to leave those waters and return to Bombay, then Cochin in the state of Kerala, SW India. A delightful little place, Christianity came here not with the British or Portugese but with the apostle Thomas, he who doubted. Vasco da Gama was originally buried in the church here, before being returned in state to Lisbon, his final resting place. On the harbour undecked cargo craft drifted on the tide, single spritsailed vessels with curiously raised ends, their plans sewn together with leather thonging – looking remarkably like the Egyptian craft on ancient pyramid carvings. A boat propelled by many oarsmen threshed across the water like a war canoe, full to the gunwales with silver fish for the market, while ancient Chinese fish traps at the harbour mouth all show that people came here from far away, long ago.

Twelve hours in Colombo next, where the containers on the quay stretch as far as the eye can see, then round Dondra Head (southern tip of Sri Lanka), eastwards over the Bay of Bengal to Malacca Strait and Singapore where the magnificent container terminal has us discharged (frozen Cochin prawns) and loaded (piece goods and rubber) in a couple of hours. The most interesting sea passage of the voyage comes next; our return to New Plymouth. We pass from the South China Sea to the Java Sea through Karimata Strait, past the Kangeams and the Paternoster Islands (unlit except by lanterns on the fishing canoes in the lagoon). We cross the Flores Sea and the Arafura Sea, passing islands all the time until we come to Goods Island where we embark a Torres Strait pilot for the tricky run down inside the Great Barrier Reef to Cairns. Here he disembarks leaving me to navigate the scenic Whitsunday Passage, past the Coppersmith, into the Cora Sea via Capricorn Channel, lying, as its name suggests, right on the tropic. A straight course from here brings us back to New Plymouth in four days:– six weeks since our last visit.

New Zealand Star and *Australia Star* plied this trade as regular as clockwork, usually managing to make up the day or so occasionally lost in bad weather. Blue Star had pioneered this trade alone but were soon joined by others who realised its potentialities. Now, a joint service operates very successfully; it is a box boat voyage never dull. Hard and exacting for all onboard it is, nevertheless, fascinating, and we feel – worthwhile. In a highly competitive world we are carrying the cargo, delivering the goods.

New Zealand Star in Singapore's Eastern Roads, awaiting pilot.

6. THE BEACON HILL

Helping to pioneer a new trade had been vastly interesting, increasingly profitable to the company as it developed. But not all reefer cargo – even today – goes in containers. There is still a market for frozen meat carried in the old fashioned way – in bulk rather than in box. Blue Star already had a small, efficient fleet of suitable ships and were looking round for more. Whereas most of their fleet were custom-built and had had no owner outside the Vestey Group, new vessels take time to build with escalating expenditure, (not matter what 'fixed-price' clauses are built in to the contract). At that time there were plenty of good, second hand reefers on the market, displaced by containerisation from the old trades, their owners insufficiently interested in developing new services in which these ships could work. . . The *Westmorland* was one such vessel. Built on the Clyde in 1966 for the Federal Line, she had made an impact with her new Hallan derricks swung from biped masts. I had visited her to see them when she and the *Australia Star* were new ships together in Liverpool's Gladstone Dock. The Federal Line had long been part of P & O, who decided they no longer needed such vessels and sold her to a Lebanese gentleman named Fares. He painted her hull white with green boot topping, the funnel pillar-box red over white over red – the colours of the Lebanese flag – in which she looked very smart – and had her managed for him by the Newcastle firm of Common Brothers. Supplementing his fleet of livestock carriers which brought sheep on the hoof from West Australia to the Muslim Middle East, he discovered the highly competitive frozen lamb trade from New Zealand too risky. Port delays could make all the difference between profit and loss and the *Fares Reefer* (as he named her) suffered delays. Deciding to stick with the 'quick' rather than the 'dead', Mr Fares put her up for sale, to be snapped up by Blue Star – with her two sisters – and named her *Beacon Hill* of the newly formed Dunston Shipping Company. A line of twenty two small black rectangles painted into the while funnel band was the only colourscheme change and she carried a full cargo of New Zealand lamb for Bandar Abbas in Iran when I joined her towards the end of December 1981, in Khawr Fakkan. Where?

Khawr Fakkan, United Arab Emirates, just outside the Gulf, south of the Straits of Hormuz on the Gulf of Oman's western shore. At that time the outer anchorage off Khawr Fakkan was filled with tankers awaiting orders. *Beacon Hill* had joined this illustrious company, albeit closer inshore, when I was taken out to her in the agent's launch, having been driven over the mountainous peninsular from Dubai Airport. As we passed under her stern to approach the gangway I saw her port of registry was Hong Kong and recalled that she had been just too old to be accepted by Singapore, where Blue Star's

Beacon Hill loading frozen lamb at Timaru, New Zealand.

Far Eastern Fleet was then registered. I knew she had British officers and a Singapore Chinese crew, Indian radio officer. My old friend Ian MacKillop was her captain, now heading home for a spell of leave. Proudly he showed me round his ship – the company's latest – carefully instructed me in the care of his pot plants – and went off home rejoicing. I expected to weigh anchor and sail at once, but was told to wait.

The Iranians, it seemed, were well behind with payments for previous deliveries and the New Zealand Meat Exporters were concerned. Many millions of dollars were at stake. It had been decided that when they showed the colour of their money for past shipments, the Iranians could have the *Beacon Hill's*. Not before!

So we waited. Khawr (an inlet of the sea) Fakkan had until recently been a tiny fishing port, backed by rugged desolate mountains. For most of the year these were an arid reddish brown but after the very occasional shower of rain grass grew, bushes burst into leaf and flowers bloomed overnight – before it all withered again. The Arab Ruler had realised that, strategically placed outside the Gulf, it would make an ideal container terminal for ships whose owners were not keen on sending their vessels 'inside' in such troubled times. Once unloaded in Khawr Fakkan, containers could be transhipped in feeder vessels, or trucked overland up the Gulf on the fine highways which now were being built all the way to Iraq. . .

Day after hot, sunlit day followed dawns of incredible beauty. As the sun rose 'out of a shining sea', its light crept down the mountains turning deep

66

Khawr Fakkan

purple into glowing orange. The sky remained a clear blue, the weather calm, and one morning I took our motor lifeboat in to pay my respects to the harbour master – a Scot, I found – who had been a Clyde pilot when the *Westmorland* was new. He had, in fact, been her first ever pilot, taking her from the shipyard. Surprisingly, a whole host of the Port People turned out to be British and as a result there was none of the tiresome bureaucratic formality and paperwork which surrounds so many of the Gulf States' port operations.

Finding my way round the *Beacon Hill* I saw her as a splendid vessel in every way. Main engine was the same as the *Australia Star's,* a Vickers' Sulzer, her equipment was modern and rapidly being brought up to company standards. The purser, Alan Greaves, was an old friend from previous ships, and showed me his storerooms. In the meatroom lay a considerable quantity of prime beef steak in perfect condition, not shown on any of the books. This was in addition to our already more-than-adequate supplies and we could only surmise it had been private stocks of her previous officers who had not removed it when they left the ship. What to do? Well, the obvious answer was to have a barbeque and invite the harbour master, port manager – a few others perhaps, and their wives. Sunday night? Invitations were issued and gratefully accepted:– an expat population always welcomes a little variety! The pilot launch brought them out. Our well-appointed officers' smokeroom had been provided by her past people with chairs fashioned out of old whisky barrels, varnished – there was even a tiny dance floor! Our purser was a dab hand at the barbeque, the guests bought their drinks at the bar (and paid generously) while we supplied the food free. It was a good night and became a regular Sunday fixture, for the stocks of beef seemed bottomless. A Swedish ship on charter came in, also meat-laden and likewise restrained from proceeding further, while the occasional Blue Star came and went on other lawful occasions. While with us they all became members of 'the club'.

But it was noised abroad that the Iranians may come over and help themselves to our cargo, which they saw as legitimately theirs. They might even attempt a hijack, and if they came armed (as they would) how could we stop them? At that time the Revolutionary Guard were very much inclined to attack any merchant ship which took their fancy – coming alongside in fast motorboats with guns blazing. Some of the results we had seen were horrendous. So, the meat fleet was brought into port, alongside the quay, which kept us safe and of course made it easier for the Port People to visit us

It was a strange life. I was on twelve hours' notice to proceed and a state of alertness had to be maintained – but time otherwise stood still.

The old dhow harbour at the head of the inlet was constantly busy. At low water the little ships there would be scrubbed down by their crews, the underwater areas recoated with what looked like white lead and tallow, while the topsides were oiled and varnished. The magical sound of caulking mallets hung in the air. Tiny fish laid out to dry in their millions were best avoided, walked well away from, as they rotted in the sun. One morning a two masted dhow crept in under sail! This was rare as most of these craft depended on their engines, only keeping the sails 'in case'. On passage from Bombay to Dubai however her engine had failed and she had put in for repairs, the winds being light and flukey and not to be relied upon to get her to Dubai before food and water ran out. Such Port of Refuge Procedure is as old as shipping itself. It transpired that our Indian Sparks was a relative of her owner/master, who invited us round. Stepping aboard the *Gift From God* (as her name translated) was a leap into the past. Rigging was all of hemp, set up with dead-eyes. Only accommodation was the bare wheelhouse in which the captain slept on a wooden pallet, when not using the large steering wheel, the magnetic compass, or operating the engine control lever (bridge control!). His crew slept around the decks, or in the cargo in inclement weather. The galley was a portable out-on-deck little brick and iron stove over which crouched the cook, blowing the charcoal embers into a glow beneath a pot of curry. Toilets were, of course, a pair of open thunderboxes hung over the stern port and starboard. She was employed in the ancient triangular trade between India, the Gulf and the East Coast of Africa and when I admired his vessel's sturdy construction her owner told me she was over thirty years old. He had laid her up in Bombay twenty years ago, when he went into business ashore. When this business (exporting shrimps) failed, he had returned to the calling of his fathers and refitted the old family sailing ship. But, as he smilingly told me, she did not like having an engine, and frequently broke down. . .

Khawr Fakkan's only hotel was the Holiday Inn (British manager) – a splendid sanctuary with swimming pool, the hub of social activity as Christmas approached. By tradition, Captain James Peattie the harbour master would be Santa Claus at the children's Christmas Party, but poor Jim suddenly went down with 'flu. Would I officiate instead? This was new experience! The children, mostly British but including German and Dutch, with a few from india and Pakistan, assembled in a lounge with their parents, saucer-eyed at this suitably-attired old man who, with many a 'Ho-ho-ho!' told them his reindeer had been unable to haul the sledge through the mountain passes from the North Pole this year because of insufficient snow – etc. The school headmaster knew all their names and was able to brief me with family history as each child stepped up to take a present. Sotto voce. – 'Mary, aged four, has new baby brother John, Daddy hoping to get in from his job as an outback engineer tomorrow. . .' so I was able to chat knowledgeably with Mary who – like the others, seemed to accept my bona fides quite naturally. The *Halifax Star* came in and John Greenwell, third engineer, organised his choir to join with ours and sing carols at the Holiday Inn. The Port People still tell me they had never seen a Christmas quite like it. As the old year drew to a close my orders came:– 'Proceed to Bandar Abbas to arrive 0600 January 1st.' So Khawr Fakkn had to manage its Hogmanay without us.

The long line of anchored ships all blew deafening blasts on their sirens when the New Year came in, to which we replied as strains of 'Auld' Lang Syne in many languages floated over the water. Next morning, across the Straits of Hormuz, an Irani warship addressed me in Oxford English, wishing me a Happy New Year, welcoming me to the Islamic Republic and politely requesting me to anchor in the appointed spot off the town.

The *Beacon Hill* had collected – before I joined – a considerable number of old empty 45 gallon oil drums, about which I wondered, receiving only shaken heads and I-don't-knows. Realisation dawned however when a small local craft nudged furtively along our offshore side – away from prying Revolutionary Eyes, – laden with freshly caught prawns and fish. The deal was made by our purser who had been here before; – delicious!

The old port of Bandar Abbas, now mainly a naval base – lay 72 miles east along the coast, with the white-painted ex Italian liner *Michelangelo* acting as naval barracks, a conspicuous 'landmark'. The new commercial port had been planned and begun in the Shah's time but work stopped when the Revolutionary Council decided Iran wanted no truck with Outside (Western) Corruption. So it languished for a spell, contract work only

And are you being a good girl?

A receptive audience for Santa.

resuming when the Revolutionary Council reminded itself that the Revolution had promised the people Food Not Guns. And here we were, with Food! The approach was made interesting by leading-lights and beacons as yet incomplete and there was still some dredging to be done, but we arrived eventually, alongside a dusty, unsurfaced wharf with strictly limited facilities and equipment. However, our cargo went out in twenty-ton slingloads thanks to our marvellous Hallen derricks, to be loaded into freezer lorries for the long drive up through the mountains to Teheran. To our surprise we found that many of these lorries and their drivers were Bulgarian, who had been initially employed to carry fruit and veg from Bulgaria to Teheran. In Iran they had been offered extra money to – 'Just go down to Bandar Abbas for a load of meat. . .' an offer too good to refuse. But when upon their return they politely asked for their wages they were told they would be paid after another journey: an all too common trap in this part of the world. But, in his 'back shop', Alan Greaves looked after them handsomely with food and drink helping to relieve, we felt, the drudgery of their lot.

I imagined we were living onboard under conditions not greatly different from those obtaining on ships in Russian ports after the 1918 revolution and we dwelt in daily dread of a visit from the Revolutionary Guard. When they did put in a sudden appearance – young men barely out of their teens, unshaven, armed to the teeth, they inspected our cabins very thoroughly, asked if we had any chocolate, smiled sadly when we shook our heads, and clattered off ashore. But one never knew when they would come in earnest – arrests and subsequent floggings were being made – and it was said that even the smell of alcohol drive them crazy.

The agent entertained me at his house one evening. Over the dockside gatehouse the long, green white and red banner emblazoned with the revolutionary centre-symbol, floated lazily in the setting sun. Heavily armed young soldiers suspiciously scrutinised my identity card and seaman's pass, searched me, then curtly nodded me on. The agent's driver spoke no English but drove at great speed over a dusty desert road until we came to an isolated house resembling a Beau Geste Fort rather than a civilian dwelling. Stopping outside a huge iron-studded wooden door set in a high stone wall, the driver leaned out and tugged at an ornate bell rope. To my astonishment the door was opened by a shyly smiling girl, the agent's daughter, who – in perfect English – bade me welcome; "Please come in Captain Kinghorn". Fountains played in a courtyard, in the house we sat on silken cushions strewn across the floor, ate a sumptuous Iranian meal, and watched Benny Hill on video! Upon my return to the docks the guards made an elaborate point of smelling my breath. Charming!

Cargo all satisfactorily discharged, we sailed on 13th January. I was asked by the agent to turn a blind eye to any stowaways, as to return them

71

would surely guarantee their death sentence. Memories came back of a late neighbour whose late father had been captain of a British tramp steamer loading wheat in Odessa in 1919. *His* stowaways turned out to be an archduke and family who rewarded my friend's family so handsomely for saving them from the Bolsheviks that he was able to retire when he got home . . . but the *Beacon Hill* had no such luck!

It was good to return to the relaxed atmosphere of Khawr Fakkan for another fortnight, by which time stocks of barbeque beef were getting low. I received the telex in the nick of time – 'Proceed towards Fremantle'. In mid-Indian Ocean fresh orders told me to stop and drift, while our London Office sought us lucrative employment. For ten days we drifted, without satellite navigator but taking sights daily. We drifted – final position was 421 miles NW of where we had stopped! Our Singapore crew were keen fishermen and caught sharks daily. When one shark gave birth to a baby shark while being hauled aboard however, even our hard-nosed Chinamen felt sorry for her, and let her go.

After our long drift I was re-ordered to Fremantle where Captain MacKillop rejoined and – pot plants intact – I flew home. He subsequently took the *Beacon Hill* to Valparaiso to load fruit for Europe. By sailing far south of Cape Horn he avoided the Falklands War unmolested, but the old ship went to scrap four years later when the Iranian meat contract expired, some time later. She had been a profitable, if short term, investment.

7. ROLLING DOWN TO RIO

The Falklands Conflict was drawing to its close when I joined Lamport and Holt's SD14 *Browning* in Liverpool on 7th June 1982. British ships had ceased visiting Argentina for the duration but trade with Brazil was booming. Having completed unloading and secured for sea, we sailed for Glasgow on 11th June, arriving next day. Since I had last sailed up the Clyde fourteen years previously, unbelievable changes had taken place and now grass and trees grew where mighty ships had once been built. Apart from Yarrows where considerable naval construction was in hand, the river presented a truly rural appearance. We were the only cargo ship in King George V Dock, where blackberry bushes encroached all around and rabbits came out to play in the evenings, on what had once been a busy quay.

For the next two weeks we loaded bagged malt for Brazil's Brahma Brewery, general cargo and cased whisky for Recife and Salvador. The pace was leisurely, no overtime being worked and there was time for my wife and me to visit old friends in the city and walk the famous banks of Loch Lomond, especially bonny in the bloom of summer.

The SD14 represented the last batch of 'Liberty Replacement' standardised construction to come out of Sunderland and as such helped to prolong the port as a shipbuilding town well into its final decade. It was appropriate that this replacement for the original vessel be built here, for it was in Sunderland that the original Liberty Ship concept was born over forty years previously.

The *Browning*, built in 1979, was one of four sisters owned by Lamport and Holt, the last ships built for this old Liverpool company. Her class sisters *Belloc, Bronte* and *Boswell* were identical but by mid-1982 *Belloc* had already been sold abroad and it seemed only a matter of time before the others were also displaced by fully cellular container ships. As we sailed from Glasgow on 25th June, despite a gloomy wet evening with even gloomier weather forecast, we all felt a sense of relief induced by the Argentine surrender in the Falklands.

The *Browning's* funnel was not quite authentic according to the company's ancient rules which stated that colours must be 'blue for three sevenths of its lower part, white and black for two sevenths each above the blue'. But as the mate remarked, "Those rules were probably made for coal-burners with woodbine funnels. . ." and ours certainly looked fine, one seventh black over three sevenths white over regulation three sevenths blue. There was no doubting her proud ownership and she was maintained like a yacht – our Liverpool bosun saw to that! We carried the L & H badge on our stem and always flew the City of Liverpool coat of arms flag as stemjack in

Lamport & Holt Line's *Browning. (FotoFlite)*

port. The British crew of thirty were keen as mustard. Predominantly Liverpudlian as befitted her port of registry, they came also from St Albans and South Africa, Glasgow and Sunderland, York and Salford, Birmingham and Yarmouth, Barry and Lambeth, Chester, Darlington and North Shields – a good mixture! We came complete with one of those hardy Poles who became British during World War II, in the engineroom.

Main engine was a Sulzer – a quaint little motor in the eyes of those accustomed to the power of larger vessels but quite capable of driving her along at 16.3 knots over a passage on a mean daily consumption of 24.2 tons of heavy oil. She was able to manoeuvre on heavy oil into and out of port and was the first ship to have the company-designed Star Blender, an invention which enabled heavy oil to be mixed with the lighter diesel oil on demand, for the ship's auxiliary engines thus contributing greatly to fuel cost savings. Heavy weather from ahead, I found, tended to cause her to slow down without being asked but her overall performance compared well with the turbine steamer *Dunedin Star* of similar size in which I had sailed as chief officer twenty years previously and which burned 46 tons of the same fuel per day for slightly less speed. The *Browning* also evaporated ample fresh water for her daily need of ten tons per day though of course this facility was not employed in coastal waters where pollution exists, organic if invisible.

Navigation equipment included gyro compass and radar but lacked that modern marvel, satellite navigator, so distance steamed was measured on a

Walker's Patent Log – an age-old device which streams a 65-fathom line astern, at the end of which is a bronze 18 inch long streamlined rotator with curved fins so designed that its revolutions caused by the ship's way through the water measure distance travelled. Read on a special clock fitted to the taffrail, this transmits electrically to a similar clock in the chartroom, on the bridge. Nineteenth century sailing ships carried similar equipment and I was delighted to find that *Browning's* was as accurate a measure of our progress through the water as could be desired. And the absence of 'satnav' brought us back to basics, using the sextant whenever a sighting of the heavenly bodies coinciding with a sharp horizon made astro navigation possible.

The *Browning's* accommodation, though below the best of modern standards (juniors shared a bathroom between two for instance, and there were no baths, only showers) was far above that in the basic SD14, tastefully appointed and nicely finished. As with cars, you get what you pay for, if you're lucky.

For carrying cargo she was right up to date, with a total capacity of 689,278 cubic feet in five holds, the forward four of which, before the bridge, had 'tweendecks, with sliding steel hatchcovers and Velé swinging derricks, one to each hatch. The biggest, with a safe working load of 26 tonnes was at No.2 hatch; number one, three and four had 22-tonners, while Number 5 was served by a pair of 5 tonne derricks in union purchase. A handy vessel!

Crossing the Atlantic from NE to SW showed the SD14 to be a great roller – she rolled all the way and the first trippers – once they got used to the motion – insisted that "this one would roll on damp grass" (as first trippers always do).

On 7th July we came to Recife – Pernambuco – and anchored for the night, to be granted entry next day at first light. Recife is Portuguese for 'reef' – the reef sheltering the entrance to the port of this colourful city which has a population now of one million. Skyscrapers stretch for miles along the palm-fringed shore, up and down the coast. But despite the modernity I was pleased to see a couple of *jangada* the ancient traditional balsa-wood sailing fishing craft beating in from sea as we approached. The port was busier than normal (at Argentine expense?) and urgency was stressed as we tied up at ten am. Approaching the berth – according to port custom – we let go the port anchor to act as a brake to check the scend which would otherwise have ranged us constantly back and forward along the quay. Even the sheltering reef does not keep out all the South Atlantic rollers.

During our two days there I had time to look around. A few miles north is Olinda with its conspicuous ship-in-a-bottle black-and-white-striped lighthouse towering above the palms on the crest of a headland. In its lee shelters a small village with thriving market place. In a glorious sunset the ornate pastel shaded buildings provided a perfect backdrop for the glowing costumes of the people and their stalls, a scene enhanced by cathedral bells across the square tolling in deep-toned Angelus. From here the view of the sea and the city was breathtakingly beautiful in the evening light – a vista which quite compensated for the minor discomforts of rolling out from the Clyde.

When we came to leave Recife I had first to heave the anchor home. It was now I discovered another SD14 characteristic:– you can heave the ship up to the anchor but not the anchor up to the ship, until you are vertically above it!

Twenty four hours later we entered the Bay of All the Saints and came to Salvador which was probably more famous when it was Bahia, the ancient capital. Over a century and a half ago the Portuguese Viceroy seized the opportunity of current liberal feeling and proclaimed himself the Emperor of Brazil, establishing brief popularity by freeing the slaves. This part of South America – and it will be seen on the map – borders the narrowest part of the Atlantic, less than 1,650 miles from the bulge of Africa. It is almost certain that people crossed here habitually long before the white men came, which probably explains the rich mixture of races entwined in the modern Brazilian population.

At each port we saw SD14s under various flags and at one time found ourselves alongside a quay with Argentine SD14s for and aft. During the previous voyage, when the Falklands War was at its height, local newspapers had tried to arouse antagonism between ships of both sides – without effect. We like to think that merchant seamen have more sense than to become stooges of any local press – and so it turned out to be. Each simply pretended the other was not there.

Salvador is indeed a beautiful city, as our Basque agent showed me. Parking his car in one of the numerous picturesque squares, he was immediately approached by two boys who offered to guard his car while we went sightseeing. After lively discussion they cheerfully agreed a suitable fee for this service and off we went. When I asked the agent why he agreed to pay anything at all he smilingly told me that had he not 'played the game' we would indubitably return to find a car minus its wheels!

Built largely in Portuguese colonial style, Salvador has at least one church with high altar wrought in pure gold from floor to ceiling. Restaurants provided traditional Brazilian food served by black 'slave girls' dressed all in white. In the harbour local sailing craft took visitors on colourful trips around the bay. Tourism was booming. To me, the gulf existing between rich and poor seemed to be bridged by a united determination to enjoy life to the full and I have rarely seen such cheerful people.

By the time we left Salvador most of our cargo was out and we rode high and light in the water. The vast size of Brazil became apparent when we set off for our next port, Rio Grande do Sul, over 1,400 miles to the south. South-westerly gales up to force 10 combined with a heavy swell to force us well out into the South Atlantic. She seemed to want to head for the Falklands rather than coastwise to Rio Grande – and for the first time for many years I was unable to make my ship go in the required direction. Speed had to be reduced to avoid pounding – the slamming of a ship's forefoot onto the sea which can cause untold structural damage if allowed. At five knots we were making more leeway than headway – rolling of course! – sliding sideways out to sea. Potted plants shot in all directions depositing soil and foliage overall, freely across my carpet and furniture, but at first light on 14th July, the cloud lifted and the chief officer, keeping the 4-8 watch, got good star sights. We were forty miles off course. As the sun rose in splendour over a tumultuous sea, wind and swell moderated to allow us to head in – only a day late – to find that, after all, we had to anchor for another 36 hours awaiting our berth. The tugs here had Lamport and Holt funnels and to an imaginative observer we must have resembled a duck with her brood of ducklings as we came alongside the quay. The chief engineer and I went down onto the quay to inspect the propeller, while a junior engineer turned it slowly from within on the electric turning gear. It pays to inspect your prop frequently on this coast as plenty of huge logs washed down the rivers present hidden hazards, floating awash as they do. But this time all was well – no sign of cracks or damage.

Argentine bulk carriers lay alongside a nearby mill pumping out soya beans through elevators amid clouds of white dust. The beans are processed into many diverse manufactured foods, mostly re-exported to Third World countries and are big business here. In the wild marshlands across the river I watched numerous waterfowl and heron fishing. Persons seeing my binoculars thought I had discovered some exotic nudist bathing beach . . .

Here we began loading in earnest for Liverpool – tobacco and timber, most of the latter in the shape of fashioned doors and household furniture Industria Brasilia!

I tried to exchange our Walport Films here – three 'feature films' of three reels each in a galvanised box. But although exchange facilities were advertised, – , for reasons known only to themselves the Customs would not allow a transaction to take place. The era of such films lasted about twenty years in the British Merchant Navy but was clearly drawing to an end. The films were played upon the hired Bell & Howell projector onto a large, usually homemade screen, and Movie Nite was an occasion with time for social chit-chat and a drink from the bar in between reels. But the ubiquitous video was taking over. With no projector or screen needed the video is simpler – probably the reason it now plays non-stop! But it constitutes less of an evening 'occasion'.

A day's run took us up the coast to Itajai where we anchored-off for five and a half days in heavy swell, rolling steadily, awaiting our berth. 'Ours' was occupied by a Brazilian ship with salt from the north, another major coastwise cargo. But her salt had become damp and congealed into solid rock

Browning at Paranagua, Brazil, loading for Liverpool.

necessitating pneumatic drillwork to break it out chunk by chunk – a time-consuming process which could not of course be undertaken out here at anchor. And there were no spare berths where she could have laid-by. Alongside at last we loaded Brazilian hardwoods and sailed on 28th July for Paranagua – 'Paddy M'Graw' to our Liverpudlians.

We berthed there on arrival next afternoon, without delay. Coming alongside a mooring rope jammed, then jumped off the bitts, striking a sailor on the ankle, causing a multiple fracture. There was no doctor onboard of course, but the shore doctor pinned and plastered. Our lad knew Paranagua well and had no objection to a short spell in hospital there. No matter how careful everyone is, a ship is always a potentially dangerous workplace, liable to move unpredictably through all three dimensions. Our man expressed the feelings of all of us – his injury could have been much worse had the rope caught him, for instance, amidships instead of across the ankle. The cook slipped in the mud at the foot of the gangway and returned five stitches later The purser was treated for gout. Medically speaking, it was a quiet voyage.

As we came in I had espied a neat little white clipper-stemmed yellow-funnelled survey ship alongside, near our berth. I read her name, *Almirante Saldanha* and the pilot confirmed she was formerly the four-masted schooner schoolship of that same name. Her still-rigged sisters are Spain's *Juan Sebastian D'Elcano* and Chile's *Esmeralda* compared with which she now seemed strangely small and insignificant. But perhaps Brazil has lost interest

78

in sail training. Her three masted barque *Guanabara* which passed to Brazil after the war, a sister to the USCG *Eagle* and other's of Hitler's Kreigsmarine, was sold to Portugal and is now their *Sagres*.

Our next port was Santos where we anchored in the bay on 30th July. This anchorage is notorious for the activities of pirates who board ship by night and plunder cargo, ropes, tarpaulins, personal possessions and money – especially money. They come aboard armed and prevention is much better than cure. Hang lights over the side. Floodlight your decks, maintain a constant deckwatch, keep hoses at the ready, be prepared to blow deafening blasts upon the ship's siren. This has been found to instil panic into pirate hearts, for the modern pirate depends upon stealth and will rarely board if he knows he has been spotted. After all, he doesn't know we are unarmed – a fact which many shore-abiding law-abiding citizens find rather hard and not a little disappointing to accept. But the 'Captain's Sixgun' is strictly Hollywood – and could easily create more problems than it solved were it really carried. In British ships, that is – I cannot speak for the others.

Having successfully eluded pirates – a wet, stormy night probably helped – we moored to Santos's long riverside waterfront quay next day and loading completed with a swing. All was for Liverpool discharge.

Some was consigned to Manchester but *Browning's* high superstructure and fixed funnel precluded her passage through the Ship Canal, unlike the steamers of an earlier era with their telescopic topmasts and removable funnel-tops specially designed to pass under low bridges. Probably road haulage is now handier and cheaper, a contributing factor to that famous waterway's demise.

Our cargo included bales of silk and rayon, cotton, wool and timber in the raw and fashioned, including one hundred tonnes of broomsticks! Peanuts and Brazil nuts – of course – corned beef and coffee, much of it securely locked in containers carried three high on deck as well as down below, giving the impression that we were now a box boat.

Whilst in Santos one quiet, sunny afternoon before the shift returned from its mealbreak, we watched a small green boat rowed by two lads cross the river from the far shore and park alongside the Argentine vessel *Marfrio* which lay eastern of us. As we watched a grapnel on a line was flung up and over her rail and the two young men shinned up it with amazing agility. It dawned upon us that they were probably up to no good and forthwith one of our number shot out on deck and bellowed at them "loud and clear". They may not have understood English perfectly but some expressions are international and, as in an old silent comic film, the villains dropped back into their green boat and rowed with desperate haste across the river whence they had come. By the time we had alerted the watchman they had, of course, vanished, but at least the *Marfrio* remained unmolested, on that occasion at any rate.

Browing approaching the Brazilian island of Fernando de Noronha

We left Brazil on 4th August with compliments ringing in our ears. The chief officer had run a particularly efficient cargo operation and we had committed none of those disastrously accidental crimes caused by pumping oil into the harbour or smoke from our funnel into Brazil's clear air. We counted our blessings and with our little ship fully laden, looking a picture of smartness, sailed for home.

Still rolling she crossed the Atlantic in fourteen days, passing the curiously lop-sided mountain on the island of Fernando de Noronha, once a Brazilian penal settlement, now – we were told – a holiday paradise. Another sunny afternoon saw us passing through Gladstone Lock Entrance into the Royal Seaforth Dock on 18th August. We seemed to be the only working ship in the port. Our two remaining sisters, *Boswell* and *Bronte* were laid up – forlorn ships awaiting sale in a forlorn setting. We felt the docks somehow resembled England as it had been fifteen hundred years before, after the Romans left – with elegant buildings and complex systems falling into ugly desuetude.

After a few more voyages *Browning* herself was sold to the Chinese, having filled her intended purpose of bridging the gap between the old, break-bulk cargo ships and the fully containerised 'mode'.

I saw her last year at Shanghai, now named *Fortunate Star* and she must still have a good bosun – she looked immaculate!

8.   THE FALKLANDS

I was enjoying home leave in between ships when, on April 1st 1982, Argentina invaded the Falklands. My first reaction was total disbelief, followed by dull astonishment. Of course Argentina had – in theory – coveted those wild and lonely islands for generations, using the doubtfully valid argument that since they took independence from Spain last century, all that which had been Spanish should now be theirs.

On my first trip to Buenos Aires over thirty years previously the General Post Office was decorated with a handsome mural map of Argentina, on which the 'Malvinas' were, of course, prominently depicted. I recall good humoured discussion over this with local persons and soon came to realise that – sure, they said, the 'Malvinas' should be theirs, but the Argentinian is strictly an urban person, a lover of the bright city lights – in no way a pioneer of the wide open spaces far from home as a permanent way of life. And the Falklands offer as much sophisticated Nitelife as the average Hebridean village which Port Stanley so closely resembles. I was told by a reliable source that some time during the nineteen thirties, London offered Argentina the Falklands lock, stock and barrel in return for a new British Embassy in Buenos Aires – to be politely told, "thanks but no thanks!".

But, like many another ruler seeing a sudden overseas conquest as a successful means of distracting his population from its own considerable homespun grievances, President Galtieri took the big step. At least, his armed forces did. They went, they saw, they conquered – and soon were chased back home – with few of their lads who did the fighting ever wishing to return. Led to believe they were liberating an Argentine population from the hated British yoke, they were astonished when – as their heavy armoured personnel carriers rumbled through Stanley's little streets – they found a British population speaking English, smoking English cigarettes – so different from their own brands – and who looked upon these 'muchachos de la guerra' with a mixture of concern and pity. The Argentine officers took comfortable billets in town, posting their inexperienced rookies (stiffened by a hard core of marines battle-hardened in Argentina's own internal struggles) to the rugged terrain swept by snow, rain and biting winds, to fend as best they could until the avenging British returned. It became not uncommon for a Falklands back door to be knocked upon of an evening and opened to find a group of tired, frightened, shivering young men from the conquering army asking – "Please can you spare us cup of tea, Missus?"

To remove this extraordinary invasion Britain mustered her forces in a remarkably efficient manner. To provide transport much of our Merchant Navy became STUFT – Ships Taken Up From Trade – one of them the

Avelona Star with "camouflaged" funnel in Port William, Falklands, 1982.

Avelona Star, currently unloading Cape apples at Sheerness. Swiftly transformed into a Garrison Rations Supply Ship at Portsmouth, a small helipad was erected aft while portacabins on the bridge deck provided accommodation for the dozen or so MOD civilian staff who would see to her cargo. This now included not only the residue of the Cape apples and other refrigerated foodstuffs, but a ship-full of everything a modern army needs to survive in the field, from Mars Bars to toilet rolls.

The striking Blue Star funnel was dramatically toned down as a form of camouflage. Grey paint was intended but a sudden shortage in Portsmouth at the time led to white paint being substituted which, beneath the black funnel-top and over the white superstructure and grey hull melted uncannily well into the Falklands landscape.

Captain Hugh Dyer took her down south, often blacked out and in convoy (where her normal speed was found too much for her escorts) – not using radar in case echoes were picked up by the enemy, to arrive in the Falklands soon after the Argentine surrender. Hugh was already overdue for voyage leave and I was sent down as a passenger in the *Norland* to relieve him. Pot plants were, of course, committed to my care, and a brief appraisal of the current situation given. At the time it was felt the Argentinians may make a savage come-back – not in their previous armed might but in the form of commando raids, which would have been all too easy to carry out on that wild, indefensible coast. . . So we still practised blackout and kept on a semi-war footing. But as time passed and the situation in Buenos Aires became

82

Avelona Star unloading in a snowstorm, Port William, Falklands, 1982.

less clouded it was felt that no further attacks were imminent and life grew more relaxed. The famous Falklands Weather kept us on our toes. Ships occasionally blew ashore in blizzards but none of those keeping a proper, seamanlike watch did; – and life settled down – unloading our cargo day by day as required. At first we were anchored, with many other ships, in the outer harbour of Port William into which the South Atlantic frequently rolled, adding interest to our work of transferring cargo onto the long, oblong flat barges known as mexefloats. As the ship rolled, our own crew drove the ship's cranes while the MOD lads acted as stevedores, slithering around our snowy decks. Occasionally a Wessex helicopter would hover overhead, hoisting a load on a 60 foot strop, taking it to some urgent destination inland. In those early days – only a few weeks after hostilities ceased – there was much coming and going of helicopters. I was taken to the dentist in one – a Sea King – and another time was taken for a ride in a little Scout, over the Yomping Trail to San Carlos Water and back. Our purser Alan Greaves, of *Beacon Hill* fame, soon established our reputation for hospitality, which instantly paid us all kinds of dividends. The permanently stationed deep-sea tugs *Irishman* and *Yorkshireman* provided us occasionally with fresh water while we supplied them with beer. . . On one auspicious occasion we were visited by an Admiral accompanied by SNOFI (Senior Naval Officer Falkland Islands – a fully fledged RN captain). Over lunch I mentioned that we had discovered that while our armed forces were now being quite well provided for – the civilian population were less fortunate. The Argentine invaders had indiscriminately slaughtered their cattle, sheep and most of the poultry, while fresh fruit had faded into memory of what seemed like long ago. . . The Admiral looked at SNOFI and was sure we could help here, couldn't we? After all, the war had been fought for the civilians. So, of course we helped. The little passengership *St. Helena* was coming to the end of her Falklands work and her captain kindly passed on to me his grey fibreglass whaler,

Part of "that class" aboard the *Avelona Star* in the Falklands with
Miss Hands, their teacher.

originally the property of HMS *Fife*. This we overhauled and painted, white
above and blue below, varnished within and carrying Blue Star mermaids on
her bow badges, with the new name *Starlet* in Old English lettering. Tiddley!
She was faster than our motor lifeboat and anyway the Department of
Transport were growing tired (they said) of "ships' lifeboats being in constant
use as jollyboats". So in our little *Starlet,* entrusted to the care of Second
Officer Bruce Campbell, a New Zealander full of the required keenness, we
took provisions ashore, sometimes to church but usually to the school, whence
they were effectively distributed around the town. I even acted as school
milkman once, trundling a barrowload of cartoned Long Life up from the
Public Jetty to hand out in the schoolyard at playtime. . .

Thus we came to know and like the civilian population. We soon
discovered there was one class in the school who were Naughty. A last-
minute Argentine scattering of land mines, completely indiscriminately, had
effectively put former playgrounds – hills and beaches – out of bounds; live
ammunition was still turning up in the oddest places, from garden sheds to
hen houses, and with no television to provide home entertainment it was not
surprising these children were bursting with frustrated energy. We learned
they had been taken aboard one of the anchored ships one afternoon as a treat
– by two schoolmasters who promptly accepted the ship's officers'

Andalucia Star taking over from *Avelona* Star in Port William, 1983.
Camouflage no longer considered necessary.

hospitality, leaving That Class to its own unsupervised devices. Well, of course a certain amount of mayhem broke out, heated words were spoken, and That Class were never allowed out again, on ship visits or any of the other little functions laid on from time to time. That Class was in disgrace! Recalling our own less than blameless boyhoods, we felt a sneaking sympathy for That Class – so issued our own invitation to them.

Two lady teachers brought them out in a naval pinnace specially laid on by SNOFI. Met at the gangway by the chief officer and purser, they were escorted to the officers' lounge and told the captain would arrive in a minute. I (waiting in the wings in best uniform) entered on cue, whereupon the pupils rose smartly to their feet. A good start! I welcomed them aboard, explained what the *Avelona Star* was doing here and then they split into groups to be escorted right round the ship, from engine room to helipad, including all the storerooms. The gear stores were found fascinating, especially as our lamptrimmer had decorated his paint locker with beautiful miniatures of the funnels of all the ships which used to visit Liverpool. The circular steel discs which must by port order around the world be affixed the mooring ropes to keep off rats brought forth much merriment. Why couldn't the rats walk up the gangway like everybody else? Good question! The MOD staff entered fully into the spirit of the visit by preparing a stall in No.2 'tweendecks where each child was given a little white canvas bag containing a few apples, oranges, sweets and a Mars Bar, to their wide-eyed delight. Back, then, up to the lounge for lemonade, jelly and icecream in abundance before the pinnace returned to take them home. That Class were no longer deemed Naughty!

85

The *Avelona Star* made in all five Falklands voyages and occasionally visited San Carlos Water as well as Stanley, spending up to six weeks 'on station'. Our twin sister *Andalucia Star* made three voyages so that there was always one of us down there.

Then, in October 1984, I was appointed to command Her Majesty's last troopship, the *Keren*.

* * * * * *

The first *Keren* was built for B.I.* as the *Kenya* in 1930, becoming HMS *Keren* in 1941 after a two month spell as HMS *Hydra* following conversion to an infantry landing ship used for assaulting enemy-held beaches. She won battle honours at Madagascar and North Africa in 1942, Sicily in 1943 and Southern France 1944. Eventually she became Sitmar Line's famous emigrant liner *Castel Felice*, well known to thousands of New Australians who sailed in her from war-torn Europe to their new homeland. The name *Keren* lapsed until March 1983 when Sealink's *St Edmund* was bought by the Ministry of Defence (Army) and placed under Blue Star Management after a brief sojourn as HMS *Keren* in which the Royal Navy took her to sea from the Tyne, whither she soon returned to complete her refit. She proudly wore the Merchant Navy's Red Ensign thereafter, unique in that she was an MOD-owned vessel under private civilian management and operation. Blue Star won the management contract on open tender – rather to the chagrin of some of our friends in the Royal Fleet Auxiliary who deemed her "theirs by right". But Blue Star were able to run her far more cost effectively (as today's expression is – it means "cheaper"). But why *Keren*? In 1941, before the British could bring full weight to bear upon the enemy threatening Egypt and the Suez Canal, it was first necessary to clear the Italians out of Eritrea. Not only were they a thorn in the British southern flank but they were disrupting British shipping in the Red Sea out of the port of Massawa. A concerted attack from the south on the Italian held town of Keren was to be the answer, fought hard and long by both sides, a bloody conflict which resulted, after eight weeks of mountain warfare – attack and counter attack – in the victorious British entering Keren. The battle, fought largely by colonial troops with British and Italian officers respectively, was not the last of this campaign but it was decisive. The Italians never fought so determinedly again. So the Battle of Keren, 2nd February to 27th March 1941, paved the way for British victory in North Africa and ultimately for allied victory in Europe four years later.

Since becoming the second *Keren* (albeit MV and not HMS) the former *St Edmund* made in all 27 voyages north and south between the Falklands and Ascension Island, covering over 90,000 ocean miles, carrying almost 18,000 passengers, mostly military but including many Falklands civilians and merchant

---

*B.I. – BRITISH INDIA STEAM NAVIGATION COMPANY

navy crews. Her only break from this service was a return to the Tyne in May 1984 for a rapid refit at North Shields, a job completed well inside allotted time. I had the honour of commanding this fine ship on her last trooping voyages.

Built at Cammell Laird's Birkenhead in 1973-4, she was delivered for service on the night run between Harwich and the Hook of Holland on January 19th, 1975. Being a *night* ferry she had many cabins, which made her so suitable for her work in the South Atlantic a decade later. In her North Sea life she carried thousands of civilians on the six-hour run, also many British troops on furlough from Germany. Not a few soldiers later in the Falklands recalled crossing the North Sea in the *St Edmund*. As *Keren* she retained her Sealink topsides (a bottle green paint of amazing durability!) but changed her funnel colour to yellow with black top. She, too, as the *St Edmund* had been STUFT in 1982, one of the 66 vessels which included passenger liners, tugs, trawlers, tankers, repair ships, a cable vessel, general and refrigerated cargo liners – and car ferries. At this time she was still owned by Sealink, chartered by the Ministry of Defence. She carried British troops south, then, after the surrender, Argentine troops back to Argentina, including their commander General Menendez (Sealink gives you Freedom!). Returning then to the Falklands she took up a static role as a floating barracks anchored in Port Stanley with two others, *Rangatira* (Union Steamship of New Zealand) and the *Baltic Ferry* (Townsend Thoreson).

It may be worth explaining here that the little town of Stanley lies on the southern shore of Port Stanley, an East-West lying natural harbour almost five miles by half a mile wide at its broadest, only saved from being an inland lake by The Narrows which lead out of the northeast side into Port William, slightly larger though parallel and similarly shaped, which opens at its eastern end into the South Atlantic. When the car ferries took up their barracks role there were at any one time up to six large ships anchored in Port Stanley which surprised many of the inhabitants who had not realised their harbour was deep enough. Outside The Narrows in Port William were more ships in dedicated anchorages, mostly too deep of draft to enter Port Stanley where the maximum depth was 22 feet – tankers and supply vessels with an unfortunate Elder Dempster ammunition ship lying furthest east of all, rolling at anchor to the ceaseless ocean swell.

Gradually the ships left, while the three accommodation ships were replaced during 1983/4 by three 'Coastels' – barge-like accommodation blocks moored to the shore with heavy chains connected by road ramps; all three situated at the far eastern end of Port Stanley.

When first 'Taken up from Trade', *St Edmund* was fitted with a large helicopter deck, big enough to take Chinooks, those twin-rotored port-holed monsters which would have saved much yomping had not so many been sunk in the *Atlantic Conveyor* when she went down on 25 May 1982 with Captain

Ian North and eleven of his men, victims of an Exocet missile.

When she first entered her post conflict trooping service with the *Uganda* as running mate, she would anchor in her old spot in Port Stanley and lower the stern ramp, thus enabling troops to embark and disembark by mexefloat – whose twin outboards made them so useful for such work – if not the height of comfort for passengers on a cold, wet, blustery day!

Early in 1984 another marvel came to the Falklands – the floating port. Falklands Intermediate Port and Storage System – FIPASS – alias the Flexiport – came out in sections and was assembled west of the coastels, connected to the shore by a road bridge able to take heavy lorries. A road was built to connect these new establishments with Port Stanley and out to the Mount Pleasant airport, then under construction, thirty miles away over the hills. FIPASS came complete with roll-on, roll-off sections, warehouses, offices and machinery spaces, proving most effectively that the concept of Mulberry Harbour 1944 lives on!

When standing on its steel quayside surrounded by recently offloaded containers it was difficult to believe this whole structure was afloat, capable of being taken elsewhere when no longer needed here. Once FIPASS opened, *Keren* was able to go alongside, making operations much simpler. There was no pilot so one had the privilege of being allowed to handle one's own ship into and out of port. On two occasions when the wharf was busy I berthed the *Keren* in a Mediterranean Moor, stern on to the quay with both anchors out and leading ahead. Ships have tied-up thus in the tideless Mediterranean since the Old Testament was written – hence its name. It made an interesting evolution in a ship *Keren's* size (though with her twin screws, twin rudders and bow thruster all operated by the captain on the bridge, she would park like a mini). The first time I tried it, 'Mediterranean Moor' suddenly became "In Words" in Stanley society, and I was glad I had not made a hash of it, or the expression would have taken on a very different meaning. . .

We played our part in various military exercises but most voyages were straight trooping runs and I found the little North Sea ferry took to the mighty South Atlantic rollers like a seagull. Her stabilisers helped to keep mal-de-mer at bay and despite having at any one time over 500 passengers and 80 crew aboard, she never seemed overcrowded. She also carried a permanent military staff with an army major as Ship's Commandant in charge. Fortunately he and I hit it off rather well. A North Sea overnight ferry's facilities are, however, limited, as of course some passengers pointed out. "No swimming pool? *Uganda* has a *lovely* swimming pool!" But at least our lot were housed decently in cabins. "*Uganda* has dormitories – from her former schoolship days". Nine days at sea were no real hardship to anyone, and army commanders, especially, relished this rare chance of travelling by sea with their men. Getting to know and like our armed forces (most of 'em) was a great experience and they in their turn seemed glad to be meeting their Merchant Navy, "at home", so to speak.

The armed forces of the crown are adept at providing entertainment, usually with a delightfully self-mocking slant, and many concerts were put on for us (at my suggestion) by them to an enthusiastic audience. The Royal Navy Fleet Air Arm even treated us to a Floral Dance, as put on each year at Helston, Cornwall, near their Culdrose base. Brave men in top hats and frock coats (outdated ship's charts, paint and the ragbag came in useful here) danced gracefully with fair maidens dressed ravishingly in haute couture and gumboots. All these 'damsels' had enormous bosoms and many sported beards. . . After dancing to 'that tune' – the Floral Dance – all through the ship, the way was led to 'C' Car Deck, transformed into a fairground with hoopla, coconut shies, 'Penguin' racing, cake-weight guessing, etc etc, an effort which pulled in over £400 for charity. There was deck hockey, and darts, tugs of war and rifle shooting. When the Commandant worried that his troops' rifle practice would disturb the watch below's sleep, we decided the best way round this problem was to invite the crew to participate – an offer taken up gladly. Targets from the ship's stern were kites and balloons, boxes of rubbish and empty beer cans; – the rattle of gunfire and reek of cordite intoxicating, and some of our best shots turned out to be young stewards who didn't know they had it in them. A mock man-overboard one morning had all hands in a high state of trepidation as only a select few knew it was only an exercise. The ship was turned in the classic Williamson manner and a great shout went up when, an hour later, our 'man' was spotted right ahead. That he was only a dummy dressed in red did not, by this time, seem to matter.

In heavy weather passengers were escorted in small parties to the bridge to watch open-mouthed from the wheelhouse the whole wild panorama of the South Atlantic in majestic mood, from ringside seats. Almost miraculously the storm abated in time for the ship's Remembrance Day Service, Sunday, November 11th – a most moving ceremony on the afterdeck attended by over 600 troops, civilians and crew members. As our wreaths were cast on the still quite stormy waters, the sun came out and a lone bugler, high on the flight deck, played the Last Post, followed, after a brief pause, by Reveille. Like the Lord's Prayer, this seemed to us to say it all, as two albatrosses wheeled in our wake.

Back in Stanley we occasionally helped local pensioners with such little tasks as gardening – a delightful break from sea life. Thus, one afternoon I was happily pulling up weeds from a flower bed and tossing them into the dustbin with – it must be admitted – a fair amount of soil attached. Bringing me my cup of tea my hostess observed, rather sharply –"It has taken us 150 years to get decent solid onto this gigantic peat bog" (by which she meant the Falklands) "Please don't just throw it in the dustbin!"

At Ascension Island there is no port, ships lay off at anchor when weather

Alternative landing to using a helicopter at
Ascension Island!

permitted while passengers came and went by helicopter. There *was* an alternative – by small launch, the *Gannet,* which would angle itself alongside the stone wall from which dangled a rope secured to an overhead beam. All you had to do was catch the rope as the boat rolled towards it and swing ashore to the concrete steps Tarzan style – made a change from helicopters!

Long the base of the Cable and Wireless Company, Ascension is the centre of a huge web of undersea cables. Many of these are still in use, many more are not, being old and disused, and it is no uncommon event for a ship to hook one up on her anchor when the time comes to depart. On such occasions the practice is to pass a soft manila rope round the hooked cable (a man goes over the bow on a bosun's chair to do this) and hang it off; then lower the anchor. With a bit of luck the cable comes clear first time, but it is often a longish job especially if a high swell is running.

Ascension is a fascinating clump of rugged rock in the South Atlantic almost midway between Brazil and West Africa; an old volcanic heap of brown clinker first discovered by the Portuguese navigator Joao de Nova Gellego on 20 May, 1501, which happened to be Ascension Day that year. The British established a garrison of Royal Marines there in 1821when it was feared the French were about to mount an escape bid from Ascension to spring Napoleon Bonaparte out of St Helena – where he was imprisoned after meeting his Waterloo in 1815. The marines remained until 1922 (by which time the threat had passed) building Georgetown with its church and barrack square, its houses and, interestingly, its concrete rain catchments up Green Mountain where the drizzly damp climate makes a pleasant oasis above the parched brown rocks.

In Georgetown are still many relics of the old sailing navy – rope walks,

The sad little Bonetta Cemetery near Comfortless Cove, Ascension Island.

rigging lofts and turtle ponds concreted to hold water, for turtles are yet another of Ascension's delights and mysteries. Why would a turtle want to swim 1,200 miles from the coast of Brazil just to lay its eggs on Ascension? One fine morning, going ashore in our Gemini rubber dinghy we were astonished when a large turtle surfaced alongside, regarding us curiously as though our low, black rubber boat were some new kind of turtle. . . Wideawake airport, named after the Wideawake Tern which nests here in large colonies called 'Fairs', became one of the busiest for a few days in 1982, coping with traffic of an almost exclusively military nature. Another spot well worth seeing, even if it only fills one with pity, is the Bonetta Cemetery, a tiny twenty-grave plot in this most inhospitable cinder-like terrain where lie the mortal remains of those who died of fever a century and more ago. When a ship put in with yellow fever (usually from West Africa) the sufferers were appointed desolate habitation at the aptly-named Comfortless Cove, one mile from Georgetown. Food was left at an appointed spot, the carrier then firing a rifle shot as dinner gong, rapidly retiring before he, too, became a victim. Even those who recovered were not allowed back in town but eked out the remainder of their days caring for the sick. There are several such cemeteries on Ascension Island but Bonetta is the best preserved.

So, having disentangled our anchor from the seabed's debris we headed south again for the Falklands. *Uganda* was somewhat slower than *Keren* and as the speed of a joint service, like the speed of a convoy, is governed by the speed of the slowest ship, *Keren* usually had a day or two in hand each voyage which enabled us to slow down and save fuel. It could be that I was directed, first, to San Carlos Water, just a hundred miles by sea from Stanley, at the north western corner of East Falkland, which was where the returning British first landed (fortunately while the Argentine sentries were asleep). We would go alongside an anchored tanker to take fuel (still called 'bunkers' long after the days of coal) in the now-silent inlet, so like the English Lake District. Hard to realise that only three years ago this was 'Bomb Alley' through which screamed Argentine aircraft with their deadly loads; or that that old derelict frigorifico over there in Ajax Bay was Surgeon Commander Jolly's hospital, his Red and Green Life Machine where every man, British and Argentine, who came in injured but alive went out alive – no mean feat under the attack conditions prevailing at the time.

Our ship anchored near the buoys marking HMS *Antelope's* grave. Blue Beach Cemetery was close by – where Colonel H. Jones V.C. and his comrades sleep now in peace – a touchingly beautiful little plot lovingly maintained by the managers of the nearby farm.

Up anchor and down Falklands Sound, then, where fabled wrecks containing hoards of copper ingots lure the brave and hardy to fit-out salvage expeditions back in Stanley; to Fox Bay where Geminini took us to visit the gentoo penguins. Round to Stanley next, that now-familiar little town with its neat houses, brightly painted corrugated iron roofs, red-roofed grey stone cathedral, and the neat little white wooden Catholic chapel of St Mary which I shall never forget seeing in vivid silhouette from the harbour against the flaring glow that dreadful night of 9/10 April 1984 when the hospital caught fire, killing more civilians than had died in the conflict.

But the new Mount Pleasant Airport, a truly remarkable feat of civil engineering, had been opened by Prince Andrew and wide-bodied jet airliners had, at a stroke, rendered yet another troopship redundant. *Uganda* had retired earlier – the termination of her long and interesting career.

Where next? We lay alongside the FIPASS for a while, providing bed, breakfast and meals for the news reporters out to cover the airport's opening. Detachments of troops whose airport accommodation was yet to be completed waited with us, Paras and Gurkhas among them, soon to deploy elsewhere. We were *Mother Keren* to one of our submarines at a buoy in the harbour. The submariners were delighted to savour *Keren's* space and comfort – for even a modern submarine is cramped by comparison – to have their washing done and wallow in hot baths with unlimited fresh water.

What next? The answer came soon. "You are going to South Georgia!". I should say here that many of us had been wanting to go to South Georgia for the previous three years – since we heard there was a chance! In the conflict's beginnings many ships went there, not least the *Queen Elizabeth 2*, though because of her size she only anchored on the Submerged ridge outside King

Edward Cove, in Cumberland Bay. Now *Keren* was to go right in, alongside the wharf if possible, to deliver much needed stores for the British garrison.

Having borrowed a line-throwing rifle (though not the helicopter requested!) *Keren* sailed from Stanley for the last time, after a 'lap of honour' round the harbour attended by many who had helped to make our time in the Falklands so pleasant, including Sir Rex and Lady Mavis Hunt, those two wonderful people who epitomized the Falklands Spirit. Out through The Narrows for the last time, appropriately enough in a blizzard, our passengers were disembarked into the tug *Irishman*. A Falklands veteran, she it was who went after the smouldering *Atlantic Conveyor* through fog, eventually following her oil slick until they found her, took her in tow – only to lose her when she sank on passage back to the Falklands.

My first appointment was to go to Bird Island, South Georgia, and take off from the British Antarctic Survey hut a British scientist who had broken a collar bone. But when we arrived off Bird Island, rags of cloud tore at the snowy mountain peaks and such a southwesterly swell was running into the Sound that launching our boat could have been disastrous. Instead, our doctor was able to speak to the scientists in the hut by radio telephone and find that the fracture had been correctly set and was healing well. So I turned out of Bird Island Sound and headed for Grytviken, in King Edward Cove, off Cumberland Bay. We arrived next daybreak through floating ice in the shape of small bergs which are called "growlers" and "bergy bits". A few large bergs lit by the morning sunshine were radiant in the distance but I was assured by the garrison commander that the cove had cleared of ice during the night – Splendid! Extra lookouts had been posted all night as we knew – from a talk specially given us before we sailed from Stanley – that growlers are old, almost transparent ice, carved from glaciers. Awash, they make poor radar targets. Although South Georgia (same latitude south as Carlisle is north) is little south of the Falklands, which enjoy a temperate climate not unlike that experienced on my own north-east coast of England, the 726 miles on a course of 100 degrees true (East by South) from Stanley take a ship through the Antarctic Convergence Barrier and so, climatalogically, into the Antarctic. Temperatures plunged below zero, for this was mid winter, June.

Slowly the vessel entered King Edward Cove with my deck officers checking bearings and position as I conned the way in – no pilot here, either, of course. The tiny, almost circular cove is surrounded by 2,000 feet high mountains, snow covered at this time of year. At the far end lies Grytviken (Pot Cove in Norwegian, from the trypots of the early sealers) – now a ghost town, complete with white wooden church, 'kinema' and the whale factories which flourished, then died in the early 'sixties when there suddenly became no market for whale products. The whalers left, expecting to return, but never did. Grytviken was, then, like a shore-based *Mary Celeste* with jobs waiting to be completed, stores waiting to be unpacked. On this strange little scene of man's folly, the awesome snow clad mountains looked down with immense disdain. Opposite Grytviken, on King Point, stood Discovery House, a green, two-storied red-roofed building housing troops and scientists, with a few scattered buildings and a wooden wharf – looking about the size of a soap box! At this I would now moor Mediterranean style (in the practised manner) and discharge our cargo through the stern door in what we estimated would take a couple of hours, using the ship's fork trucks. The line-throwing gun was used to get our first line ashore. In pleasant weather our pre-arranged plan went smoothly – too smoothly. No sooner had our stern ramp been lowered onto the tiny jetty than all hell broke loose!

It was as if the Elements were outraged that this North Sea Ferry should have the temerity to come here. Katabatic winds of hurricane force screamed at us suddenly from, it seemed, all directions, blowing snow off the mountains in blinding flurries. The stern door was immediately raised and secured and after five further unsuccessful attempts at berthing, *Keren* clawed her way out into the cove's centre and re-anchored. My horror at finding I had punched a 21 inch hole aft in the steering flat was only tempered with relief that this gash was above the waterline – just! The soap box had taken a battering, too. As our second engineer welded over the hole and the mate and carpenters applied a cement box for good measure, we meekly worked our cargo out through the stern door, lowered once more, into the ship's motorboat for ferrying ashore. In this our crew pitched in with a zest that was heartening to see. The cement would take twenty-four hours to set hard.

A force 10 blizzard blew all that night but the anchors held, with a little assistance now and then from the engines, and it was almost as though the Elements felt we had passed their test, for next day dawned in ethereal calm and beauty which lasted until we sailed the following morning. Everything, ship included, lay under a thick mantle of snow and that night under a full moon every detail of every mountain was mirrored to perfection in the glassy waters of the cove.

When next morning we came to sail, the stern door could not be raised. Had I damaged that, also, in my grapple with the soap box? Fortunately the chief officer and I together found that ice had formed in the channels and once we had chipped this away the door was able to be raised and secured. Phew! (No ship repair facilities existed in South Georgia).

By the time we sailed King Edward Cove had frozen over and seabirds walked and slipped like tipsy sailors on the ice – but our anchors came up without trouble and we moved out, marvelling at the intense turquoise green of the glacier's edge – as we headed north to Ascension and Portsmouth, Homeward Bound!

The *Keren* anchored in King Edward Cove, South Georgia, 1st June, 1985.

9.   THE SAILOR'S WIFE

Since earliest classical times countless volumes have been written about the sailor's life – very little about the sailor's wife. But then, compared with her husband's, her life is prosaic, lived largely Alone.

When the starry-eyed bride takes on a sailor husband she little realises that she is letting herself in for a life spent largely Alone. She is distressed to find that suddenly she has become socially not quite acceptable in mixed company, for even today an attractive lone married woman is seen by other wives as a thinly veiled threat to their own domestic security. She finds she has been classified and labelled. When other wives bewail the fact that hubby has to go ABROAD for a whole FORTNIGHT and she calmly replies – "Mine's been away four months. . ." the stung rejoinder is, "Ah, but YOUR husband goes away to SEA!"

Alone she keeps her husband's house, tends his garden, bears his children and Alone she struggles to bring them up decently. If she takes a job she finds she still has to come home to the housework, a cold and lonely bed with no cheerful male coming home telling of *his* day, no one to hear how *her* day has passed. . . Alone she copes with the family finances and budgets for what can be afforded. . . We were lucky in our time that at least seafaring jobs were secure – as long as one kept one's nose clean and worked hard. Even so, many a marriage foundered on the rocks of extravagance. When the sailor came home with a fistful of dollars he completely upset his wife's hard-won family routine, spoiled the children atrociously, demanded total attention, and was not always keen on taking the family off on holiday. After all (he reasoned) *he* had been pitting himself against the perils of the sea for months that they may live in this house, wallow in all this luxury. . . Now, he would like to wallow in it himself for a space. . . But when the inevitable rows had been made up – and few things are sweeter than making up after a row – life became gloriously happy again – until he was once more called away. Towards the end of his leave she came to dread the telephone's ring, hoped he would get the Joblist completed in time. This comprised all the little jobs around house and garden which shore-abiding husbands take in their stride. In his cowardly way he fervently hoped to himself that whatever he was fixing, be it doorlock, cabinet, hinge or bracket, would not fall apart – at least until he was safely back at sea. . . When he had gone, she picked up the pieces and started life again, Alone..

She probably benefited from her pretty stern Methodist upbringing and did not take to drink (as she so easily could have). Taking the plunge into matrimony with a Blue Star Line third mate little older than herself – but whom she had known since their schooldays together – she found they had just enough cash to afford the deposit on a 27 year old three-bedroomed semi, enough to pay the modest mortgage, and enough left over to furnish the dining room, one bedroom, lay a strip of carpet on hall, stairs and landing:.. the wedding-present carpet-sweeper sufficed for these which was just as well as they had no vacuum cleaner. No fridge either, no electric sewing machine, no TV, no washing machine and certainly no hope, then, of ever affording a car. The dining room fire was lit each morning with sticks and paper. When the coalman arrived and dumped his load in the coalhouse under the stairs the whole house acquired a layer of black dust. But, Alone she kept the house, herself, her children and the garden immaculate. No matter that half the rooms remained unfurnished bare boards, pretty curtains she had made were hung at each sparkling Windowlened window. When she had put the children to bed and heard their prayers (after he started school our five year old son insisted on *singing* the Lord's Prayer) she returned downstairs and did the mending. It was indeed a life which few modern young wives would countenance.

But as time passed, things grew a little easier. In sickness and in health she persevered, raising her children into happy, caring, responsible young adults, earning the love and respect of all around her. The little luxuries of life – considered absolutely necessary by today's brides – came gradually as they could be afforded, appreciated all the more because of this. She never got into debt, always had that little nestegg tucked away in the form of insurance. Her cooking became legendary and she made clothes and knitted with the style of a professional dressmaker.

Until her husband rose to the dizzy rank of chief officer there was no question of her spending even a night aboard his ship legally – Company Rules were strict. But as soon as he got the mate's job she could spend a few days with him in port in London or Liverpool, even venturing on short continental voyages leaving grandparents in charge of the children. Abandoning all three to kith and kin she ventured on a voyage to New Zealand while her husband was still chief officer – a not entirely satisfactory arrangement because so much of his time was taken up with work in which she could not assist. But this voyage provided valuable experience for us both. When husband eventually obtained command, things improved. The two younger children were able to accompany us on a round-the-world voyage to New Zealand and South Africa. Elder daughter was at the time deep into her 'O' levels so stayed at home and looked after widowed Granny.

Eventually of course, the children grew up and left home, still, thanks to their mother's hard work, a happy family, interested in each other and their parents. For the first time in her life Mother felt almost footloose and fancy free! She could accompany her husband on a long voyage – if she so wished – with no family to worry about. The house was old enough to look after itself, with a little help from kindly son and neighbours.

Thus, in January 1986, Brenda and I flew from Gatwick with chief officer Alan Brown to join the *Afric Star* at Gibraltar. Having recently carried oranges from Casablanca to Marseilles, our ship now awaited further orders, for the *Afric Star* is a Reefer Tramp.

A Reefer Tramp?

A refrigerated cargo vessel – not a container ship – engaged on world-wide charter voyages carrying perishable foodstuffs, able to take cargoes at different temperatures simultaneously, she can often be recognised for what she is by her ship's side cargo doors.

A splendid ship, first of a class of six, *Afric, Avelona, Almeda, Almeria, Andalucia* and *Avila* (built Denmark) Stars all but one of which were built at Middlesbrough during the middle 'seventies, the *Afric Star* had for some time been dogged by troubles. Mechanical troubles, crew troubles, cargo troubles – some ships get like that. I had been told to sort them out.

As our plane roared in to land, bringing the Rock into picture-postcard focus, our ship looked like a toy alongside the mole. On-the-spot troubles were dealt with at once and thereafter a happy atmosphere prevailed, in no small measure due to my wife's quiet, unobtrusive way of treating all hands as though they were members of her family. Our crew numbered 32, all British, hardworking and cheerful. Brenda was the only woman onboard.

Where our next charter would take us we did not know. Back in Blue Star's Reefer Trading Division in Leadenhall Street, charters for the fleet were continually being sought and 'fixed'. The start of the southern hemisphere fruit season turned our thoughts towards South Africa, Australia and New Zealand. Chile also entered our speculations. Meanwhile, we explored Gibraltar's famous caves in which our primitive ancestors eked out the great ice age, marvelled at the huge concrete rainwater catchments, and walked sombrely round the little Trafalgar Cemetery (now appropriately and beautifully maintained by Trafalgar House). Here lie the men who were killed at Trafalgar, or died of wounds after the battle, after their wearied ships struggled into port to refit for the voyage home.

After four days I was ordered to Las Palmas, in the Canaries, on charter to the giant Japanese NYK Line for frozen fish. This would be a part cargo, probably to be topped up with citrus fruit from Tampa, Florida – all for Japan.

Anchoring off Las Palmas to await a loading berth, the weather blew up and heavy seas pounded the sea wall, hurling columns of white water over the promenade, sending holiday-makers scurrying for cover. It was time to up-anchor and put to sea before we began dragging towards the lee shore. Clear of the land, engines were stopped to save fuel and we drifted, safely and not uncomfortably until the storm abated. On 1st February I was called in and we went alongside, to be advised that the cartonned frozen octopus and cuttlefish we had hope to load were in short supply. We would have to wait – perhaps a month! Spain had recently joined the Common Market and, it seemed, was no longer allowed to operate Las Palmas as an international Billingsgate. Although the port was full of trawlers, cargo for Japan was elusive. After several days we loaded a trifling amount, before I was suddenly summoned to the agent's office to be told to proceed to Nouadhibou (pron. Noo-AH-dee-boo). Where's that? Yes, I asked the same question!

Formerly Etienne in the French colony of Mauritania on the western bulge of Africa, south western corner of the Sahara Desert – when independence came in 1960 Mauritania declared itself an Islamic Republic and Port Etienne reverted to its ancient tribal name. Tucked away behind Cap Blanc on the Bay of Tiredness (Cansado) is the Bay of Repose with a large fishing village of quite Biblical appearance whose dark-skinned inhabitants dressed in coloured robes, turbans and curly slippers. Some 25 years before, the French had built and developed an iron ore terminal, since which time trainloads of this heavy cargo had poured continuously into enormous bulkships under a constant cloud of dust. Over the years this had stained Cap Blanc a dull rouge. Sadly, the great lighthouse has been well and truly vandalised and no longer guides the mariner. None of the port's navigation lights worked either, we found, though they were still marked on my newly-obtained chart as 'light buoys'. The old port is several miles from the ore terminal, its harbour shallow and crowded with small ships. A cluster of large Russian and other East European factory trawlers were lying in the deepwater anchorage surrounded by their catchers while 2,000 ton freighters worked cargo into barges. Small reefers waited either to load or sail. More trawlers lay alongside a refrigerated packing plant and a wooden quay 125 metres long catered for larger ships. *Afric Star's* length is 155 metres and there are no tugs. A ship was already loading alongside when we arrived, we would have to wait a few days, but the agent wanted me as close to the quay as possible so that he could conveniently come aboard and use our marine telex facilities and international telephone. Theirs, it seemed, were 'out of order' with 'no spares available'.

One of our sailors had been hurt ashore in Las Palmas in a scuffle with the police who tried to arrest him in mistake for someone else. Although at first he seemed to be recovering satisfactorily a head wound must never be taken lightly and when he took a turn for the worse I decided to send him home. Taking the ship in as far as the echo sounder deemed prudent, I put him off into the agent's launch, accompanied by the chief officer (to make the necessary arrangements), and a cadet who would accompany him back to England, then rejoin us later at Panama. Brenda's support in my decision-making here was invaluable.

It soon became apparent that anchored where we were – a big fish in a small pool – we could easily find ourselves aground at the extra low tide of

The old wrecks at Nouadhibou!

the night's new moon. As we watched, the ebb revealed wreck after skeletal wreck grinning wolfishly from the sandbanks now drying out all around us. As the ebb continued to pour water out of the bay a wild sunset sky full of windy promise made me decide to weigh anchor and proceed outside – at once! As we raced down the unlit waterway into the deepening dusk we counted over thirty wrecks around the bay, one an airliner which had missed the runway in a sand storm.

I returned at daylight, having anchored outside, but that afternoon a small blue-painted Dutchman, registered in Curacao, who was anchored ahead of us working long steel girders out into barges, suddenly began to drag down towards us. Her master and I exchanged brief VHF conversation. Yes, he said irritably, he *knew* he was dragging and No, he could do nothing about it – his engines were not working. . . It would have taken several valuable minutes to raise our anchor and try to get out of the way, but Alan Brown, chief officer on the bridge, put our wheel hard a starboard which, on the strong ebb tide rushing past, sheered us out of the dutchman's way. By the Grace of God she missed us narrowly, the whole floating circus of ship and barges dragging rapidly past – still unloading steel girders! It is indeed true that you never see a Dutchman but what he's working cargo! Thereafter I remained outside in the deepwater anchorage until called in to load,

A trip ashore from the *Afric Star* at Nouadhibou.

maintaining contact with the shore by VHF and our motor lifeboat, which made several trips, giving our crew some valuable opportunity to practise that most basic of seamanships – how to handle a small boat.

We had all seen all our collection of Walport films and time was beginning to drag – so at Brenda's suggestion we invited all hands up to our dayroom for a party one evening. Smartly dressed and well behaved our lads showed us they were perfect gentlemen. 'Teabags', the second steward, produced his mouth organ and the evening became a sing-song, very pleasantly, and helped to pass the time until we were called in next day. The pilot here remained French and in many ways seemed to us to be the only shoreside person who really understood what was going on. He and his lovely Parisienne wife entertained us handsomely (I always get better treatment when Brenda is with me!). They drove us out to where the desert meets the sea in endless struggle – weirdly contorted rocks on the seashore a graphic demonstration of the forces of nature eternally at work against each other. He warned me about stowaways.

Before leaving I told the crew I would give a pound for every potential stowaway they found before we departed, with the natural provision that they pay me a pound for every stowaway who made it out to sea. Nine pounds later we sailed but seven eventually appeared after we had sailed, so my expenditure was not colossal. They were set to work around the decks and happily, thanks to smart work by our people in Leadenhall Street, were landed without too much difficulty in Panama.

The day before we entered the Caribbean, late in the afternoon watch, an upturned boat was spotted drifting. The air bubble under fore cabin may just have been supporting life so I rounded-to and took the ship alongside. A light breeze ruffled the surface of a gently heaving swell as, without much difficulty, a cargo crane was raised, swung out, and a pilot ladder lowered to the water. The bosun accompanied Alan Brown down the ladder to secure the drifting boat. A ship becomes amazingly silent when her engine is stopped at sea which made the splash seem louder when the first lifting attempt failed. Numerous denizens of the deep promptly came up to watch the fun. Shoals of brilliantly coloured fish nosed around inquisitively, larger ones followed and finally, circling cautiously, came several grey sharks, flicking over to show white bellies, and teeth. At the third attempt the rope strop passed round the boat held and it was landed, spewing water, on the foredeck, right way up. Our stowaways thought I intended casting them adrift in it. . . Eighteen feet long, it was a fibreglass outboard runabout, heavily barnacled, stinking to high heaven, containing nobody – and no body! Two orange lifejackets with faded spanish markings were the only clues – perhaps she had drifted down from the Canaries? The throttle was jammed at full ahead and the tank was empty. Had some joyrider taken his girl for a spin, taking the waves offshore just a little too fast perhaps, to both be thrown out into the water, without their life jackets on? Had they drowned as their boat roared away – until all its fuel was spent? Her name was *Maye* with presumably identifiable numbers clearly engraved on the Mercury engine block, but although I contacted the nearest US Coastguard Station at Puerto Rico, *Maye* – for us at any rate – remained one of the sea's many unsolved mysteries.

After initial inspection, Brenda would not go near it.

Due to all our delays Tampa had been replaced as our next loading port by Puerto Bolivar in Ecuador – south from the Panama Canal, and after a day at anchor in the river there we went alongside to load almost 4,000 tons – a lot of bananas! In fine weather this took almost a week. On the other side of the single finger pier was a ship loading for the United States whose people told us the sad story of how last voyage they had suffered a small fire in the cargo at sea. When this was extinguished two charred bodies were discovered among the ashes; – stowaways who had probably unwittingly started the fire themselves by smoking. . . As stowaways from Ecuador seemed plentiful we advertised that we were bound for Japan, where stowaways were, of course, beheaded on the wharf on arrival by the harbourmaster wielding a big sword with due ceremony.

Loading depended on the arrival of lorries on which the cartons were wrapped round with banana fronds to help keep off the hot sunshine. We were taken out to the plantation and shown the fruit cut from the 'trees', the stems cut into hands, washed, sprayed and packed in 14kg cartons. A gang of tough little boys grinned at us shyly, looking as though they would run for their lives if necessary. We were told that these were the Mountain Men – boys from the neighbouring hills who formed into Fagan-type bands, fending for themselves as best they could – up to all sorts of pranks. Back at the ship the two large holds were loaded by portable electric conveyor belts while the other two were loaded by chains of men running up wooden ramps through the ship's side doorways each carrying two or three cartons on their shoulders. Hard labour, perhaps, but these dockers were, like most Ecuadorians we met, decidedly cheerful, full of fun. The quay, even late at night, was a bustling scene of lorries backing up to the ship to be boarded by men tearing away the protective banana fronds, setting up the gear, leaping around, working hard, laughing and joking while little boys – great businessmen – sold cakes and meringues their mums had made, individual cigarettes and plastic bags of coconut milk. My wife thought it would be nice to ask the office girls down to the ship for an evening – an offer gleefully taken up by half a dozen very pretty, beautifully turned out young ladies wearing identical white blouses and wine-red skirts. That their English was almost as limited as our Spanish did not matter once we'd all had a couple of drinks. The purser had laid on tabnabs (a small cake made onboard, origins of the word unknown but tabnabs they have been since the days of sail!) Suddenly a silence fell on the girls and there, standing beaming in the doorway, was Mr. Bong! Mr. Bong was the Chinese Ecuadorian who owned the banana plantation and much else besides, and was now delighted to inform us that his cargo was to be taken to Dalian, in China. As far as he was concerned, that was Home! To his girls' delight he joined in our little party, and next day laid on an outing for all our lads not actually 'on duty' while Brenda and I and one or two others looked after the ship. A bus took them on a 'picnic', lasting from mid-morning to early evening. Visiting plantations, a zoo, swimming pools – with as much to eat and drink as they could manage – an old-fashioned and much appreciated gesture. Next day Mr. Bong arranged for Brenda and me to fly to Guayaquil in his own light aircraft – we were the sole passengers. Sixty miles to the north of Puerto Bolivar, Guayaquil is Ecuador's business capital (though the seat of government is at Quito). Elegantly Spanish in the city centre, colonnaded pavements provided cool shade from the equatorial sun, and even the park benches were of marble, while petrol was selling at the equivalent of 20p per gallon!

One evening after dinner I was visited by local police, very stern. One of my crew had 'stolen a docker's bicycle and wrecked same'. Oh dear! The sailor, readily identifiable by his shock of red hair, was summoned and explained that he had asked the docker if he may have a short ride on the bicycle, to which the docker agreed. But the docker did not tell him the bicycle had no brakes! Our man had been lucky not to end up drowned in the dock. . . but of course this charge was resolved by my asking the policeman – "How much?" The docker suggested a figure – not unreasonable our sailor thought – hands were shaken and I gave an advance on wages to the appropriate amount. Our sailor promised the docker a ride on his own bike next time he came to Liverpool – 'and *my* brakes work!' He also told his mates afterwards he doubted if the Old Man would have been so lenient had not the Missus been there.

Late on March 10 loading completed and we sailed early on next morning's tide, bound in the first instance 8,227 miles across the Pacific to Tokyo. No stowaways!

The route took us past Clipperton Island, a low, now uninhabited coral atoll formerly quarried for guano. The last diggers sailed away in 1917 leaving the white sand beaches and nodding palm trees to clouds of seabirds. It looked idyllic in the sunshine but the Pilot Book warns that the water in the lagoon below a depth of 15 metres is poisonous. By international agreement the sea around the Galapagos Islands is now out of bounds to prevent pollution there. A pity, as a trip between these fascinating islands always gave opportunity to admire the many creatures which abound in the water rich in plankton brought up on the cool current from the south. Whales, dolphins, seals and birdlife are plentiful, as are the great flightless tortoises which give the island their name. Instead, we headed towards the Hawaiian Isles, a 1,400 mile chain discovered by Captain Cook who named them after his worthy mentor, Lord Sandwich. But when we passed it was raining and Honolulu had her head in the clouds. Local radio told of floods caused by the recent downpours and the sea was grey and rough. No sign of the famous rainbows – not like the travel posters at all. Southwest of Honolulu, bowling along before the steady NE trade wind, we came upon a modern commercial sailing ship – a new, gleaming white Japanese trawler with two masts, main and mizen, each setting a large rectangular metal alloy squaresail trimming to the wind automatically. She was making a good ten knots and with no sign of propeller-wake, clearly she was under sail alone. And I, who had sneered at reports of these modern sailing vessels as being little more than government-grant-catching gimmicks whose owners would take the money but still rely on their engines only, was impressed. Perhaps there *is* something in the notion after all!

By crossing the International Dateline on my birthday I omitted it (the secret of eternal youth; but Alan Brown the chief officer went one better. Born 29th February he is still little more than a toddler!

The only really heavy weather of the whole voyage struck us several days before we arrived off Tokyo, but abated as we joined the throng of shipping which hurries about its lawful occasions in Japanese waters. Fleets of fishermen were like toys on a park lake – each boat painted white with a traditional gaff spanker sail in red, green or bright blue. Unloading our octopus and cuttle fish took two days: we wondered how long before it was all eaten. By this time I was worried about our bananas, some of which, as George Hall the chief engineer pointed out to me, were turning yellow in the stow. Bananas should be landed as they are loaded – green. But bananas are a tricky cargo. Like all fresh fruit they are continually ripening and ship's application of cooling and CO_2 extraction merely retards this natural process. Despite all care taken bananas can ripen unpredictably fast in stow, and thirty five days – as these would be by the time we reached China – is a long time. I mentioned my concern to our charterers when they took my wife and me out to lunch. "Do not worry, captain", they smiled. "You will find the Chinese prefer there bananas on the ripe side – if not actually black!"

For all of us, China in 1986 was something new – behind the Bamboo Curtain – to be regarded with apprehension. Huge fleets of fishermen working in pairs and small brown Christmas-tree shaped net markers were all carefully avoided as we came to the large almost landlocked harbour amongst sundry anchored vessels, mostly large bulkers. The ice of winter had departed but the night wind still blew chill as port officials came aboard in their green uniforms. I had lowered the lee gangway, the port side one, but they insisted loudly that what they wanted was not the gangway but the starboard side pilot ladder. Thus delayed for several minutes our six or seven boarding officials came aboard in a furious temper, which soon melted into smiles when they found themselves surrounded by warmth and congeniality with food and drink to hand. Formalities were completed smoothly and thereafter we enjoyed our visit to the People's Republic, which seemed determined to put the long horrors of war, civil war and the dreadful excesses of the 1966-76 Cultural Revolution behind and join the real world. Proclaiming the economic necessity of hard work, foreign investment and export, their Communist propaganda read like good Conservative Party manifesto material! They were pleased to see our bananas and told me Dalian receives a monthly shipment – some from South China, mostly from the Philippines. Ours was only their second Ecuadorian cargo. And yes, they prefer them over-ripe!

Dalian used to be part of Imperial Russia, taken by the Japanese in the 1905 war, after which it was laid-out in its present form, with wide streets radiating like wheel spokes from the town centre and quite elegant buildings as it grew into an important industrial and commercial centre. In 1945, following Japan's defeat by the Allies, Dalian became part of China, the People's Republic since 1949.

Discharge of our cargo proceeded steadily, shore cranes supplementing our own, using the upper hatchways rather than the ship's side doors. One hundred cartons per sling were tallied out by girls using metal 'tallies' – on triangular metal hook-plates, an accurate system dating back to ancient times. Loaded onto rail wagons, these were towed away by a magnificent black shiny steam locomotive with red wheels, burning coal, the pride of its driver and fireman. We were allowed ashore without let or hindrance, taking photographs. Dalian's four million population seemed a cosmopolitan distillation of the Eastern Races, and most were friendly. More than once we were spoken to from across the street. . . "Hullo – Good Afternoon!" in purest BBC English. It was spring cleaning time and even on the main streets, and the roundabouts of busy intersections, lines of washing flapped in the sunshine, as though the sudden rise in temperature was a sure sign that winter was over. Children wandered home from school (six days a week) playing in the streets. The boys played marbles with earnest dedication while their sisters skipped complicated routines which my wife recognised from her own girlhood. The Dalian ladies were wearing mostly black that season, black trousers and black jackets, so my wife's clothes drew much admiration, especially her blue stockings. Older folk clung to the blue and black denim of the Mao Tse Tung era but the youngsters were just beginning to dress more daringly. At the seaside we found the newly made cliff paths and steps had been paid for by the local brewery. As we walked down these to a beach we met a crowd of young people coming up, red banner to the fore. To our surprise they were led by a couple of American schoolteachers and during the course of our ensuing conversation invited them to come and visit the ship. Sadly, China had not relaxed *that* far, and our application at the dock gate was met with a very final, terse No!

The country was booming, by order – for strict totalitarianism held firm – and this three years before Tiananmen Square – but we detected a note of hope and optimism in the air, akin to that prevailing in Britain during the late 1940s when post-war austerity was still with us but the future could only be better, bright with promise. With rich uranium deposits in the hills China was proclaiming that the secret of unlimited industrial power had been unlocked, and nuclear power stations were planned and building. No mention was made, we noticed, of nuclear waste or the problems of accidental fallout.

One morning, sitting in our room at coffee time, we heard a loud BANG! followed by a mighty rushing wind. Dashing out on deck the remarkable spectacle of a rapidly inflating liferaft presented itself, getting uncomfortably wrapped round awning spar and stanchion, while in the distance two scurrying figures were spotted disappearing round the corner of the shed. Whether they had pulled the line which inflated the raft by accident or design we would never know, but of course I had to have it repacked and a new certificate issued which – surprise surprise – would cost extra as weekend

106

overtime would be incurred! We suspected that forty years of Communism had done little to diminish a keen Chinese eye for business. . . However, the firm which repacked the liferaft presented Brenda with a handsome shell picture in frame. These pictures, three dimensionally depicting rural and coastal scenes, are cleverly worked in coloured pieces of sea shell – by white – coated damsels in the Shell Factory. My wife was taken to see them in action, painstakingly working with tiny shell fragments, wearing masks to protect their lungs from the dust arising when the shell was ground into the required shapes.

As our last bananas were unloaded a gale sprang up, closing the port until next morning, when we put to sea in a rapidly thickening fog; – just as Sparks handed me an incoming message. Sarah Liege Kinghorn, our first grandchild, had arrived in this world safe and sound back home in Northumberland, mother and child both doing well. More of this young lady will appear later. The *Afric Star* was now bound 'towards New Zealand', and each day my orders changed as booking developed on the international reefer market. First idea was to go to load apples, pears and kiwi fruit for Seattle, but it transpired that NZ weather this season had not favoured heavy enough cropping of select fruit to fill the ship, so my directions changed to "fruit for the Persian Gulf" (Less choosy there, perhaps?). This soon altered to a cargo for the UK, and hopes onboard soared, only to return to earth with firm orders:– "Load apples in Napier for the Delaware – but first just nip round to New Plymouth for 3,000 tons of butter for Algeria". At this, the height of New Zealand's fruit exporting season, no other ships were available to carry butter to Algeria, but that – and a like amount of Granny Smiths – would fill us nicely. But why would Algerians wish to buy New Zealand butter when mountains of it were cheaply available just across the Mediterranean in Europe? It seems they prefer not only the NZ flavour but also the fact that it came in the small-pack wrappings the EEC would not provide.

Our fortnight's loading in New Plymouth provided plenty of interest for all hands, time to meet old friends and make new ones, while lorry loads of butter trundled down daily from the cold store up the road. Rain stopped play several times and only occasionally could we see the peak of Mount Egmont which, at 8,255 feet, dominates the Taranaki region. It is difficult to describe how lovely is New Zealand, especially compared with some places we had visited; – beautiful, unspoiled countryside – beautiful unspoiled people – and even for the old married couple it was quite a wrench to depart, blowing our three deafening long blasts of farewell on the whistle on 7 May. Passing through Cook Strait by night we arrived at Napier in time to begin loading next morning. The deepwater port, resculpted here by the great earthquake, is tucked away under creamy white cliffs topped by the HM Prison, one of the few buildings to survive the 'quake intact – stoutly built mainly of kauri timber last century as a barracks for the British garrison during the Maori Wars. Loading of 138,409 cartons of Granny Smiths proceeded apace, leaving us time, however, to drive a hirecar up through beautiful scenery to Lake Taupo in the centre of North Island. Here we had been advised to book in at a certain motel which would ensure we awoke to a good view over the Lake. The snowcapped distant mountains, we were promised, would be reflected in the water in all their majesty and splendour. . . this room cost extra but who cared – this was a once-in-a-lifetime visit! Next morning we looked out in eager anticipation, to find the lake completely blanketed in a dense fog!

Three more blasts said our final farewell to New Zealand, and off we set for Panama, 6,431 miles away. It was nobody's birthday on 13 May, which we had twice as we crossed the Date Line. No passage from New Zealand to Panama would be complete without a call at Pitcairn Island, and I had obtained our Japanese charterers' permission to stop there for an hour to pick up mails. At one time it was common for British ships to call at Pitcairn and lie off for an hour or so, but with the demise of our Merchant Navy such calls were now so few that I discovered none of our crew had been there. When I mentioned that next day we would stop off at an island for a chat with the locals they thought I was pulling legs. . . and were consequently astonished when a tall, rocky island hove into view ahead. The Pitcairners' new aluminium longboat was already on its way out to us as I rounded – to 2 mile off Adamstown and soon men, women and children were scrambling up our pilot ladders – the ship echoing to the clatter of tiny feet. These descendants of the *Bounty* mutineers were old friends, though it was twelve years since Brenda and I had last called – and we were well received. As the children dashed excitedly around, their elders joined enthusiastically in what had become an instant party. Only for an hour, however, as I had to press on to Panama; and with six bags of mail and enough fresh fruit to furnish a Harvest Festival we took our leave; – the Pitcairn songs 'Sweet Bye and Bye' and 'Goodbye' ringing in our ears.

In Napier we had embarked a young New Zealander who was to work his passage to Britain, and Rob fitted in very well. This, of course, did not excuse him from Crossing the Line in style, and great were the preparations for his ordeal. A pillory was gleefully constructed on the afterdeck, a drum full of vile Initiation brewed. Fancy costumes were, of course, fashioned out of anything which came to hand out of the ragbag. King Neptune came aboard tastefully draped in a Blue Star houseflag (where did he get that?) and his helpers looked suitably piratical. Rob was dragged to the scene, firmly pilloried, and initiated well and truly. Plastered in foul-smelling goo, he defiantly sang 'God Bless New Zealand' throughout to the entertainment of us all. Afterwards he was allowed to buy King Neptune and Co a beer in the bar and order was restored.

We arrived at Balboa, the Pacific end of the Panama Canal, early on 29 May, in a respite from heavy weather which had put two ships ashore. Bunkering here left us time to visit the ruins of Old Panama City, sacked by Henry Morgan and his buccaneers in 1672 and never rebuilt – and the modern Panama City where over one hundred international banks testify to current prosperity.

The new Panama Canal Commission was determined to preserve efficiency and we made a good seven-hour transit, clearing for Wilmington, Delaware at half past midnight on 30 May. Passing east of Cuba we made up through the Windward Passage and Crooked Island Passage, in sight of Watling's Island where Columbus made his New World landfall in 1492. Early morning on 4 June saw us entering the Delaware River, taking pilots to Wilmington, below Philadelphia. The docking pilot and his wife took us out to lunch in Newcastle, nearby, and Granny Smith was unloaded by highly efficient stevedores. We had, however, time to visit Philadelphia – the City of Brotherly Love founded by Quaker William Penn in 1682. We saw Independence Hall, the Liberty Bell and other hallowed shrines, wandered tree-lined cobbled streets 300 years old – all beautifully kept red brick and white paint, and inspected Admiral Dewy's 1898 flagship USS *Olympia*. Also on waterfront display were an elderly barquentine Grand Banker, the WW2 submarine USS *Becuna* and a tall ship, at one time the world's largest, heroine of Eric Newby's 'Last Grain Race' – the *Moshulu*. A fine, four-masted barque, she was, now, too old to go to sea and served as a well-patronised floating restaurant.

Next day, 5 June, we sailed, crossing the Atlantic in fine weather, speaking one afternoon to HMS *Glamorgan* – and it's not often the red ensign meets the white at sea these days! We found dense fog off the Azores and pitied the tourist there. Algerian ports of discharge were declared as Oran, Algiers and Bejaia and, planning to arrive at Oran early morning 15 June, I stopped for a few hours while still out in the Atlantic. While we lay drifting an enormous whale came up and after circling the ship several times, obligingly posed for photographs taken by an excited ship's company crowding the rails. Scratching its back luxuriously on the corner of our transom stern, he remained with us until passage resumed. Then, with a last flick of his giant tail and a noisy final spouting he was gone, and we headed for the Straits of Gibraltar.

The US Navy did not perhaps intend to escort the *Afric Star* through, but on the afternoon of 14 June, pitching into a force 6 easterly, we found ourselves accompanied by an aircraft carrier and two destroyers. There was something very impressive about a squadron of warships at sea in heavy weather, their stars and stripes ensigns board-flat streaming aft, lit by occasional shafts of sunshine on a blue and white sea.

June 15, a slow dawn breaking over North Africa and before us – Oran, scene of one of WW2's saddest naval engagements when, for the first time since Trafalgar, a British fleet fired on the French. That the French had spent a great deal of money in beautifying their colony was obvious, as was the fact that the splendour was fading with independence. We celebrated our thirtieth wedding anniversary exploring some of Oran's less exclusive residential quarters (looking – unsuccessfully – for somewhere to buy ourselves a celebratory drink!). We were startled when the all-male contents of a mosque poured out and we suddenly found ourselves surrounded by Islam. But people were friendly and several addressed us in French. Many stood in groups in the evening sunshine chatting and laughing while children played World Cup football on every suitable space. (The adult World Cup series was about to commence).

After a week in port our fresh water was getting low – the ship's distillation plant could only be used at sea and there was no tap at our particular berth. So the harbourmaster obligingly shifted us one evening to the one quay where water was laid on, right under the wall of his office. We continued unloading and sailed for Algiers on 24 June.

A dozen of us were to be relieved here but our reliefs flew out on Thursday and nothing, but nothing, happens in Algiers on Friday, the Muslim sabbath. After considerable verbal wrestling (no other word for it!) with our less than helpful agent, we obtained tickets as far as Marseilles where a kindly and efficient Air France took us under its wing and got us home, via Paris, on 29 June.

Five months and 33, 206 nautical miles after leaving Gibraltar, visiting a dozen countries, our cargoes – with the exception of some of the butter – would all have been eaten long ago. It would soon be time to go and fetch some more.

I was glad my wife had been able to accompany me – the first voyage on our own together since I became master. It was also our last voyage in a British registered ship with an all-British crew. Times were changing rapidly and my next voyage was going to be very, very different.

10. FIVE DAYS LATE!

Blue Star Line had always concentrated on employing good British crews, but usually, in addition carried one or more foreign crews on certain of their ships. In the early 'fifties when many liner companies were building a tanker or two, the *Pacific Star* had British officers and Indian ratings from Bombay. The *Queensland Star* class of four ships built a few years later employed British officers with ratings from Singapore-Chinese, many of whom had fled communist persecution on the mainland of China: while the *Canterbury Star* class of six ships were manned by Barbadians. The 'Chinese' ships carried huge crews which more than made up the difference between British and Singapore wage bills, while the Barbadians – employed as a form of Commonwealth Aid to alleviate unemployment on the island – were on British wages. So no one could accuse the company of 'crewing cheap' – and all these nationals were not only experienced men but were also familiar with the running of British ships.

So when it was announced in 1986 that some of the reefer tramps would henceforth be manned by ratings from the People's Republic of China, few eyebrows were raised. The first such vessel I joined was the *Perth* (formerly *Almeria Star* of 1976 – last of the *Afric Star* class to be built). She lay alongside in the Emirates Port of Fujairah awaiting her next charter and the new crew arrived the same day as I did, in September 1986. Fortunately we did not sail – for Genoa – for another three weeks, during which time we (the British Blue Star officers) began to realise just how ignorant this new crew was! All complete novices – we had sailors who could neither steer nor tie knots, who had never seen a ship at close hand – cooks with not the faintest of culinary notion – and the engineroom staff's total mechanical experience hitherto seemed to have centred on their communal farm's tractor. . . Sure, every ship is a schoolship – but when *all* your pupils are New Boys, intensive instruction must be carried out – fast! Entering the Suez Canal I put the man I thought was the best of the bunch to the wheel – for him to burst into tears in claustrophobic panic as he saw the steep sandbanked sides of the Canal looming on either side. The pilot was not impressed. Fortunately our third mate could steer – until I sent for the bosun. The Chinese bosun wrung his hands and said he would TEACH the sailor to steer. . .

Having weathered this baptism of Chinese Fire I was next appointed to the *Limari*, a fine looking ship – a big white reefer built in France as the *Snowflake* in 1972, for the Swedish Salen company. Since then she had been the *South View, Blue Sea* and *Santos Star* and perhaps we should have wondered why such a fine looking ship had changed hands so frequently. . . Her charterers were now the old-established South American Steamship

Company – the C.S.A.V. – of Valparaiso who had – as was their wont – renamed her after a Chilean River – Limari. Her charterer's red, black topped funnel indubitably enhanced her white-hulled, yellow masted, green-decked appearance – and I knew this company only chartered first class ships. . . She was employed to carry quick-frozen fresh fruit from Valparaiso to Philadelphia for the booming U.S. market – returning empty unless 'sufficient inducement' was made to put her into Ecuador for Valparaiso-bound bananas. Speed was of the utmost importance at all times for the carriage of fresh fruit but, unfortunately, our advertised 22 knots soon proved impossible to achieve and performance of her main and auxiliary engines became a perpetual nightmare. These facts did not emerge, of course, until after we took over on December 15th 1986, at Philadelphia. The chief engineer, chief officer, electrician and I had joined six days earlier in Panama for 'familiarisation' – and of course we saw exactly (and only) what we were shown. Coming up the Delaware overnight she arrived at 0400 hours – an icy cold morning to wake us up as we participated in our new ship's berthing. By six pm that day we had changed the ship's shoreside management, all 34 personnel, unloaded all the fresh fruit cargo, taken bunkers, fresh water and stores, effected the few repairs upon which I insisted – and sailed. A busy day!

Disembarking our pilot and clearing the Delaware at 0100 next day, I headed south for Crooked Island Passage into the Caribbean for the Panama Canal, Guayquil and Valparaiso. Fortunately the weather remained fine as all hands found their way around the ship, learned the ropes – and began to realise something of what we had taken on.

The new Chinese crew proved vastly inexperienced, keen and willing but almost without any English apart from their chief steward – who had been a dredging engineer before coming to sea with us. Dimly and slowly we realised that the Chinese government was using us to train the men for their rapidly expanding merchant fleet – now one of the world's largest and one of the few employing 'own' crews in 'own registered' ships. At the same time we were helping solve China's growing unemployment problem – brought on by modern techniques of industry – bully for us! The new hands were (of course) unfamiliar with such basics as steering and had to be closely watched at all times. Like most modern ships the *Limari* employed auto-steering when at sea but in busy traffic or close waters she was hand-steered. The eight hour passage down the Delaware and ten hours through the Panama Canal provided the seaman with practice and the captain with grey hairs. It was not uncommon for the officer of the watch to have to take the wheel in moments of near crisis.

The four alternators which provided our electricity began giving trouble as we came down the Delaware and before we entered the Caribbean one of the three brine pumps exploded, wrecking itself and the brine room door but fortunately injuring no one, although flying jagged metal chunks would have killed or maimed anyone unfortunate enough to be in the brine room at the time. Never mind – we had two additional brine pumps and the holds were already cooled ready to load bananas – and we'd get that pump's motor rewound in Guayaquil. . . Despite their desperate ignorance the crew remained cheerful, until they realised that a large proportion of their wages was creamed off for their government as a form of tax. But I felt I could rely upon the chief steward, whose English was good. An important part of his job was to supervise catering – ensure we were well fed without undue extravagance – and write the all-important Catering Book. To help him understand this a Blue Star purser had flown to Philadelphia to sail with us to Panama and go – with his Chinese counterpart – "through the books". By the time he left he was satisfied that all was comprehended – as the Chinaman had smilingly answered "Yes" to his final every question. It was only later that I realised that all this well-intentioned instruction had been so much water off a mandarin duck's back.

"Have you completed the monthly catering returns?" I asked when he came to see me just as I was busy taking the ship through the harbour entrance.

"Yes", he smiled.

"Good", I said, taking action to avoid an outbound tanker.

"Have you kept the officer's and crew accounts separately?" I asked next.

"Yes", he smiled. The tanker passed us with yards to spare.

"How many dollars a day are we costing the company in food?" I asked.

"Yes", he smiled. . .

I tested the ship's manoeuvring characteristics before entering the anchorage, feeling that *Limari's* controllable pitch propeller might provide interesting results. It did. Her bow thruster would have been useful here, enabling me to push the ship's bow to port or starboard in confined waters when stopped, but some thoughtful superintendence in the past had sealed this off. Whereas a normal right-handed fixed-pitch propeller can usually be relied upon to kick the stern to port when the engine is put astern, this 'controllable' propeller behaved totally unpredictably – French you see. Coming to anchor surrounded by shipping was fraught with interest – every time! We had several hours to wait in Limon Bay before, with pilots aboard, (two pilots, she was very slightly wider than the maximum for one pilot) – I received VHF orders to weigh anchor and commence canal transit. The main engine would not start. How long would repairs take? asked the pilots. The chief and his engineers had toiled manfully with the machinery ever since we took over but tracing this particular fault to a jammed air-valve took an hour, by which time the pilots had left for another ship and I had been put back to the end of the queue – involving a twenty four hours wait. The charterers were not pleased. As soon as the engine was ready to go I endeavoured to take transit but the laws were inviolable – I had to wait.

The Panama Canal is always a memorable experience; rising through the locks 85 feet above the ocean, traversing exotic lakes and jungle-hedged narrows, past waterfalls and towering cliffs to eventually descend through more locks fifty miles on. . . with erratic engines and unskilled helmsmen it was unforgettable!

Clearing Panama Bay at 0200 on 22nd December after 23 hours on my feet, I returned to my cabin and sank into an armchair to read the letters from home, unwilling to turn-in as strange nagging doubts insisted the night was not yet over. An hour later the engines suddenly stopped. Lights went out and all power failed. No alarm bells rang – there was total blackout, and silence! Fortunately we were away from main traffic lanes by now – just – lighting and sending up red "Not Under Command" oil lamps took time.

From the bridge I carefully made my way down into the engineroom, shining the beam of my torch on the steel ladder steps as I went, to find the chief and his men calmly trying to locate the cause of this latest stoppage. Meanwhile the radio officer coaxed the emergency generator to life and some essential lighting returned. Running true to form, the emergency 'jenny' had failed to start as it should, automatically. A faulty fuel gauge registering adequate fuel supply in a tank which was in fact empty – fuel 'starvation' – was the cause of our stoppage but when after two hours hard work below, the engines sprang back into life, both remaining brine pumps blew their remaining shreds of insulation and burned out. In equatorial heat we now had no means of cooling and maintaining cool the bananas to be loaded at Guayaquil next day. With luck, however, we could now get all three motors rewound there. But of course this proved impossible – all works ashore were closed 'for the Christmas holiday!'

The exporter of bananas had already cut his crop, which faced ruin through deterioration over Christmas, and he urged me to please accept his cargo. Both the company and I agreed we should accept it for carriage 'under air circulation but not refrigeration' – the best we could promise. But the banana man pleaded, so in these hardly ideal conditions, in light rain, we loaded 30,000 cartons and sailed on Christmas Eve on the five-day passage to Valparaiso. After our mid-day Christmas dinner the chief and I accompanied by the chief officer went down to take a look at our cargo. To our horror the heat below was stifling – those bananas would never turn yellow, they would just turn rotten! So, our ever-resourceful and quite brilliant chief engineer found an electric motor similar enough to those which had blown on the brine pumps in another part of his engine room. Part of the auxiliary blower, it was removed with great difficulty and fitted to one of the brine pumps. Cargo temperature, which was soaring into the high nineties (F), reduced at once. Our bananas arrived in Valparaiso on 29th December in perfect condition. The importer had anticipated a write-off and was delighted. Sometimes you win. Despite considerable time and no small expense put into righting our mechanical problems – rewinding motors does not come cheaply – *Limari* seemed malevolently determined and, despite all efforts, engine trouble persisted.

However, delivering the cargo in good condition is the name of the game and our northbound peaches, apricots, plums, melons, nectarines, pears and 'garlics' arrived at Philadelphia in first class condition, if not quite as early as would have been the case had we managed 22 knots. By this time however, the chief had got her up to 21 on a good day – we lived in hope. We seemed to be getting on top of the job now. The charterers still lamented, but the seamen had learned to steer and, apart from daily minor problems, the engines presented no unsolvable puzzles. Morale soared. We collected a couple of young stowaways in Valparaiso – a pair of hopefuls who thought the streets of North America were paved with gold. They hid at first under the forecastle, tucked away in the anchor recess – and only came out after Panama by which time boredom had clearly set in. Thereafter they were a constant headache, as I had to keep them under lock and key in the States – on pain of a multi-thousand dollar fine – and when they did in fact make a break for freedom in Philadelphia I was glad our Scottish second mate had the wit and agility to pursue them until caught. We tried locking them up but Houdini must have been their ancestor.

Light snow was falling in Philadelphia as we made ready to sail. The charterer's representative – a retired Chilean captain, and his charming English wife, always made me welcome in Philly – a brief respite which I truly appreciated. As they brought me back to the ship after a delightful evening out, forecasts were glumly telling of one of the worst storms the Middle West had seen for years – "Coming your way soon!" With a rapidly falling barometer I proceeded down the Delaware in an awesome glassy calm beneath a leaden sky. If we could get south fast enough we might just get clear before the gale struck. All was made doubly secure, just in case. Before noon a breeze whispered from the east, steadied and strengthened, heaping the waters of the Gulf Stream Drift into a short, steep swell. Already dangerously low, the barometer now took a nose dive and continued falling as the wind veered steadily through south to south-west, increasing in strength until by nightfall a violent storm, wind speed over 60 knots, was hurling itself upon us straight off the coast – due west. In the shallow seas off Virginia this produced a dangerously steep short swell right on our starboard beam. *Limari* began to roll heavily. Unlike every other ship I had ever sailed in, she had no bilge keels; and we had recently discovered that her built-in roll-damping tanks were unsafe to use due to metal wastage – to use them risked cascading a deluge of several tons of water into the engine room! In light condition the ship was very stiff, and rolling became rapid, jerky and vicious. Conscious of the fact that the charterers would scarcely understand why, I altered course and speed to ease the motion – safety must come first.

Despite alterations and speed reductions however, the rolling worsened as the weather deteriorated. By midnight the ship was throwing herself over, 60 degrees off the vertical to port and starboard in a ten second cycle. At 0130 the chief telephoned the bridge from the engineroom to advise that a 1·2 tonne piece of spare machinery, a piston crown, had broken loose from its mounting in the flat high above the engine and that a man had been injured trying to secure it. Could I do any more to ease the rolling?

The only way was to alter course to due east – ninety degrees off my required course – to run before wind and swell, which I did while the piston crown was rescued and engineer officers got the injured man into the Neil Robertson stretcher and up into the ship's little hospital. We carried no doctor and only limited basic medical equipment but fortunately this included morphine which I administered to ease the pain. The injured man seemed to have a badly broken leg. He was the leader of a team of four sent by the company from England to Philadelphia to help our own engineers rectify alternator deficiencies and had offered his assistance freely when the crown broke loose. I found the exact nature of the injury difficult to assess, sufficient to realise however that it was serious and that he required skilled medical attention as soon as possible. The chief engineer himself had narrowly escaped being crushed to death, surviving with deep body grazes as the piston crown hurtled past him. At this moment an engineroom switchboard fire broke out, soon to be extinguished. We had enough on our plate without a fire! Sparks made radio contact with the US Coast Guard base at Portsmouth, Virginia and I was able to speak with the duty officer on radio telephone, while Sparks held me in his chair (the ship, even on this easterly heading was still performing wondrous gyrations). After I had explained our situation a helicopter was promised at first light and I gave silent thanks for my helicopter experience in the Falklands. If I could turn round and head back towards the coast, the helicopter would take our man off about 0830.

Everyone hung on as I made our turn, and continued to hang on as we thrashed into the teeth of the gale at best speed conducive to the patient's comfort. Though in considerable pain despite morphia, he remained amazingly brave and cheerful, quipping that he didn't care for flying when I told him he was to be flown ashore.

The sun rose that morning on a marvellously wild and wintry ocean – a watery wilderness of green, blue and white stretching to a ragged horizon with spray rainbows everywhere. I decided to disembark our patient from the port side of the foredeck, clear of funnel smoke and other heli-hazards if the pilot could hover there. Portsmouth advised that the 'chopper' had taken off, I told them the patient's present medical condition and gave an estimated 0830 position. Eagerly we scanned the western sky.

For long minutes we saw nothing as the ship pitched into the still-rising

116

swell. Wind screamed and spray drove in sheets over the bow, rattling like hail against the wheelhouse windows. I would reduce speed when we were spotted.

"There she is!"

"No, that's a seagull!"

Then – like the U.S. Cavalry galloping over the hill to save the covered wagons from the redskins in the old movies – USCG Sikorsky 1483 hove into view, at first a speck in the sky, wonderfully soon a great red-striped white whirlybird circling the ship. The pilot and I exchanged information on VHF Channel 16.

"You sure make a great sight down there Captain!" He was a great sight to us, also!

With consummate skill he angled his helicopter into a hovering position sixty feet up, just off the port side of the foredeck by number 2 hatch – and sent down his aluminium 'basket' on a line. Without delay our man was tenderly placed in the basket, still strapped into the Neil Robertson stretcher, to be winched aloft, followed by his bag on a line. Within an hour he was safe in hospital ashore his injuries diagnosed as compound fractures of fibia and tibula. He was better off there than out afloat with us. The good ship *Limari* resumed a southerly course and we hoped the weather would now improve.

Instead, it grew much worse, as by heading back towards the coast I had brought the ship into the path of the eye of the storm. I later learned we had come very close to the eye of one of the worst storms to cross the eastern states for many years. It was a bad winter over there, in which several ships were lost. We were lucky. The sea was wonderful to look upon; occasionally we passed craters, almost like bomb craters in the tumult, a phenomenon of which until then I had only read. Hurricane force wind for several hours over the shallow water of the Gulf Stream Drift produced weird results. Maybe there *was* something in this Bermuda Triangle nonsense after all!

Everything, including the maverick piston crown, was resecured but as the swell steepened and rolling increased its ferocity I realised we were reaching that degree of synchronisation which can roll a ship right over like a toy in a bathrub. I decided to heave-to. By this time objects broken loose were flying around the wheelhouse at every roll. The Scottish second officer and the Chinese wheelman were marvellously calm amid the chaos – always reassuring to see such response to what can be quite terrifying conditions – but philosophic mediation ended abruptly when a large jar of Nescafé shot past my face to shatter against the steering console.

"Dead slow ahead, starboard easy".

As she came round to bring wind and sea fine to starboard, the ship suddenly faltered and fell off into the trough. Our good old 'controllable' pitch propeller had casually put itself *astern!*

She rolled once – God, would she ever come back?

"Hard a'port, full ahead!"

She rolled twice, gathering momentum – next roll she'd go over. Instead, she surged ahead, turning to port out of the trough. The chief engineer, at the controls below, had realised what was happening and threw the engine (and propeller) full ahead at once. We got her round onto an easterly course and I held her there. Those two and a half rolls on top of her previous gyrations had left the impression of a ship plucked from the sea by some evil giant who shook her upside down a few times, then dropped her back, by chance, right way up. Another piece of spare machinery, a heavy cylinder cover, sheared its holding down bolts, swiped free the recently resecured piston crown and smashed a lubricating oil pipe. With oil spurting this well-lubricated collection of heavy metal had begun hurtling from side to side, too dangerous to approach until rolling eased. As soon as they fetched up in a corner, they were pounced upon by engineer officers with ropes, chains, steel bars and planks, at no small risk to life and limb and fully conscious of the injuries sustained last time. But had they not secured these heavy items it was inevitable that sooner rather than later they would have either crashed down onto the main engine or gone straight out through the thin plating of the ship's side, throwing the engine room open to the sea. . .

On her easterly course the ship was now reasonably steady and free of potentially dangerous vibration. Two days run ahead lay Bermuda. I would make for this Port of Refuge and in the safety of a peaceful haven we would repair our damage and secure those spare engine parts. Port of Refuge Procedure is almost as old as seafaring, and of course I informed the company and charterers what I was doing and why. The company approved. The charterers did not. Too bad.

As we entered the narrow cleft in the rocks which opens into the lovely harbour of St. George's it was Sunday morning. With church bells ringing in our ears we wondered in our dazed way if we had reached heaven!

By this time all hands were pretty near exhausted. Neither the chief engineer nor I had slept except for catnaps for four days and four nights. The surveyor coming aboard said in all his years – and he was not a young man — he had never seen such chaos. The engineroom was a shambles, the saloon a wreck. The office shared by the chief and myself was ankle deep in papers, well mixed with broken glass, ink and the contents of a self-discharged portable fire extinguisher. Doors were smashed off their cupboards, drawers had shot open depositing their contents over all. And oh – we still hadn't completed filling in the Catering Book!

Two days later we were able to sail for the Canal and enjoyed serene weather all the way to Valpo – where far from being pleased to see us the charterers were furious. After all, as they pointed out, time is money – and I was FIVE DAYS LATE!

Limari at St Geroge's Bay, Bermuda, 25 January 1987.

The Lairg at Auckland.

11.   CHRISTMAS AT SEA

The Crusader Line was formed during the 1950s by a consortium of British shipping companies to develop trade from New Zealand around the Pacific; at first with three purpose-built ships, later with vessels from the parent companies, who completely took over from Crusader during 1970. For several years afterwards, Crusader containers bearing their distinctive badge – yellow sword vertical on a St George's red and white shield against sable background, were to be seen as far afield as the Persian Gulf until it was realised this may cause offence in a Muslim land: Shaw Savill Line took over Crusader's West Indies Service; P & O the run to Japan, while Blue Star Line settled for the West Coast of North America, which soon became known as the WECNA trade. Via Suva and other Fijian ports, Hawaii and American Samoa (Pago Pago) it became, from the seafarer's point of view, the pleasantest of the Company's services. For many years it was maintained by the *Southland Star* and *Wellington Star*, both built during the 1960s by Bremer Vulcan as twin-Stulcken conventional refrigerated cargo liners, converted to box boats at their builder's yard in 1977. As the trade developed it was decided that a third ship was needed, able to carry the old-fashioned break-bulk cargo (not in containers), especially steel and lumber. Able to work this cargo in and out with her own derricks, the *Lairg* was chosen and put on the service.

Built as Andrew Weir's *Rudbank* by British Shipbuilders at the Wearside Deptford yard in 1979, she had been bought by the Vestey group and placed with Lamport and Holt as their *Romney* in 1983. As such she earned good freight by regularly carrying much of the necessary building equipment from Avonmouth to the Falkland Islands for the new airport. Her floodable No. 2 hold was ideal for carrying diesel fuel in bulk for the construction vehicles while holds and upper decks were crammed, trip after trip, with every item needed to built a large military airport over 7,000 miles from home. Mount Pleasant Airport was formally opened by HRH Prince Andrew in May 1985, which saw the beginning of the end of *Romney's* Falklands work. By no means the least difficult part of this was getting into East Cove – handier for the new airport than Stanley. A temporary jetty-head had been provided by mooring the *Merchant Providence* close in – with a connecting road ramp to the shore. An ex-German cargo liner, she initially provided accommodation for airport workers. Her Denham's chief officer had himself charted the cove and laid the buoys marking the entrance channel – a most useful work in a shallow harbour wide open to Cape Horn gales. The bottom according to the old chart was clay (good holding ground for an anchor) but in fact turned out to be only shallow slurry over rock (NOT good holding ground!) which made the necessary evolution of dropping the port anchor to turn sharply on it fraught with interest. Northbound, *Romney* picked up the traditional Lamport and Holt Brazilian loadings for Dublin and Liverpool. On completion of her Falklands work she was laid-up in Liverpool for a while before setting off for Singapore via the Mediterranean, Suez Canal and the Red Sea with cargo for India. In 1986 she emerged from Singapore drydock and refit in the new colours of Lion Shipping Ltd, which incorporated her L & H black hull minus white line, with a black and white topped funnel emblazoned with a white forward-facing rampant lion on red. This was the Company which employed the new Chinese crews, but by the time I joined the *Lairg* (as she was now named) these lads had been well-trained by her British officers; and I found a well-found, well-run ship. Of 12,213.98 tons gross she had four cargo hatches forward and one aft. Her cargo was handled by Velé derricks and propulsion was provided by a 12,000 bhp Doxford four cylinder engine. She had been built with endearingly old fashioned non-bulbous bow and wooden-sheathed decks on bridge and boat decks.

After my first voyage in her, from Los Angeles in September 1987 to New Zealand, my wife joined at the end of October. Next morning we moved round to Long Beach which shared its commercial port with the US Navy. One of the newly-recommissioned *Missouri* class battleships lay at anchor – an impressive sight by the dawn's early light. Impressive, too, was RMS *Queen Mary* which, together with Howard Hughes' spectacularly unsuccessful plywood flying boat *Spruce Goose* was advertised as 'The World's Biggest Double Feature and Fantasy Adventure'. The *Spruce Goose* became the largest plane ever to fly when she took to the air in 1947 – for one minute at a height of 70 feet for one mile. Since 9th December 1967 *Queen Mary* had dominated the Long Beach waterfront and we found our visit to her well worthwhile. Part hotel, part showpiece, she still retained much of her original style and elegance.

Sailing from California north to Cape Flattery, we came through the pine-scented strait of Juan de Fuca which separates the USA from Canada – down Admiralty Inlet to the most southerly deepwater port on Puget Sound, Tacoma, in the state of Washington. Less than a day here was spent discharging and loading – we took containers and earth-moving machinery, before setting off on the twelve-hour run to Vancouver. Sheltered waters most of the way – it was only crossing Juan de Fuca Strait in dense fog that a swell coming in from the Pacific caused the ship to roll slightly. The mate had his crew cleaning holds ready to load lumber – strapped bundles of sawn red cedar – and paper. This latter came in enormous rolls in delicate shades of blue, primrose and pink and yes, they were destined for toilet purposes, to be cut down to size, we understood, at their destination, Suva.

Vancouver is a lovely city and one night we took the cable car up snowdeep mountains to a hilltop restaurant. The ride was enlivened by a .303 bullet zipping through the window just behind my wife, to fall spent and harmless at her feet. We were hastily assured by the gondola staff that this was probably the act of some wayward nutter. . . and on the house we enjoyed a large drink, and our meal at the restaurant, to find our bullet-holed car had been removed from service for the (uneventful) downward trip.

As we sailed from Vancouver on a glittering calm frosty night the city's lights were perfectly reflected in the harbour, silhouetting the Narrows as we passed under the elegant tracery of Lion's Gate Bridge at the entrance. Clearing the numerous fishermen lying to their nets in the straits, we headed south for the tiny port of Coos Bay, in Oregon.

Occasionally heavy breakers on the bar precluded entering Coos Bay but we were lucky. There was only a "moderate swell". The pilot boarded outside, to surfride us through the entrance, turn hard a'port inside the breakwaters – and take us fourteen miles up a winding creek. Past Empire and North Bend, where lumber mills were "going like steam" in the densely wooded countryside – to Coos Bay itself.

The longshoremen here worked at great speed – we had only the briefest time to go ashore shopping. Items in the shops were remarkably inexpensive and a must for visitors was Myrtlewood. The myrtle tree grows in two places – we were advised – Israel and Oregon – where its wood is fashioned into everything from necklaces to cuckoo clocks. Laden with parcels, the tourists repaired aboard and we sailed, south again to Oakland, San Francisco's container port, with no time to go ashore. Then we sailed back to Los Angeles, where a superb evening meal lacked the excitement of .303 fire, but beautifully ended our spell On The West Coast.

For this was where the coasting ended and deep water began; after six days of cool, grey, blustery weather we approached Honolulu, on the southern side of the island of Oahu, where steep valleys are constantly brightened by rainbows. We called here to load a dismantled sugar mill – pretty old by the looks of it – for Suva. Hawaii, it seemed, was getting out of sugar in favour of pineapples and tourism, while Fiji was now focussing on sugar production. Honolulu is the 50th state's principal port and a great deal of traffic has for many years passed up and down the West Coast of North America by barge and out to Hawaii. In the late 'forties and early 'fifties Liberty ship hulks were towed two at a time grain-laden over these routes. Today's barges are even larger.

Against the skyscrapers of downtown Honolulu stood the tall masts and spars of a vessel whose rig was rare even in the days of sail – the four-masted full-rigged ship *Falls of Clyde*. A rare bird not only in rig, this remarkable vessel was once a sailing oil tanker and later became one of Captain Matson's first ships, her memory perpetuated in one of his houseflag's seven white stars. She was the first deep-vessel to be registered in Honolulu, a sailing passenger-carrying cargo liner by then, operating between San Francisco and the Hawaiian Islands. She must have been a wonderful ship to work in – and was now in an advanced state of loving restoration. Of course, we visited her first, then the town. Strolling along Waikiki Beach as to the manner born. Next day we visited Pearl Harbour, still an important US Naval Base. The USS *Arizona* Memorial, operated in conjunction with the National Park Service, was a touching and awesome reminder of that dreadful day in December 1941 when, without any warning or declaration of war, the Japanese attacked. *Arizona's* young men were enjoying a "long lie-in" that Sunday morning, as a reward for having come second in the previous night's Band Contest – so were mostly drowned in their bunks when the battleship sank at her moorings. The memorial itself, in gleaming white concrete, spans the sunken vessel, parts of which are still visible in the green water. There were many Japanese visitors that day and we wondered how they felt. . .

From Honolulu next morning we sailed south by west for Pago Pago. Several of our Chinese crew members had visited the *Arizona* and were deeply moved, sending postcards home which they gave me to mail for them. We were impressed by the film-illustrated talk given before our boat trip out to the memorial – all without cant – simply giving an account of the ships life and Pearl Harbour as it happened.

The weather improved as we headed into the tropics and soon our small ship's pool was in constant use. Friday night was barbeque night – quaint western custom in which our Chinese crewmen did not seem to wish to participate. Not one of the South Seas coral atoll islands, American Samoa rises in steep, majestic jungle-covered hills 2,000 feet high, the harbour of Pago Pago situated on the southern side of the island of Tutuilla. The Polynesian pronunciation is PANGO PANGO, which village lies at the upper end of the inlet while the deep sea wharf lies nearer the sea, at Fagatogo, the seat of government. A US colony in everything but name, Samoa is a delightful spot, a yachtperson's paradise, far from the madding crowd. The Rainmaker Hotel celebrates Somerset Maugham's 'Rain' and its dubious heroine Miss Sadie Thompson, while down the road the equally touristy Sadie's Bar was under construction. But so far, genuine tourists were few, the trickle not yet the hoped-for stream. They were mainly elderly Americans who tottered from their ship along to the Rainmaker, sank into deep cane chairs for a coke, announced how hot it was, and made their way back as soon as they could to their air conditioned cruise liner. Some years ago an aerial cableway was erected – said to be the Southern Hemisphere's longest at one mile, spanning the harbour from Solo Hill to Mount Alava, 1,700 feet – a superb vantage point on a clear day. Built to facilitate the construction and service of a space station, when the big silver domes were shipped away, no longer needed, the station fell into desuetude and the cableway opened to the public. In 1980 an air display ended in tragedy when a plane crashed into the cable, killing the crew. But the cableway survives.

We had taken timber and other building material to Pago Pago and also the large skiff of a tuna clipper, one of the yachtlike fishermen under the U.S. flag:– so different from the rustbucket tunamen from Taiwan and South Korea which fish the same waters. This 'skiff' was a large, bluff, praam-shaped boat of fibreglass construction, such as are carried piggy-back on the clipper's stern ramp, used for laying and recovering nets. Built in Los Angeles, we first spotted her lying in the river near our berth. But her engine refused to start – she could not come down to us.

Full of resource, three of our officers offered to help and lowered our motor lifeboat to tow the skiff alongside so it could be lifted aboard. On passage to Pago Pago they fixed the engine, to deliver it to a happy consignee. All part of our smiling service!

The International Dateline was crossed between Pago and Suva, making our two-day passage three on the calendar. The Fiji tourist trade was struggling to repair its reputation since the recent coup, in which the Fijian ethnic minority prevented the Indian immigrant majority from attaining political power (but because this serious conflict between peoples was a strictly dark-skinned affair it received not half so much publicity as it would have had the minority been white, perhaps?). Signs of the quite bloody takeover were mercifully few. Several Indian shops were having closing-down sales in Suva streets reminiscent of Bombay, other shops were selling T-shirts emblazoned with "Coup – what coup?" But when Cunard announced the *Queen Elizabeth 2* would call at Suva on a Sunday, the strictly Methodist government said "No way!" And it remains a fact that no business of any kind may be conducted here on the Sabbath. Cunard cut Fiji out of their flagship's itinerary and the Fijian businessmen went to Church. . . by order.

Three Indians came to inspect our sugar mill and supervised its unloading into a barge. They pronounced their satisfaction at our prompt delivery etc and advised that the various parts would be fitted into sugar mills around the islands – they hoped we would bring them some more next trip.

Suva market is always a bustle of activity and our Chinese chief steward asked my wife to accompany him and the chandler to purchase provisions. Catering for seventeen Chinamen, fifteen European officers and two Fijian cadets calls for understanding, common sense and patience, as well as skilled catering. The pennies must be watched, our people adequately fed – achieving this balance occupied us more and more. As every sailor knows, the quality and quantity of his food are of prime importance in sustaining ship's morale!

From Fiji's steamy heat to the pleasant semi-tropical summer in North New Zealand, we spent eight December days in Auckland. This, by modern standards, is a long time – enough for everyone to have a break, and time for the mate to get the funnel painted. In any port it is good practice to have a couple of sailors over the side in the punt, touching-up paintwork, while down in the engineroom, such time allows the chief and his merry men to draw a piston, open an alternator for Lloyd's surveyor to inspect as part of the Continuous Running Survey, and carry out modifications to the holds' ventilation system thus accommodating self-sustaining reefer containers of beef. Though not built as a refrigerated ship (a reefer) the *Lairg* was made able to carry reefer containers, (provided each of these carried its own refrigerating motor). All that was needed was a convenient source of power, adequate ventilation and a keen efficient chief engineer – instant reefer!

Surprisingly we loaded steel coils in Auckland for the USA; and in the Bay of Plenty, Tauranga – our next port – vast quantities of newsprint in reels, for Long Beach, California. Smacking of coals to Newcastle, perhaps, but providing employment for ships (and those who man them!)

Tauranga has at its harbour entrance the celebrated Mount Maunganui, a green extinct volcano dotted in December with the red flowers of the Pohutikawa Tree, called in New Zealand the Christmas Tree for obvious reasons. When during the early 'sixties New Zealand's trade with Japan began to boom, one of the first exports to "take off" was the log trade. The Pinus Radiata tree grows rapidly in New Zealand and Japanese eat their meals with disposable wooden chopsticks. If 120 million Japanese eat three meals a day. . . But not only log ships line Tauranga's waterfront. Butter and kiwi fruit are exported in abundance. On one of our sorties ashore we watched lorries laden with beehives moving from one kiwi fruit farm to another – an essential part of the pollination process.

Leaving Tauranga we passed White Island during the afternoon. An active volcano, now uninhabited, the rock was once mined for its sulphur deposits. As we steamed by on a calm Saturday sea, gaseous cloud darkened the sky and a mighty rushing wind passed over the ship, drawn in by heat from the crater. It was an awe-inspiring reminder of the seemingly casual forces of nature. . . Only the older generation now remember the earthquake which devastated Napier in 1931 – photographs taken then show similarities to a recently suffered air raid. The harbour was "restructured", so that the deepwater port now lies at the foot of the creamy coloured cliffs. Until the breakwaters were extended during the 1960s vessels moored alongside had to "slip" moorings and proceed to sea if a rising swell made the port untenable. Even now a special mooring gang boarded on arrival, setting up special coir "springs" with quick-release senhouse slips, to cope with any swell and make instant departure safely possible. But we spent less than a day in Napier, loading containers full of frozen beef in our newly 'reefer enhanced' holds.

It had not been intended to call northbound at Pago Pago but a ship which regularly loaded canned tuna fish there had got into collision and was now in a Korean repair yard. Could we load 2,000 tonnes, in containers – mostly on deck? Calculations made by the chief officer, our stability calculator, and yours truly working individually decided stability would become no problem, so we took it – a bonus on our freight that voyage!

We sailed from Pago Pago on 17th December – bound for Los Angeles where our estimated time of arrival was 29th. Christmas, therefore, would be spent at sea roughly 1,000 miles east of the Hawaiian Isles. Our Chinamen had not seen an English Christmas and while the two cooks could now roast and carve turkey, they were unfamiliar with the "trimmings" and the way we would want it done. Could my wife help, please, and show them how? She was, of course, delighted. Coming to the company group from Bank Line it seemed our ship had gone too long – said our catering superintendent in London – without a proper stocktake. Would I "just see to this, please?" Well, everyone else had their own work to do; the Chinese chief steward was not really up to this kind of thing, yet – but it would be (I felt) a good job for the master and his wife to tackle. Imagine stocktaking everything in a small hotel with 34 persons living therein, (only afloat), in hot weather. . . It was in fact great fun, in which everyone cheerfully co-operated. Questionnaires were made out and issued (fortunately we had a small photocopier) – translated where applicable into Chinese by the chief steward. All hands wrote on it how many of everything they had in their cabins on a certain Friday, with conditions of their mattresses, towels, pillowslips, sheets, etc. Carpets, curtains, teaspoons and mugs were counted. That took care of cabin contents. We measured each cabin:– that too, was part of "request". The cooks emptied their lockers – everything was examined. Some items of Bank Line's Indian cookery were unidentifiable and really unsuitable for further use. Gleefully our cooks gave these items the "heave-ho" into Davy Jones's locker. . . Items which had not seen the light of day since the ship's initial storing in Sunderland eight years previously – still in their packing cases – were unpacked, counted and listed. Several large stainless steel oval carving dishes, a full set of mint condition Bank Line coffee cups and saucers, jugs and sauceboats – these would come in for Christmas!

We had of course purchased many of the necessities in Canada, Coos Bay and Auckland on our shopping expeditions, but we made the streamers ourselves out of crepe paper. Two good-quality artificial Christmas trees came to light during our stocktake, their boxes stencilled *Romney*. There were also decorations – even a box of crackers. Our own purchases included a green circular wreath for the captain's front door. The chief steward, astonished by our preparations as were all his men – fingered this plastic wreath wonderingly and proclaimed it "Almost like really!" Shyly he told us that his sister, back in Tianjin, was "A Religious" and had asked him to send her the words of our Christmas carols. As Christmas approached the ship took on a festive air although decorating the saloon was left until Christmas Eve itself. Bread sauce was made in our bedroom on a small electric heater discovered during stocktaking. The sherry trifles were also made in our

Christmas party in the Captain's cabin, *Lairg*, at sea, 1987.
Our Chinese crew had not seen Christmas before!

Brenda helping cooks, *Lairg*, Christmas 1987.

cabin, likewise the shrimp cocktails, which the third engineer's wife helped my wife to prepare. Reams of instructions were carefully translated for the cook, by the chief steward into Mandarin. Questions were answered, such as "When to make the rum sauce?" "When must potatoes be ready?" etc etc. . . Lack of space precluded all hands eating Christmas Dinner in the same room so the Chinese ate in their festively decorated messroom, the officers in the saloon. Same meal, commencing 1300.

Christmas dawned fine and clear but heavily overcast with a fresh north-easterly whipping whitecaps off a grey swell, coming from right ahead. The ship was pitching but, fortunately, not rolling. With time in hand I could afford to ease our speed to ensure nothing would be spilt.

White tablecloth, red table decorations, tall red candles, gleaming silver and glasses, crackers at each place, streamers overhead and Merry Christmas in snow upon the large sideboard mirror. . . Her Majesty the Queen smiled upon us from her picture on the bulkhead. First came the shrimp cocktails in stainless steel coupés, then steaming hot soup. The turkeys, carved to perfection in the galley only a few steps from the saloon were placed in two heaps, white meat and dark, upon a large oval dish and brought into the saloon. Dinner plates came hot from the galley with parsnips, potatoes, carrots, brussels sprouts to be placed two by two on the sidetable. The captain's wife transferred turkey slices and chipolatas to each plate, two by two, whilst the captain bore these plates, two by two, to each person sitting – service with a smile! Stuffing, bread sauce, cranberry sauce and gravy were all to hand, as was the wine the chief engineer in charge of it. Thus, everyone got their main course hot and together, followed by Christmas pudding with steaming white rum sauce. At a get-together on Christmas Eve in our cabin nostalgic comments were passed about the puddings of long ago with silver threepenny bits. So today's portions included a 20p piece each, wrapped in greaseproof paper. We were touched to discover that somehow our portions, miraculously, contained a pound piece each.

Christmas dinner at sea is always a time for toasts. The first, always, being –"the Queen", drunk remaining seated, naval fashion. (In the wooden walls of England this was to prevent heads cracking on low deckhead beams). Wives, sweethearts, absent friends – all were toasted in turn and not all of us remained dry eyed. Coffee in hitherto unused Bank Line cups completed the meal. My wife had in the past catered for many Christmas Family Dinners, but here she surpassed even herself – everyone said so.

The weather improved as we approached Los Angeles, and as we made our way into the harbour the smooth sea was crowded with yachts, almost as though they were escorting us in. In Californian shirt and long shorts, smoking a big cigar, our genial pilot climbed aboard from his cutter.

"Compliments of the season, Cap – how was Christmas?"

12. FRESH HORIZONS

Our Christmas voyage in the *Lairg* was my last with the Blue Star Group after 37 years, but I did not yet feel ready for the pipe and slippers of retirement. Yet I soon found, after casting around, that no British shipping company was interested in an old codger of 55 – especially one who had no experience of oil or gas tankers. Blue Star however came to the rescue. They had long been associated in Australia with a small family company based on Singapore, now running their four ships on a regular cargo liner service – one per month – from Shanghai through Singapore to Colombo, Karachi and ports in the Persian Gulf. On the strength of Blue Star friends' recommendations I was offered a master's job by return of post.

After years of container-carrying I found a way of life which had more in common with Conrad's day than the rush and bustle to which I had become accustomed. . . Leisurely voyages lifting not the all-concealing Twenty-Foot Equivalent-Units of boxboat jargon but real cargo one could actually see. A fascinating object lesson for me – on how things could once again become after the box boats had priced themselves out of existence. . .

Beginning at Singapore, 19th February 1989 –

The company launch thudded out from Clifford Pier across the sparkling sunlit water of the Eastern Roads where lay at anchor enough ships to satisfy the most ardent ship-spotter. Several miles to the east, silhouetted against the bright morning sun lay the tankers; closer in, dry cargo and container ships; near at hand, short sea traders in abundance. One even had the bar stem and counter stern of long ago, her midships bridge and funnel aft bearing the unmistakable stamp of the Straits Steamship Company of which she had once been part. There, beyond a pair of fish factory trawlers lay the *Tomoh Satu* of Labuan, her Vestey-shaped bridge and funnel clearly identifying her as one of those fine vessels built for the Blue Star group. Sure enough, I found in Lloyd's that she had been Booth Line's *Cyril*, formerly Lamport and Holt's *Sheridan* built in 1961. A gleaming white ship with many lifeboats, rows of portholes and bristling antennae was our old friend the Soviet research ship, while beyond a brace of oilrig supply boats a North Korean log carrier was being towed in by a Panamanian deep-sea tug after engine failure at sea.

Eastern ensigns predominated but the ubiquitous stars and quarters of Panama flew at the stern of many a vessel whose only link with the isthmus republic is her port of registry. The once familiar Liberian flag was becoming rare, since Liberia raised her standards and tightened her regulations, but where one flag of convenience furls at least two more are broken out and the banners of Malta and the Virgin Islands were here, with many Greek now under the white flag of Cyprus. As befitted, there were plenty Singaporean

The *Golden Haven* with white forecastle.

ensigns, not a few from the People's Republic of China. A sky-blue Dane and a green West German showed that Europe is still into deep sea ship owning – just – but although an Australian container ship was putting to sea – of the British flag, not a flutter. My own ship eventually hove into view beyond a huge Bulgarian bulker.

The *Golden Haven – Jing Gang* in Chinese – was built at Flushing by De Schelde as the British flag *London Advocate* in 1964. Her clipper non-bulbous bow, graceful sheer, streamlined bridge-and-funnel amidships and neat cruiser stern were those of a ship which looked like a ship, a true lady surrounded by today's functional uglies. Lloyd's Register states that she was specially strengthened during building for heavy cargoes, an undoubted contribution to her longevity. There were three cargo hatches forward, two aft. Deep tanks for water ballast or other liquids were situated abaft Number 3 hold. A single tween deck ran through each hold and cargo handling gear comprised – rather unusually – 5-ton SWL derricks to port with 10-ton SWL derricks to starboard. A 60-ton jumbo at No. 2 and a 40 tonner at hatch 4 were now not in use. Propulsion consisted of a six-cylinder Sulzer 6RD76 of 7,000 bhp, turbo-charged to give an original $15^1/_2$ knots. Since slow nozzles were fitted her service speed had reduced to $12^1/_2$ knots, economically adequate for the service. Each round voyage from China to the Gulf and back takes approximately four months; – general cargo westwards, bulk cargo east. When I joined to relieve Captain Harvey her crew of 34 included an Irish chief officer, Singapore Chinese chief engineer and Chinese chief cook. That the cook and I had sailed together in Blue Star Line at one time seemed to ensure I was well fed. The others came from Burma, Bangladesh, Ghana and

Indonesia. There was a Singapore Chin Chew.

What's a Chin Chew?

Nowadays, he's the purser, attending the ship's paper work and accounts of wages, housekeeping and victualling, but in the good old days before radio he was the Chinese Owner's Representative, booking and arranging cargoes from port to port, telling the British captain where to go next – a very important person. He still is, of course, though now the British captain receives his orders direct by radio from the Singapore office and our Mr Yeo was in fact the last Chin Chew the company employed. He kept a pair of pigeons in a disused shipboard laundry (laughingly referred to as the Emergency Radio Room) though as far as I know they were never used to send messages.

Headquartered in Telok Ayer Street, a charming backwater of Old Singapore where crowded pavements and low buildings are surrounded by the skyscrapers of the modern city, Guan Guan Shipping is an old established Chinese family company. The very name, Guan Guan means, in Chinese, continually flowing gold, hence the Golden Line. Owning at one time round fifty ships, including passenger liners and short-sea traders, the Golden Line's distinctive black-topped blue funnels with matching blue masts and derricks over black or grey hulls, red boot-topping and gleaming white superstructure, are well known in Eastern waters. In the pre-boxboat era they ran in conjunction with Blue Star a service to Australia and occasionally New Zealand but this ended when box boats began and has not been resumed.

After storing, bunkering, watering, effecting a few repairs and changing a few crew members, we sailed next day for Shanghai. The pirate-infested waters east of Singapore were perforce traversed by night, cargo lights over the side, decks illuminated, constant deck patrol maintained and a vigilant lookout kept, not only for lawful ships but for small boats shooting out from any of the numerous heavily wooded islands, to cast grapnels over our sternrail. It was only weeks since the company's *Golden Harvest* was boarded in these waters by pirates who made off with personal valuables, radios and cassette players but little money. The captain was bound hand and foot but otherwise no attempt was made to cause personal injury. It was only when his steward came in in the morning that anyone else realised a robbery had taken place. To some poverty-stricken Indonesians piracy became a way of life. Unless caught in the act detection was virtually impossible as they melted into their village communities, unarmed except with the long knives used by fishermen. Prevention is the only satisfactory way of avoiding attack. They rarely inflicted personal injury and doubtless seemed as romantic nautical Robin Hoods to those not subject to their visits. Piracy, however, became Big Business, with the inevitable involvement of guns and killings – high-value cargoes of electronic and other dutiable goods being prime targets. As we headed north the northeast monsoon strengthened and remained with us for the next week, bringing cold weather, rough, white-capped grey seas, a heavy swell and frequent sweeping rain. Our British-made Navstar satellite navigator proved invaluable, giving accurate positions in weather which rendered use of the sextant impossible. As the head-on swell increased I reduced speed to prevent heavy seas coming over the bows. 'Shipping it green' may look spectacular and features well in nautical fiction but in real life one 'greeny' coming aboard can do untold damage. I found the old ship was a splendid seaboat, rolling easily and comfortably in seas which would cause many a modern vessel to perform the most violent gyrations.

The Japan Current sweeps to the north-north-east around Taiwan, stronger to the east than through Formosa Strait at that time of the year, so I took the eastern route, outside, which also allows more searoom if a serious storm develops. Though this route to Shanghai was a few miles longer, it was safer, and in the long run, just as quick.

In murky weather early on the 1st March we came to anchor in the Chanjiang Kou, the mouth of the great Yangtze River, some 65 miles below the city. It was the time of the quarter moon, neap tides – highest low and lowest high – and our 31 feet (9.39 metres) draft was too deep for the bar so I was ordered by radio to await further orders, at anchor. Twenty four hours later the tides were making and we weighed anchor, when thick fog descended, closing the port. Next day the fog began to lift and I was ordered to embark a pilot at No.9 buoy five miles up from the sea where conditions were less dangerous, the sea calmer. He came to us in a small open launch from a big white cruising pilot cutter. This was my first visit to Shanghai and I was naturally filled with anticipation and not a little apprehension – as one always is when entering a 'new' port for the first time in fog.

Creeping up the mist-shrouded estuary we were at first unable to see either bank except on radar. Our pilot was a smartly-uniformed cheerful 32 year old (the chinese discuss age almost with their first greeting, I found; eg: "Full ahead Captain, steer 265 – and by the way, how old are you?"). Expertly he directed our course and speed between buoyed shoals and, as traffic grew busier he carefully avoided the numerous ships and fishing vessels crossing our path. A sudden, strident commotion on the VHF in rapid chinese told of a collision ahead between a deep-laden Chinese collier and a Polish container ship. We soon came upon this chilling scene, realising that "But for the Grace of God there go I". The collier was beached on a mid-river sandbank to prevent her sinking in the channel, with the Pole's bulbous bow buried deep in her port side. Fortunately there were no human casualties and by the time we left Shanghai six weeks later both ships had been repaired and were back in service.

Swinging to port at the small hill which dominates an otherwise flat landscape we left the Yangtze behind and entered the Huangpo (has various spellings) – the river on which stands the city which has been a port for thousands of years. I soon realised this must be one of the world's busiest waterways. Most of the ships were Chinese but by no means all carried the familiar yellow funnels with star-and-waves over the grey hull with green boot-topping. Numerous 'private' companies now operate within the state system, with their own liveries, an expanding fleet currently owning over fifteen hundred vessels, increasing as trades develop. With a 'well-paid' Chinaman earning less than the equivalent of £300 per annum it is difficult to see how the rest of the world could compete. . . At the time much Chinese tonnage was second hand and quite elderly. Ships built for British and particularly German owners during the 'fifties and 'sixties were common, but shipyards all the way up the Huangpo were busily engaged in new construction. A large container ship for Hapag Lloyd was on the stocks that first visit – several months later she was fitting-out alongside, the *Berlin Express*. New ships for Cuba and Hamburg Sud were also on view, but most seemed destined to sail under the Red Ensign of the People's Republic.

In the lower reaches were container berths where huge box boats arrived in the morning and sailed at night having worked in and out more cargo in that time than my own ship would handle in a week. But these ships were trading to 'The West' where, for various reasons, conventional trade has become impractical. My own ship operates between ports where labour and port costs are relatively low priced and the risk of pilferage and delay-through-strikes practically unknown. In other words, if costs can be kept low without impairing efficiency there is no need for the enormous expense of containerisation. *Golden Haven's* cargo was 11,000 tonnes of bagged urea from Ruwais in the United Arab Emirates, the most southerly of the Persian Gulf ports. Urea carried from New Zealand was a final product of protein decomposition (dried animal urine) but in the Gulf it is yet another bi-product of the oil industry. Both natural and synthetic fertiliser is in increasing demand in China if she is to feed her billion-plus population. When one considers that China has one quarter of the world's population but only one sixth of its arable land, it will be seen that China's main concern is to Grow More Food.

Destined up-country, our cargo would be transhipped in barges which may take weeks to reach their destination, such is the extent of China's inland waterways.

Carefully we made our way up through the murk, then the sun came out, burning away the morning mist to reveal outlines of ships working cargo in and out along miles of wharves, with more ships lying tier upon tier to buoys midstream, surrounded by clusters of barges. On either side of the buoyed ships a mighty traffic plied ceaselessly up and down this multi-lane highway.

A maximum string of barges (12) in tow on the Huangpo river, Shanghai.

Stately white passenger liners came and went on regular services to Japan and Hong Kong. An increasing number of Western cruise ships now included Shanghai in their itineraries. Ferries scuttled in all directions. Some were large coastal ferries, passenger liners in miniature, for air travel had, as yet, hardly impinged on Chinese life. Ultra modern catamaran ferries plied the estuaries, almost as large as the coastwise vessels, while smaller traditional ferries carried commuters and served ships at the buoys. Cheerful green, white and orange were the traditional ferry colours though vehicular ferries were in battleship grey, rushing lorries, vans, cargo and foot passengers across the strongly running tide. At night the ferries carried a flashing masthead orange light to distinguish them from the myriad other craft. Tugs pushing huge rectangular barges carried a blue light. Coasters large and small passed continually. Grimy colliers from North China, deep-sea tankers and cargo ships enormous floating cranes – even the occasional junk, picturesque under her bamboo-battened sails with large eyes painted on the bows. Sailing craft and supertankers, they were all here – and barges. During the afternoon we passed Shanghai's business centre, the Bund, whose solidly Thames-Embankment-like substantial buildings complete with ornate street lamps and flashing neons came as something of a culture shock when rounding the bend of the river. Everywhere else the river banks were crowded with heavy industry stretching for miles, tall chimneys, power stations, factories of all kinds (including the Smart Shirt Factory). New blocks of flats arose under their skeletal cranes everywhere one looked with, crouching behind, the quaint high-peaked roofs and dormer windows of an earlier China. It was dark by the time we came to our berth between Buoys 73 and 74 after a river passage where we had twice to drop anchor and several times stop engines, then go astern to avert collision. Before our ropes were secure to the buoys a dozen barges had swooped down and made themselves fast alongside. Steel, round-bowed craft with neither engines nor sails – what are quite mistakenly known as "dumb" barges, they clamoured for our cargo. Each had a small house aft in which lived her people; parents, beautifully dressed children, dog, cat inevitably a few chickens. The vegetable garden grew on the roof, smoke drifted from the small stove-funnel and washing dried to windward strung out on a line. A home afloat, but a home without electricity or power of any kind save the two hand capstans on which the whole family could often be seen working. Their water supply, all purposes, is the river on which they float. If father and son are walking round the capstan, mother and daughters tend the mooring wires as they work their way around the ship from hatch to hatch. China's stern one-child-per-family rule (to break which incurs severe penalty) seemed to be ignored On The River, whose people were a law unto themselves.

As soon as our hatches were opened by our sailors work commenced. Dockers drove the electric winches to lift the straw-coloured nylon-weave 50kg bags out of the hold forty per sling, over the side and down into a barge. More dockers assisted the family to stow their craft's long, single hold. Work proceeded day and night with great clamour while the brown tide swirled past. From where we stood it was easy to count a hundred barges without trying, on our own reach of the river alone – the waterborne population must run into millions. They are cheerful, hardworking folk and their life is often cold and always dangerous. Not surprisingly they wear lifejackets at all times. One slip into the rushing water could mean a swift watery grave trapped beneath a barge or ship.

One morning one of 'our' barges accidentally slipped astern and jammed beneath our mooring wire, which began to prise the roof off the little house to the screams of women and children, tinkle of breaking glass and the crack of splintering wood. More serious was the alarming list to port the deep laden barge was taking, trapped against the six-knot tide. She would have inevitably been forced under had not my own crew taken prompt action to avert disaster by passing her a line, slacking our wire, and hauling her clear. On another occasion, from my cabin, I watched a junk tacking her graceful way past a string of deep-laden barges on one of which a person was suddenly running aft, leaping from barge to barge with a long boathook. Splashing in the water could only mean one thing – man overboard! By the

135

Above:
Girl welders, *Golden Haven,* Zhanghua Shipyard, Shanghai.

Left:
Trimming the coals.

time I had turned to grab my binoculars the barges had passed behind a tier of moored ships. . .

After four days unloading we were moved upriver into shallower water, at Buoys 78/79, on 8th March, continued for another ten days, then, holds swept empty, went alongside the Zhonghua shipyard for "Small Lepair". By the time a working cargo ship is a quarter of a century old her steelwork needs constant attention – much of which here was attended by young women welders. Feminine despite their drab overalls they stood no nonsense from their male comrades who seemed to regard the girls with amused kindly tolerance. As our "Small Lepair" neared completion a party was given for us in the shipyard canteen, a Chinese meal par excellence over which looked a huge red and black banner reading (in Chinese) 'the Harder We Work The More We Earn'.

The weather in Shanghai was cold in March and passing continually from cosily heated accommodation to the icy conditions on deck may have caused most of us to catch' 'flu. I spent a couple of days in my bunk feeling very sorry for myself but our Chinese Second Engineer felt so unwell he was admitted to the Seamen's Hospital. His death the following day (of more than mere 'flu, I was told) cast a gloom of sadness over the whole ship as our ensign was lowered to half-mast until after his funeral.

At the shipyard we lay near a coal wharf where large colliers unloaded. Much of their cargo was then transhipped into barges for transport up into the counties. When laden, the barges assembled into trains of six pairs, right under my bedroom window. The wives worked as energetically as their husbands using long-handled shovels to trim the coal into the far corners of their barge's hold. On completion, wooden buckets were dipped overside and decks washed down to remove all traces of coal dust. At night lanterns danced like fireflies as the barges rocked gently in the water of a passing tanker. Capstans clanked, dogs barked, cocks crowed and people called out to each other as the barges bumped and clanged along our ship's side. Eventually the assembled "train", secured together with ropes and chains, hitched up to a small green diesel tug which assumed its position as "locomotive" at the head. More toots on its whistle and off they went into the night accompanied by much cheerful banter between those leaving and those awaiting the next train.

Other barges in similar trains swept past continuously carrying all manner of cargoes. Some were full of bright red bricks, others piled high with sheets of Indonesian plywood. Deep-laden craft, their deck awash, carried cement and sand, gravel and rock, coils of steel wire, iron pipes, bales of cotton and paper, bags of rice. One resembled a floating haystack. Logs and concrete beams overhung the ends and sides of some barges so it was a wonder they could remain float. Some craft were self propelled and travelled singly, or towed another barge. Twin inboard-outboard engines on deck right over the stern belt – drove them along in fine style, emitting small clouds of steam from the water cooling in the frosty air. Each morning a varnished sampan drifted past manned by father, mother and teenage son. They seemed to be fishing, dragging a net along the bottom. They WERE fishing, I was told, but for coal spilled from the barges!

From the shipyard we moved on 27th March to Buoys 44/45 and began loading sacks of beans (which looked like dried peas). Our sailors had cleaned the holds and the port surveyor had inspected and passed them Fit for Food. Soon after our arrival at Shanghai I had been handed several large sheets of rice paper on which was typed our Shipping List itemising all the cargo booked to be loaded for Colombo, Karachi, Dubai, Dammam and Kuwait – six thousand tonnes of general cargo, "Made in China". I found myself back before the boxboats at once, discussing with the mate how and where to stow it all. Once our broad strategy had been decided he shut himself in his room for a day and, free of all interruption, loaded the ship on paper, item by item. Many of the manufactured goods – industrial, domestic and medical – were similar to those I'd helped carry thirty years before from Britain to New Zealand and Australia:– steel, chemicals, paint, paint brushes, glassware, crockery (china!) cutlery, textiles, toys, musical instruments, machine tools, bicycle parts, diesel engines – as well as the more exotic bales of silk and green tea packed in small burlap-covered chests. Our 'clean' hatches were numbers two and four so all food cargo always went in there. 'Dirties' went into number three. All had to be stowed so that Colombo cargo would be accessible at Colombo, Karachi at Karachi, and so on. It had to be stowed so that cleaning may commence as soon as the first port's cargo was unloaded, as time in the Gulf was critical and to spend too long hatch cleaning after completion of discharge could mean missing the next eastbound charter.

When completed, the mate brought me the proposed stowage plan, the "allocation", as two heads are better than one, and it was important to make sure we had not 'stowed' heavy cargo over light cartons, for instance. . . When we were satisfied, I handed our plan to the agent who translated it into Mandarin for his stevedores and tally clerks. While we had been unloading urea and repairing in the shipyard our cargo had begun assembling on Gonpinglu Wharf under green tarpaulin covers, called by the Chinese "warehouses". But another ship was delayed in our berth by rain, the dockers staged a one day strike, so we were moved out into Yanggzte, to the Wusong anchorage for a couple of days. Here, in clear weather with no wind one fine Saturday afternoon we suddenly began to drag anchor at the turn of the tide. Fortunately we were able to re-anchor before any damage was done, but it was a salutory reminder that NO anchorage can be considered entirely 'safe'. At last, on 8th April, we went alongside and loading began in earnest, day and night.

One dark, wet evening we were required to shift a ship's length astern to allow another ship alongside – an evolution known as warping in which we eased ourselves along using mooring wires and ropes, hauling on winches and windlass, with main engines on stand-by as the tide was strong. As our gangway was partly hoisted ready for the shift, the chief cook – well into his seventies – returning from the shore, thought we were about to sail and made a run for it. Jumping for the raised gangway he missed it, slipped, and fell into the river between ship and quay. At once our Burmese third mate and an Indonesian sailor dived in and rescued him, hauling him aboard shaken and shivering but otherwise none the worse, uttering thanks to his rescuers and apologies to me for putting us out. From then on he had to take much banter about 'long-distance-swimming', but when he retired upon our arrival in Singapore his family wrote to thank our lads for Saving Grandad.

Elsewhere they would probably have qualified for a medal but in Shanghai it was all part of a night's work!

On Saturday afternoon, 15th April, we finally took our departure, passing a smart Chinese frigate in the estuary with whom we dipped ensigns. Back in Singapore eight days later we went alongside Keppel Wharf and topped up with bundles of sawn Malaysian hardwood, drums of latex, steel and more general cargo for Colombo. Our Irish chief officer went home on leave as did several others, new faces joined, stores, water and bunkers were taken and we sailed on 28th April for Colombo.

Beautiful weather attended our passage up Malacca Strait and as we crossed the Bay of Bengal an early Southwesterly light breeze brought showers of rain. Rounding Dondra Head, Sri Lanka's southern headland, we berthed at Colombo on arrival on the evening of 3rd May. Cargo work began next day and a squad of labourers appeared to chip rust off and paint the ship's side. Under the new Burmese mate's direction they did a good job, making the old ship gleam like new.

I now found myself for the first time in my life alone on board with a ship's company of foreigners, our complement being as follows:–

British	1	(me)
Burmese	14	(all the deck officers, radio officer and several ratings. The Burmese Mafia!)
Indonesians	14	(Deck and engineroom ratings)
Bangladeshis	3	(Third engineer and both electricians)
Ghana	1	(Second engineer)
Singapore Chinese	2	(Chief engineer and cook)
Total	35	(An excellent crew with whom it was a pleasure to sail)

The engineers from Burma, Indonesia, Bangladesh and Ghana, *Golden Haven* 1989.

Seamanship class, *Golden Haven*, 1989.

Fortunately for us British, English remains the language of the sea and a ship is a hierarchy in which the captain (master) rules through his senior officers who, in turn, operate through the juniors, petty officers and ratings. So long as everyone knows what has to be done and gets on with it, language itself is not of paramount importance. Most spoke or understood enough English to get by and the seniors sufficient to carry out limited conversation. At first I had thought our Able Seamen were unable to steer – shades of *Limari!* But then I learned the helm orders in Indonesian – and LO! they could steer! Everyone acquired a smattering of other tongues and a cheerful atmosphere prevailed. Most, though not all, of our Burmese were Buddhists and most of the Indonesians were Muslims while a couple were Catholics from the Portuguese Timor days. There were other less prominent religions and I was impressed by the good-natured tolerance of each one for the others. For instance, the fast of Ramaddan was staunchly observed by the Muslims, the main meal of the day being cooked by the non-Muslim catering staff so that the Muslims could eat it well-cooked and hot after sunset, as required by the faith – while at the same time catering for us non-Muslims at ordinary meal times. Ramaddan ended in Colombo and, in company with a PIL* ship astern of us, a great party was held to which we were all invited – a splendid evening! Life on that ship – indeed, I have since found, in all Guan Guan's ships – is an education in communal tolerance and encouragement. I was able to take eight or nine crew members for seamanship lessons on the bridge in the evenings using home-made models. My class was very keen and the models helped overcome language difficulties. My chief officer taught navigation: all in the best seafaring traditions where every ship is a schoolship!

From Colombo we made up to Karachi where we had to anchor for five days awaiting a berth, in another busy, crowded port. In past times I had always anchored west of the fairway but I found here that the approach chart had been pencilled in by my predecessor – "Good fishing here" – east of the fairway. There had been no fish to be caught in the western anchorage but, following this advice, I had fresh fish for breakfast every day here thereafter.

From Karachi we sailed on the evening tide, 24th May, passing through a quiet Straits of Hormuz two days later to berth in Dubai on 27th. On arrival my ship was promptly arrested!

I discovered this was a mistake, of course – the result of a dispute between an Arab shipper of cargo and a Chinese importer. It had nothing to do with our ship but as we were the only vessel on that trade around I was held until Singapore sorted matters out. Dubai is, without a doubt, the pleasantest port in the Gulf, none of us complained about our detention as there was no physical arrest – Only a restraint called an attachment order

---

* PIL – PACIFIC INTERNATIONAL LINES – another Singapore Company.

which the police would enforce if I tried to take my ship away. By 1st June however, all was settled and – after a pleasant break – we sailed for Dammam, where such are the 'security' measures taken that not even our agent was allowed aboard. He (on the quay) and I (on the ship's gangway) had perforce to carry out our daily business *al fresco*. Only two days were spent here before departing for Kuwait, at the head of the Gulf. That night I was diverted from my course by a Saudi warship who called on VHF and told me to give him not less than three miles clearance. Later, a 'US Navy Warship' (her own signaller's description) diverted us again. Clearly, the situation in the Gulf was tense as a result of the Ayotullah's death the day before. It was quite on the cards that the Iranian Revolutionary Guard would embark on a grief-stricken rampage of carnage – as they frequently had in the past when they attacked innocent merchant ships. But even near the Farsi Islands, long used by them as a base for their speedboats, all was quiet. Sighs of relief!

Kuwait laws also prohibit shore-going so none of us were sorry to leave when our last cargo was unloaded. Now I was free to proceed to the loading port – but I had as yet received no orders. No port had yet been nominated, perhaps as a result of further world tension caused by the Tiananmen Square massacre, which had very recently demonstrated to the world that while China may be embracing capitalism as a means of economic survival, that in no way meant any democratisation of their political processes. But despite having nowhere to go, Kuwait ordered me off the berth and out to sea forthwith. I could not even linger at anchor within Kuwaiti waters (rather than in the still-simmering Shatt Al Arab waters outside). I took the hint and departed, steaming south through the stilly night at easy speed (no point in wasting fuel when you are not going anywhere!). Next morning dawned fine and clear and having safely negotiated our way between minefields and oilfields I espied an un-named light beacon some 20 miles off the Saudi coast. Not even a fishing dhow was in sight so I anchored, roughly equidistant from most of our probable loading ports. To give this empty place a name for the logbook I pencilled on the chart 'Min's Anchorage', after the third mate whose watch it was. Later I perceived the chart also bore curly Burmese next to this which I took to be his name in his own language. I was wrong. The second mate had written in the name of the third mate's fiancée.

There was no fishing here, only sharks who sneered at our hooks – so no bathing either though the water looked delicious. On 12th June I received orders to proceed at once at maximum speed to Ruwais, near Abu Dhabi, for another load of bagged urea for China.

A fresh northerly breeze helped the old ship on her way – we averaged fourteen knots! – and by the time we arrived off the port it was blowing a gale. Of course, a gale hereabouts soon brings sand, forming a haze which changes a ship's colour scheme to light brown. Because of the sandstorm the port was closed and I was ordered to anchor. Four large tankers were also anchored awaiting berths but I found a suitable spot, laid out plenty of cable (more than five times the depth of water) and – satisfied that the ship was safe for the night, turned in. During the early part of his middle watch (around 1.30a.m.) the second mate discovered we were dragging. He had noticed the light buoy's bearing changing appreciably and walked forward, placing his hand on the anchor chain where it passed from windlass to hawsepipe. It shuddered, was still, then shuddered again, as the sandstorm howled around him. No doubt!

He called the chief officer who confirmed his suspicions and called me. By this time a full gale was blowing and we were dragging close to one of the tankers. We spent the rest of the night weighing and re-anchoring, an interesting evolution as the ship, empty, careered around on the water like an inflated paper bag, propeller barely submerged. With the dawn the wind died but the haze remained in the air for days, brought down from the deserts to the north.

Berthing the following afternoon, we loaded bagged urea for the next eight days. Ruwais was originally an oil terminal only – jetty protruding from the desert. Several years ago the urea terminal was built, able to load in bags or bulk, and soon after along came the sulphur terminal. No shore leave is allowed, all that can be seen from the berth is the oil terminal, silver tanks and desert sand, with the overhead conveyor belting in its steel trunk housing sighing overhead in the wind, the odd loose piece of corrugated iron rattling intermittently. But at least one could stroll along the jetty here and admire the numerous seabirds while watching the spectacular desert sunsets. Desert foxes dwelt in holes among the concrete tetrapods of which the breakwater was built, and it was while watching for a fox that I noticed that our starboard anchor, hanging from the hawsepipe, was bent so that only one of its two flukes could bite into the seabed. No wonder we had dragged!

An uncanny silence attended our loading at Ruwais. There was no quayside clamour, no swinging cranes or derricks, no visible people. The bags came silently along the conveyor belt high above the quay from the distant production plant. Two electric mechanical loaders driven by one man high up in a cab with another sitting on the delivery end down below scooped the bags off the belt, guided them down a shining steel helter-skelter to the hold where two blue-overalled dockers placed the bags in the stow, row by row. The workers were all Indians, contract labour following in the traditions of the Gulf where, for centuries, Arabs themselves have not deigned to actually do much work, preferring to delegate.

The dockers worked steadily in temperatures well above 40 degrees C, only pausing when the humidity topped 80% – as in enclosed spaces the

143

ammonia fumes made the eyes hurt unbearably. The haze gradually subsided and by the time our 11,000 tonnes were loaded visibility was excellent. We sailed late afternoon 23rd June, making way for a Greek ship.

Passing through Hormuz Strait we headed SE when out into the Arabian Sea – a straight course to India's southern tip, Cape Cormorin, taking the now-fresh SW monsoon on the starboard beam, with frequent rain falling from an unremittingly overcast sky. On 29th June we passed through the Lakshadweep Archipelago (formerly the Laccadives) – low, palm-girt atolls with the sleepy lagoons of the travelogues. Chetlat Island was passed at 10am, Kiltan at noon, Androth at 4pm – we were making a good 12.7 knots point to point. Cape Cormorin was passed at 9am on 30th June and Dondra Head 27 hours later. Until we cleared the land, fishermen were everywhere, their tiny boats difficult to see in the heavy swell. Ships were in sight continually across the Bay of Bengal as this is one of the world's marine motorways.

Entering Malacca Strait south of the lushly green island of Wé, through Bengal and Malacca Passages, we came to Singapore's Eastern Roads on 6th July and remained anchored there overnight – just long enough for me to pay my respects to the company, telephone home and do the shopping, and long enough for the lads to have a run ashore; also to bunker, water and take provisions. A new starboard anchor was delivered by barge. Then we set off for Shanghai. The NE Monsoon was over but the typhoon season was with us and weather forecasts were studied carefully, though the weather remained fine.

Summer in Shanghai was pleasant with daily temperatures in the thirties. The plane trees lining the main streets were in full leaf, flowers bloomed everywhere, girls wore pretty frocks and old ladies in black fanned themselves while their grandchildren ate icecreams. There was no outward sign of the recent Turmoil in Tiananmen Square, Beijing, and it was apparent that the Chinese people had been fed a somewhat different version of the facts than as revealed by Kate Adie and her intrepid BBC TV crew on that fateful night. But now the foreign cruise liners were absent, shipping on the Huangpo markedly less. The tourists had gone and it was almost as though China had turned back the clock to the isolation days. But the fine four-masted Chilean schooner *Esmeralda* made a welcome visit, her gleaming white hull, fairy lit masts and cheerful cadets in their naval uniforms receiving much coverage in the Shanghai media where it was stressed that bonds of international friendship established by such a ship were to be encouraged despite the diametrically opposed government systems of Chile and China. . .

The typhoon system was at its height, bearing out the saw taught in the sea schools. . .. 'June too soon, July stand by, August take care you must, September remember, October all over'. This was August and typhoons had hit north and south China respectively the previous week.

Most of our bagged urea was, on this occasion, unloaded alongside Dongchanglu Wharf opposite the city – a short drive through Chinatown streets and the clean, brightly-lit river tunnel to the agents' office for a phone call home (perfect STD line). We hoped for a quick loading alongside – a quay berth is always preferable to buoys – but once again 'our' berth was already occupied and I was directed to Buoys 16/17S, furthest from the town, nearest to the Yangtze. Two amiable green-uniformed soldiers of the People's Liberation Army Frontier Guard lived aboard, inspecting passes as we went ashore and returned onboard (by midnight, or else!) – their principle purpose onboard seemingly to brush up their English. One of their senior officers paid me frequent visits asking me to explain "Humorous Jokes", mainly from Readers' Digest, of which he was a connoisseur. The Peace Hotel jazz band of six musicians (whose average age was 64 and whose elder members had sailed in British liners trans Pacific during the late thirties) was also greatly entertaining. Mr Yeo, our Chin Chew, introduced me to them and their excellent music at a time when I was the only non-Chinese in the hotel – and they seemed quite pleased to meet this "English Captain".

A typhoon warning urged all ships to increase the strength of their moorings and a port authority motorboat came to assist. Her coxwain would not take the heavy insurance wire stipulated in the warning, and which we offered – "Too hard work!" but settled for six ropes and a slip-wire each end. Both our anchors had been lowered "onto the bottom" (the river bed). Typhoon Lola was hovering over southern Japan, creating havoc in the Amamai Islands and confounding the forecasters daily by moving in small circles instead of taking off for China. Onboard we took hourly readings of barometric pressure, wind direction and force, and temperature, feeling Lola may be coming our way. Already well below seasonal average, the barometer continued to fall rapidly and wind force increased, steady for the WSW. Lola *was* on the way! The previous day, flood waters from torrential rain inland had swollen the Yangtze which, on an exceptionally high tide, ran back up the Huangpo until many of the quays were under water. Rain lashed down, the wind continued to increase from the WSW and at midnight 3rd/4th August I called hands to stations. The mate and half the sailors went forward, the second mate took the other half aft. The chief and watch engineer officers put the engines on Stand By, while I was on the bridge with the third mate and the last sailor. Long after the high tide predicted in the tide tables the river continued to rise and our forward buoy disappeared under water. Fortunately all held fast and at 0530 the ebb began, the barometer began to rise, the wind eased and the rain ceased. Our forward buoy reappeared, seemingly none the worse for its total immersion, and Lola passed inland. We stood down. A week later we went alongside Gongpinglu Wharf, handy for the city, to load steadily day and night until completion on 12th, sailing as soon as all was secured and I had that vital piece of paper, my Clearance. Having to anchor near Zhongsha lightfloat to await the next high water to cross the shallow bar in the river, we noted with relief that our new anchor held securely.

No further typhoons came near us and we made a good fine-weather run down the China Seas, passing *inside* Taiwan Strait for a change, where the sea was dotted for miles with fishing boats and their white polystyrene floats (marking nets). The Taiwan boats were pretty little white-painted, quaintly sheered little craft with high poop houses over the stern – very different from their rather grim-looking, grey-painted, rusty ragamuffin cousins from the mainland.

The Singapore Navy was patrolling in what seemed to be a largely successful attempt to stamp out piracy and we came to anchor in the Eastern Roads – busy as ever – early in the morning of 20th August. Refreshed by six months at home, Captain Harvey was waiting to relieve me. I flew home by non-stop jumbo to Heathrow, refreshed by six months of a type of seafaring I thought had gone forever. If this was the Mystic East – it would suit me down to the ground!

Golden Wonder, anchored in Singapore's Eastern Roads.

13. CHRISTMAS IN PORT 1989

"Where will you be for Christmas?" we were asked by friends in Singapore, in between leaving one ship and joining another.

"Probably up the Persian Gulf," we replied with no great enthusiasm.

But first, before the boat comes in from China, a quick trip across the sunlit Singapore Strait to the equatorial island of Batam in Indonesia. Singapore rules insist that if the ship to which you are transferring is not yet in, you must leave the country until she arrives. Indonesia was the answer, by sleek streamlined twenty-knot catamaran *Seacat 3*. Batan is being developed, largely with Singapore funding, to cater for tourists, and whilst much work remains to be done we found a quite old-established hotel where we enjoyed two days and nights of uncomplicated domestic bliss before returning to work. The good ship *Golden Wonder* of Singapore lay at anchor in the Eastern Roads, where the sea was decidedly choppy after two days hard blow caused, it was said, by a typhoon disturbance in the South China Sea. With some apprehension we watched our launch corkscrew its way alongside the silver-painted gangway. We need not have worried, at driving his boat our Mr Suchar the company's boatman was expert, waiting a lull, seizing his opportunity to take the boat alongside. As the heaving launch rose level with the gangway bottom step, all we had to do was leap across onto it, and willing hands helped with our gear. . .

Built at Shimonoseki Mitsubishi for Swiss owners in 1968/69, the *Golden Wonder* – ex *Iguape,* later the *Corviglia* of Basle which name and rare port of registry were still visible under the paint – was a four-hatch bridge-and-engines-aft conventional ship with elegantly curved bulbless bow, nice lines and a pleasingly rounded cruiser stern. Handsome in her grey topsides, white superstructure, black-topped blue funnel with matching blue masts and derricks, she was a handy-sized vessel well suited to carrying break-bulk general cargo on the company's liner service between China and the Gulf. Gross tonnage was 10,255 on a length of 151.33 metres OA, breadth 21.2 metres, powered by a Mitsubishi Sulzer 6RD68 engine.

Singapore's old Empire Dock was gradually being filled in to provide yet more container stacking space so we went alongside Keppel Quay to top up with steel, sawn planks and baulks of the beautiful Merani redwood, rubber, latex in drums and more general cargo. Singapore is one of the world's great entrepot centres – a clean, booming, elegant and friendly city. We had time to take in the new Mass Rapid Transport System (MRT – a highly advanced urban railway) to Orchard Road to admire the Christmas illuminations. Horses featured largely in these, thus able to double, a few months later, for Chinese Lunar New Year which ushered in the Year Of The Horse.

On the road to Kandy, the elephant orphanage.

A smooth sea up Malacca Strait was overcast with frequent showers, clearing to blue sky and bright sunshine as we passed through the Malacca and Bengal passages, south of the brilliantly green island of Wé (whose principle town is Sabang, the Indonesian naval base guarding that vast country's northern extremities). To the NNW of Wé, eleven miles distant, lies the hump of Rondo Island, surmounted by a lighthouse whose light can be seen over thirty miles distant. . . To our astonishment, perched on the rocks which lie on Rondo's southern side, was the huge container ship *Kowloon Bay* (58,496 grt, built 1972) which had run aground there during the night on passage from the west. Politely she declined our offer of help – a tug was already standing by, dashing our briefly-raised hopes of Salvage – and we heard she got off eventually to be drydocked at Singapore – thence back to her builders in Japan for immensely costly repairs. It remains a fact that no matter how much sophisticated electronic equipment a ship may have, the crucial business of remaining safely afloat depends in the last analysis on human eyes, skill and common sense. She – sadly – was one of only two British flag ships we encountered in almost three months of busy shipping. Both were P & O Container Line. A light NE monsoon fanned us across the Bay of Bengal, round Dondra Head and up to Colombo's man-made harbour which we entered on arrival without having to anchor, on the evening of November 28th. Two tugs and a pilot nudged us gently alongside Queen Elizabeth Quay and for the next eight days we discharged our cargo day and

148

night, in between some torrential rain storms.

A daytrip to Kandy, the ancient capital, showed us the other Sri Lanka, away from the cities. Old red London buses, oxcarts and elephants at work, little villages strung along the roadside, over the river which was the location for making the film 'Bridge on the River Kwai'; throngs of cheerful people in vividly bright clothes, plantations of tea and rubber, fields of rice where women worked up to their knees in milky brown water; – and in the distance, always, the spectacular scenery of rolling, jungle-covered hills. One village we passed through had white streamers fluttering overhead and we learned that white means mourning here – a local dignitary had passed away and we saw his funeral pyre under construction on a large open field.

The port was, as always, busy. Our quayside berth was needed for another ship with heavy-lift cargo so, on 2nd December, we were moved out to traditional Colombo moorings in the harbour; both anchors down with sternlines to a buoy. Our remaining light cargo was discharged into lighters, passage ashore provided by the agent's launch. Kind friends and the Flying Angel Seamen's Club made us welcome. An additional bonus was the arrival of the container ship *Mulbera,* the former *California Star,* now operated by Austasia Line of Singapore. A ship in which we had, eleven years before, voyaged to Vancouver, Seattle, San Francisco. . . her captain was an old cadet of mine, her chief officer likewise, while her chief engineer and I sailed together in the *Limari.* One night we watched the Tuticorin Express come in – a three masted 'country craft' sailing gracefully up the harbour, furling sail as she came. Still under canvas her master put her neatly alongside the Pettah Warehouse at the harbour's southern end, no mean feat in that crowded harbour. Few international trading voyages can still be operating under sail with ships innocent of engines or electricity as were their ancestors a thousand years ago. This regular cargo liner service still operates, however, between south-east India and Sri Lanka, across the Gulf of Mannar between Tuticorin and Colombo. The ships – dhows to the uninitiated but 'country craft' to their own people – are broad-beamed, deep-hulled, double-ended vessels, massively constructed of local timber, with raked stems and sterns. Heavily sparred on three masts, they carry a rig which defies orthodox description. Beginning with a long bowsprit fitted with jibboom and flying jibboom but lacking the dolphin striker and headgear of northern craft, a lateen sail is rigged beneath, furled along the bowsprit when not set. I suppose this could be called the spritsail. The foremast is tallest of the three, with a short topmast – invariably crowned with a small cross, for these are Christian mariners – supporting a large lateen foresail with lateen topsail above. This topsail is a versatile garment, worn wherever necessary around the ship, but when set above the foresail is curiously reminiscent of those set by the French Napoleonic Chasse Marée luggers. At least one large jib is set, often spread to catch the breeze with a spinnaker boom to give the sail an irregular four-sided appearance, making the vessel look as though she had four masts when viewed from a distance. The mainmast, shorter than the fore, carries the larger lateen, the great yards each consisting of two or even three spars fished together to form one. The mizen, well aft, carries the gaff-and-boom-rigged spanker overhanging the heavy, wooden 'out door' rudder. 'Bonnets', extra strips of canvas, are frequently laced around the larger sails to increase their pull. The result is indeed the 'cloud of canvas' of popular nautical fiction, aesthetically pleasing, a well-balanced rig which may owe something to the Portuguese who came here long ago in the wake of Vasco da Gama. All standing and running rigging is of hemp, sisal or coir – no wire – and shrouds and stays are set up with the laniards and deadeyes of the pre-bottlescrew era.

There is no deckhouse, no bulwarks, nothing to break the graceful sheer of the gunwhale which rises jauntily towards the stern from a low waist. Steering is by massive wooden tiller – no steering wheel, and of course no wheelhouse! The anchors, wrought iron admiralty-pattern, are raised by the hand windlass, fished and catted to wooden catheads in the eyes. Navigational equipment consists of a magnetic compass – nothing else.

The vessels are painted black with name and 'Tuticorin', their port of registry, in white, as is the large registration on the side of the hull. Names, too, reflect Portuguese influence. They sail well, making the most of the SW monsoon in summer and the NE monsoon in winter, but usually covering rather more than the 150 miles between the two ports that a seagull would fly. Manned by a crew of ten or so, they carry all manner of cargo. One I watched was unloading sacks of red earth, bales, boxes, crates and cartons, an unpacked motor car. Bulk scrap iron – small stuff mostly – comprises most of their cargo home to Tuticorin. They are a warm-weather version of the British sailing coasters of the last century; of the brigs, brigantines, barquentines, schooners and ketches which, like today's 'country craft', provided employment for countless shipwrights, riggers, sailmakers and blacksmiths who were needed to maintain them, the infrastructure of a way of life now sadly lost in the so-called 'developed' world.

My favourite pre-breakfast stroll in the dim early morning light was round Pettah Wharf and inevitably, I suppose, each visit showed more and more vessels appearing as motor ships. This metamorphosis results in the stout black hull emerging in a coat of silver or pastel shaded paint crowned with a glassed-in wheelhouse and stripped of much of their sailing gear. But a few true sailormen remained and even at that early hour men were working on their vessels, caulking decks and topsides and repairing rigging, while the massive main yard of one still fully-rigged craft was being swung aloft to the melodious notes of a shanty. Not "Shenandoah" or "Blow the Man Down" but a working song nevertheless, sung with gusto by the crew straining at the large, mangle-shaped winch.

A trio of tall three-masters which I had taken to be laid-up, displaced perhaps by their motorised sisters, emerged next day in suits of brand new canvas, moved to the loading berth and sailed for home with everything set – a reassurance that sail was not quite dead after all.

There are two ways in and out of Colombo harbour, the western main entrance and the northern, through which we departed after breakfast on 6th December with a hot sun drying the night's rain puddles off the decks in steamy wisps. The pilot disembarks inside the harbour leaving you to creep out cautiously. As usual, the entrance was almost blocked with the frailest of fishing craft – looking from our bridge like two near-naked men hauling their nets aboard a pair of barely-floating planks. Even the largest were little more than outboard-powered dinghies. It is customary to warn them of your approach by blowing the siren, then head towards the widest gap in between boats at dead slow/stop to avoid tipping them into the water. Once clear, we would work up to full speed, ring Full Away and Commence Passage – Karachi here we come! But the chief officer reported from forward he was unable to heave his port anchor home into its hawsepipe because of something wrong with the windlass. Fourteen fathoms of chain and a three and a half ton anchor were trailing astern. These things occasionally happen on even the best-run ships!

After investigation the chief engineer estimated four hours for repairs, which would involve some welding. Although this work *could* be done underway on passage, dark lowering clouds and a sea of white horses troubled the horizon – squally weather ahead – so I anchored, outside port limits, well clear of the entrance and traffic. So I was surprised when, after a couple of hours, a motor launch was seen approaching at speed, full of khaki-clad figures. As they neared the ship their leader raised a white loud hailer and ordered me to lower the gangway so that he and his men might come aboard. I demurred – I had my port clearance certificate and to re-establish contact with the shore was illegal. Or so I managed to convince him, realising in my own mind that if I let them aboard they would not, eventually, leave without demanding 'compliments' in the shape of bottles of whisky and cartons of cigarettes. Such compliments are used as a form of currency – usually to curry favour with superior officers rather than to use or sell. . . He said we had no business to be anchored where we were – what was I up to?

I replied I was outside port limits, in no-one's way, and that I had stopped to repair my windlass. Then we noticed one of his men brandishing a rifle. Fortunately at this juncture the chief announced that repairs were complete, which information I passed on to my interrogator. He watched suspiciously as our dripping anchor rose from the water. He waved us on. I deemed it polite to call the Harbourmaster on VHF to explain myself with apologies for not having informed him of my intentions earlier. "Apologies accepted old boy – we have to be careful these days, y'know!" Yes, we reflected, in Sri Lanka these days, you *have* to be careful – we could have been gun runners, smugglers, terrorists. . .

We had what seemed then to be the usual four days anchored off Karachi, catching tasty little fishes – eaten whole and complete, heads an'all, when fried straight out of the water. We watched the Pakistan Navy on manoeuvres, many of our old RN Falklands friends amongst their present fleet – time passed quickly. A period at anchor in good weather provides opportunity for all kinds of ship work both on deck and below – work which is not so easily done either on passage at sea or tied up in port. The chief engineer and the mate would have happily stayed there a fortnight! Lean, narrow-gutted lateen-sailed outboard motor-assisted fishermen with curiously tall stem and sternposts, yoke-and-line steering, headed out past us in the mornings to return in the evening full of fish. One boat hove under our stern offering 'fresh fish' for sale, in which we became interested until we spotted that the goods were far from fresh – probably the ones he'd been unable to sell the day before in Karachi market!

There was a constantly changing scene of vessels arriving, anchoring, weighing to enter port or leaving. A deep-draft grain ship was being lightened into a smaller ship alongside her. When her draft had been sufficiently reduced, she too would enter port. At any one time there were at least fourteen ships at anchor, another half dozen a dozen miles to the south waiting to enter the new port of Muhammad Bin Qasim, on the Indus delta. We had deck chairs to sit in, a kindly sun not too hot and a green parrot up the signal mast who tried to engage us in conversation. We often see this parrot here – or one of its relatives. Apple green with a narrow, blood-red collar and beak to match, pale blue tail feathers, he made a handsome change from seagulls and the raucous crows which inevitably splash any washing one is insufficiently wise to hang out. . . Eventually we were called in, embarking the pilot outside making up the long curving entrance to No.21, West Quay, past the naval base to port and the tanker berth to starboard, past the container berth where the *President Taft* was unloading her five-high boxes using American President Lines' own crane. Not a container crane in the accepted modern sense but a monster mobile on caterpillar tracks trundling up and down the quay on heavy baulk timber 'rails'. This had recently been joined by its twin sister crane, but Karachi is not yet fully 'into' portainers and, along the waterfront at least, tradition holds sway when it comes to cargo. For the port was, as usual, full of ships, some lying two abreast at the wharves, working conventional cargoes. We had tied up between vessels, fore and aft of us, unloading fertiliser in bulk. Others unloaded bales of

Chinese cotton or loaded locally grown rice for the Gulf. A Russian had recently offloaded power station equipment leaving the huge crates on the quay apron awaiting collection. Most of our cargo was unloaded into stone warehouses dating from the British days, to be stored until loaded out of the opposite doorways in rail wagons and lorries. A feature of Karachi traffic is the high, ornately-painted lorries, their cabs and tailboards a mass of intricately filigreed silvered metalwork. Painted with tigers, birds, sunsets, rural scenes – anything which takes the owner's fancy and each panel an individual work of art, they rumble along like dowager duchesses wearing huge tiaras, Bedford lorries as never seen in Luton. In town swarms the mini taxi, a ladybird-like cab over a three wheel motor scooter. Emitting rich exhaust fumes – as with most of the motorised traffic – until a layer of polluted air hangs head-high over the city, it is a wonder the numerous motor cyclists do not suffer asphyxiation. Fewer oxcarts here but plenty of camel carts (heads above the smog) donkey carts (some with two abreast in harness) trotting along, a few larger four-wheelers drawn by lean horses. Cars and buses struggle aggressively for right of way to the often despairingly blown whistles of white uniformed traffic police: thousands of people throng the streets – this is Karachi on a fairly "quiet" morning.

We sailed on 19th December at 11am. Here also the pilot disembarks well inside the harbour giving the captain the rare chance of piloting his ship down the broadly curving fairway, hoping the crowding fishing craft will see the ship coming and keep out of the narrow deep channel. Past the slowly disintegrating British fort buildings and yellow stone chapel on the point, past Manora lighthouse. A stark rusted wreck on the breakwater is a stern reminder not to stray out of the channel! Out to sea we turned west and headed for the Gulf. No firing practice was taking place that day so we were able to 'hug' the Makran coast and in unusually good visibility marvelled at the moonlike white rock mountains there. This was my wife's first visit to the Gulf but I was as surprised as she to find our entrance to the Straits of Hormuz attended by torrential rain showers, thunder, lightning and waterspouts, one of which passed so close to the ship we felt we could almost have reached out and grasped it as it dervish-danced past. The low grey cloud descended in a twisting spiral to a sea surface which bore all the disturbance of a low-hovering helicopter. A mighty rushing wind accompanied these phenomena, dying fitfully as we approached Dubai on 21st December. The famous Iran frigate passed us several miles off Dubai – well outside his own patch – the same Vosper which made such a nuisance of himself harassing merchantmen proceeding on their lawful occasions during the recent Iran/Iraq war. Our own ship was one innocent he had forced into Bandar Abbas for interrogation and search a couple of years ago. The port of Dubai, in the United Arab Emirates, had been closed for several hours by high winds but was now back in business. Our British pilot cheerfully forecast we'd be well on our way before Christmas – to next port Kuwait. Fortunately our Dubai agents had arranged things better; no night labour was 'available' so cargo was not unloaded as rapidly as our pilot forecast. It was soon decided we would be ready to sail in all respects at 1400 hours on Christmas Day.

Dubai is probably the Gulf's pleasantest port and we strolled round busy streets and visited the Flying Angel Seamen's Club (a trifle chilly for a swim in the pool). Though predominantly Muslim, the shops exuded a strong whiff of commercial Christmas with coloured lights, 'snow', piped carols and Santa, with Rudolph the red-nosed reindeer everywhere.

We invited all hands to our dayroom for a drink early on Christmas Eve. As we were safely in port it was possible to relax a little and the lads trooped up wearing their best clothes at 4pm. The chief officer was from Sumatra, the chief engineer and his wife from South Korea. The second officer was from Ghana, the third – Burma. Second engineer was Singapore Chinese and the rest were the usual Guan Guan merry mixture representing eight nations in all; mostly either Muslim or Buddhist. That morning our Muslim agent had brought down a huge Christmas cake in a box. Decorated with snow icing, Santa, reindeer et al, it came with a Christmas card. More cards had been pouring in all day, mostly from the ship's company, to whom my wife had sent one each. With the cards and a few decorations the cabin looked quite festive. The Flying Angel had presented every man and woman aboard every ship in port with a card accompanied by a small present – missions to seamen indeed! Our interdenominational ship's company seemed determined to make us Ancient Brits feel at home, a guitar appeared, and 'Silent Night' sweetly sung in Burmese almost had us moved to tears. The third mate brought us back to earth by putting his all, then, into a selection of Beatles' Numbers, accompanied by himself on the guitar, sung with authentic Liverpool accent. He modestly told us he'd learned them from his tapes. At 5pm we were whisked down to the crew messroom. To our astonishment this usually strictly functional place had been transformed with flags draped around the bulkheads (walls), streamers overhead, coloured lights, even an illuminated Christmas tree! The tables were laid with fair white linen cloths and the cooks had surpassed themselves with a buffet which even included roast turkey. Home made music soon broke out, singing, even dancing – and we discovered with appreciation that these lads have not lost the art of providing their own entertainment in the close confines of a ship (by no means so common now as it once was). After a splendid Christmas Eve it was consequently no hardship to depart on Christmas afternoon, off across a bright blue sea, air temperature hovering in the upper thirties C, sunshine – bound NW between oilfields and hopefully-swept minefields. Christmas

154

dinner in our dayroom that evening was brightened with the best tablecloth, a candle, tinsel and a bottle of wine we'd bought especially in Singapore. Main course was boiled fish and vegetables, followed by Christmas pud. There was, that evening, a spectacularly vivid Arab sunset.

Merry Christmas!

Christmas buffet, *GoldenWonder.*

14. KAOHSIUNG REVISITED

Kaohsiung – the name probably means High Village – is a modern city of almost one million inhabitants. Its old port is dominated by Wan Shou Shan, the 'Hill on the Bay', which, with a height of 1,174 feet, is visible from thirty miles out at sea where it resembles an island in an otherwise rather featureless landscape. But as you approach, lighthouses appear on breakwaters and dim smudges materialise into ships anchored-off, awaiting berths.

My only previous visit had been nearly twenty years ago and it occurred to me now that while this was my second entry, I had yet to sail *away* from Kaohsiung; having flown last time from there to Taipei, Hong Kong and home, leaving my ship, the *Caledonia Star* behind for scrap. In 1971 shipbreaking was a major industry with Kaohsiung at the top of the world league. In those days the hill bristled with rocket-launchers aimed over Taiwan Strait at the mainland and a harbour boom closed the entrance under the ever watchful eye of a US-built destroyer of the *Gearing* class; – or perhaps she was an *Allen M. Sumner* of similar design, for both I found now, resting on their laurels at the naval base within the commercial port.

In 1971 the United Nations admitted the Communist People's Republic of China at the expense of Taiwan (or 'free' China, as they continue to call themselves) Taiwan feared imminent invasion and was prepared to fight. To those of us old enough to remember, Taiwan's sandbagged buildings, air raid shelters and cross-taped windows were sad reminders of 1939 Britain. But, fortunately, Chinese common sense prevailed on both sides, war did not eventuate and now all signs of its frantic preparation were gone. Perhaps the two Chinas secretly see each other now in a more friendly light, as business rivals and co-operators rather than as military threats to each other.

The port had changed, too. I again came in through the first, or Northern Entrance, a daunting 300 feet gap between cliffs opening onto a lagoon six long but only half a mile wide which, in 1971, had been a dreary water where dozens of ships lay at crazy angles in tiers awaiting their turn under the torch. There were no quays, ships were run alongside others already half aground on rough banks spiked with the masts and derricks of ships long gone, used now to dismember others, continuously. Pieces torn off were tractor-towed on low trailers across a desolate wasteland to distant steel mills, belching chimneys covering ship and shore alike with layers of fine grey ash. The depth of dust on her decks indicated how long a vessel had been waiting. The acts of final destruction took less than a month but there was an appointment list.

Twenty years ago I had anchored-off, uncertain whether our ship was indeed doomed, hoping against hope – as we all were – that another charter would be found as it had been before. For this was no scrap-delivery voyage;

T.S.M.V. Caledonia Star. First command was the *English Star* to New Zealand where the *Caledonia* became the author's first permanent command. But at almost thirty years, she was soon to go to the shipbreakers. *(FotoFlite)*

Seamen of 'Seventy one. The *Caledonia Star's* complement on the boat deck in Tokyo, before taking her to Taiwan shipbreakers.

we were still fully manned and operational. Throughout the previous year the *Caledonia Star* had served as Blue Star Line's contribution to Crusader Line, which ran three separate cargo liner services from New Zealand to the West Indies, the west coast of North America, and Japan. We took frozen meat, dairy and other primary produce north, mainly industrial and household equipment back south, a pleasant run which enabled us to savour the many differences between the Land of the Rising Sun and the Land of the Long White Cloud: – the one densely populated but lacking adequate arable land, the other with a population of three million (in a country the size of Britain) with enough rich pasture to feed all the world its needs, barring grain. . .

Before this the *Caledonia* had accompanied the *Colorado, Canadian, Columbia, California* and *Catalina Stars* trading from Britain to the Canadian and US Pacific coasts whence they were eventually displaced by container ships of the Scan Star Combine which soon became Johnson Scanstar. Earlier still, as the *Royal Star* propelled by Scotch boilers burning coal, driving twin steam up-and-downers, she had voyaged to Chile, Tierra del Fuego and Patagonia in search of frozen lamb for the British housewife. Life began in 1942 at Greenock Dockyard as the *Empire Wisdom*, painted wartime grey and managed until 1944 by the Clan Line whose immediate pre-war steamers she closely resembled, except for one interesting detail. By 1942 it was realised that U-Boat commanders would take their sights on a ship through the periscope by lining up her sampson posts. .. So in some ships, including our *Empire Wisdom* (well named!) the pair of sampson posts forward of No.3 hatch were offset, not truly athwartships. It would seem that in this case, certainly, the ploy worked! Following a spell of lay-up in the Fal – displaced by more modern tonnage – in 1962 she was re-engined with MAN diesels at which time her cargo winches and windlass were converted from steam to electrical power; though steering gear, refrigerating machinery and emergency generator remained steam powered and the chief engineer delighted in ordering several tons of galley coal each trip along with his fuel, diesel and lubricating oils. It was still part of the donkeyman's job to light the fires under galley and bakery stoves each morning and in port, with a little skill and malevolence, he could dissuade the New Zealand dockers from starting work too early by emitting clouds of yellow smoke from the tall galley funnels right under the cargo-crane driver's cab. Asphyxiating! Not harmful of course to absent crane drivers – only keeping us a little longer in Port! We and our old ship had come a long way together and were loathe to let her go. In a fine gesture of defiance, our Northern Irish chief officer used every drop of paint to 'make the old girl the smartest ship ever to go for scrap'. We had arrived off Kaohsiung empty from Moji in southern Japan where our final cargo had included three elegant horses in wooden deck-stalls, jumpers from New Zealand which would beget a new strain of

Olympic champions. Heads peering out from their stalls in well-bred astonishment, they were swung onto a barge along with the bales of wool which comprised the balance of our cargo. Then – "Proceed to Khaosiung, anchor and wait", my orders read ominously. Rumour was rife. We were to revive the pre-war China egg trade to Britain, where vast quantities of frozen eggs were imported by a certain firm for catering and manufacturing purposes. . . It was meat from Australia to Vladivostock; – no – it was fruit from Valparaiso to the States. . . But one morning without warning these dreams were dispelled by a launch chugging out across the dull grey water bringing not only pilot and the agent but the immigration officers, and – of course, the customs. These latter gentlemen took no time in consigning the contents of our medicine chest to the deep – 'to prevent drug smuggling!' As the harbour boom closed astern the pilot took *Caledonia Star* with what seemed to me unseemly haste down the lagoon's nautical graveyard, to rush us without pause or ceremony alongside a not-very-old Texaco tanker whose midships bridge was even then being burned off by an old man and a very young boy who could have been his grandson. Did it matter if our side rails were dented as we crashed alongside? Not now! Two radio mechanics swooped down and dismantled our Marconi equipment. This, more than anything else, forced us to realise that 'this was it!' but we had to wait while the business of the sale was concluded in London. For the next eight days we consumed our remaining provisions and extinguished fires daily aboard our neighbouring tanker. Her fuel and cargo tanks inevitably contained oily residue and with all the cutting and burning going on it was not surprising occasional fires broke out. No one else seemed interested but we retained an old-maidish disinclination to go up in flames ourselves.

After three days a Panama flag ship, a smartly-painted former American Mail Lines 'C3' came alongside with a resounding series of clangs, denting our stern plates and again my instinctive reaction was to claim compensation for damage caused; – of course, futile! Soon voices were heard, raised in anger, followed by her polyglot crew stamping in marked manner across our afterdeck and ashore.

Soon they came back, under police escort. Their ship, it transpired, had been on voyage with no thought of scrap, proceeding empty to load in the Philippines, when the boilers lost water and an engineroom fire broke out. Though extinguished, it left the ship drifting without power for a week. Food and water ran out and the crew mutinied, demanding to be "taken off". Fights, including knife fights involving the officers, had led the captain to notify his owner who sent a tug. Now the crew wanted wages but it seemed they were promised these would be paid when they arrived by air in Hong Kong. But some of the crew had been cheated before; on arrival in Hong Kong there was no one to meet them and no money. They now demanded to

159

see their consul who "just happened" to be out of town. . . In our comfortable, well-ordered Blue Star life we were being shown the other side of modern seafaring.

One of our favourite pastimes in 1971 had been guessing "What Ship Was That?" Many of our abandoned neighbours were old friends in disguise, sold foreign for the last few years of their lives. For instance – that one over there was certainly a Bowater's paper carrier, her original smart cream and green livery hidden under black and off-white. A couple of old ANL friends from the Australian coast were now Greeks, but there was no argument about the nearby *Empire Star*, nor the more distant *Imperial Star* and we thought it interesting that the old monarchistic order had all come home to roost together; – *Imperial, Empire* and (former) *Royal Stars*.

One afternoon with nothing else to do – it was Saturday – I had climbed over the remains of our tanker and strolled through a shanty town of former ships' timber and canvas where dwelt our shipbreakers in considerable squalor. To reach the *Empire Star* I had to heave on a soggy, weed-dripping line, step gingerly onto the thwarts of one of her waterlogged wooden lifeboats, then haul myself out to a tattered rope pilot ladder at the head of which I was met in silence by an elderly Chinese watchman. He shuffled round after me for a while but lost interest when it became apparent I was of no significance. The captain's door was locked but the chief officer's stood open. Stripped of curtains, bedding and carpet, it was nevertheless the cabin I had lived in for awhile years before. Perching on the high bunk I lit a cigarette and allowed memories to come flooding back. . . I had once stood by her refit at Smith's docks, North Shields, as chief officer – a happy time with home almost every night! Later, I had joined her in Cardiff to go round to load in Liverpool. I will say here that I do not believe in ghosts, either ashore or afloat, and have never seen one. And ghosts do not have heavy footfalls – do they?

We had anchored off Point Lynas, Anglesey, awaiting our Liverpool pilot, and the night was cold. Rather than keep me, with my crew of carpenter and one AB up on the forecastle-head waiting to be told to weigh anchor when the pilot announced his coming, the captain had kindly ordered us to wait *under* the forecastle head out of the wind. Walkie Talkie would alert me when the pilot approached and it was time to heave up anchor. . . The space under the forecastle deck was dark, used for carrying bales of greasy wool, of which it smelled quite strongly – not an unpleasant smell and empty now after unloading. We perched ourselves in reasonable comfort on coils of rope and waited. Soon the chuckle of water round the bows and occasional creak of anchor chain in the hawsepipe was broken by heavy footsteps coming up the foredeck. Who could this be? But the night was freezing cold and we were not sufficiently interested to go and see. The footsteps climbed the ladder onto the steel deck above our heads, and moved around, as though their person was looking for something. Then they stopped.

"Halloa!" I shouted. The water chuckled and the chain creaked in the hawse. And yes, the wind even sighed in our scanty rigging. I called again. Silence. Mystified, I went up to see for myself who it was, playing games of hide and seek with us. Nobody there. For certain no footfalls had descended the steel ladder to the foredeck. . . I went back to my shipmates below and said cheerfully – "That must have been Old Billy come back to make sure we were properly anchored–"

Old Billy a few years ago had been chief officer of this ship, and dropped dead on the forecastle while inspecting the anchors. . . Heart attack. Suddenly the carpenter announced he was – just going to his cabin for a packet of fags; and left. The sailor, whom I could barely see in the darkness, declared a sudden urgent need to visit the toilet; and left. Alone in the gloom I found no comfort in the cigarette my (I found) trembling hand had some difficulty in getting alight; then I dropped my lighter. "Dash it, I'd just go and get my other one. . .."

Back on the bridge the captain looked at me in astonishment. "Are you alright, Mr Kinghorn – you look as though you've seen a ghost!" But that sunny afternoon ten years later in Taiwan I felt completely at ease in Old Billy's old cabin, and hoped his ghost – if it was his ghost – had been finally laid to rest.

* * * * * *

Today shipbreaking plays a very minor role in Taiwan's economy. It seems there was eventually a public outcry at the loss of life and physical injury so frequently suffered and the pollution caused. Now the business was regulated, I found, to a few special berths newly dug at the far southern end of the lagoon. Where, twenty years ago, the *Caledonia Star* had fetched up forever alongside an old tanker, *Golden Wonder* now lay in almost exactly the same spot alongside a fine, new rubber-fendered concrete quay, – with ships working cargo at every berth. Astern of us wood chips were being unloaded from a Panama flag ship while ahead, a South Korean discharged logs, each one a tree of the Pinus Radiata family whose rapid growth marks it one of New Zealand's most valuable exports today. We, with yellow soya bean meal from Kandla in NW India, were using our own derricks, with shore-owned steel grabs attached, to unload into hopper lorries. Elsewhere in the booming port are general cargo wharves, petroleum and sugar berths and a huge new container terminal for which the Second Entrance, wider and deeper, has been made at the lagoon's southern end.

Our next port was to be Tai Chung, ten hours' run up the coast, a port which did not exist for big ships until fourteen years ago and now handled from twenty to thirty at a time, all the time. I would need charts so the agent took me across Kaohsiung City to a tiny shop, dimly lit, walls crammed from floor to ceiling with apparently ancient chart folios, while from high bookshelves Brown's Nautical Almanac, Norie's Nautical Tables and Nicholls's Concise Guide peered down. The proprietors, an elderly Chinaman and his wife, greeted me courteously, produced green tea in tiny cups with no handles while we discussed the World Situation (as though I knew something about it!) and to my delight looked out right up-to-date British Admiralty charts published in Taunton, Somerset – just what I needed.

Returning to the port I noticed the wreck of a large passenger liner high on the seaward side of the lagoon, lying right over on her starboard side. A gaping vertical split had broken the hull almost in two. Now a pale rusty brown it was apparent she had once been white. "That", said the agent, "was a British ship, the *Uganda*. After a long tow out from her last lay-up in the Fal, following her Falklands service as first a hospital ship and later the troopship running mate to my own *Keren* on the Ascension-Falklands run, she had been anchored off the port to await a suitable time to bring her in and break her up. Attempts to save her, preserved for posterity, had been doomed to failure by the daunting costs of maintaining any ship in a reasonably presentable state. Everyone had left her when the typhoon struck, causing the anchor to drag. With nothing and no one to stop her, she had been driven well and truly ashore, hard and fast.

She lay on private property and I could not approach any closer. Having been aboard her in the Falklands I knew what a beautiful ship she had been, and realised suddenly that I did not really want to visit the *Uganda* now, on her deathbed, after all.

Strange, I felt, as we sailed away that night, how memories of some ports remain tinged with a certain sadness, even twenty years on.

15.   A CARGO FOR XIAMEN

Our westbound cargo from Shanghai was usually loaded at Gaoyanglu Wharf, from the quay and attendant barges which had brought it from other points on the river, or even from 'up-country' in the counties. Crate, bale, carton, box and bag of general cargo were neatly stowed into the holds and 'tweendecks by Chinese dockers wearing basket-weave safety helmets. With no enclosed loading docks on the Huangpu River all shipping is on view, lying to tiers of buoys midstream or moored to endless quays, while a continuous procession of traffic moves past in both directions, crisscrossed by ferries moving almost sideways against a strong tidal current; – a fascinating panorama for anyone interested in ships for their own sake. Having completed loading and its attendant formalities which end with captain being presented with that all-important document 'The Clearance' (which tells his next port he has paid all his bills in this one), our vessel embarks her pilot and proceeds down to the East China Sea where he gets off into a small motor boat to be ferried over to the large white pilot cutter which cruises the estuary, to await an inbound vessel. Densely clustered fleets of fishermen keep us alert, especially if it is foggy. The inshore boats are wooden, similar in size to our own cobles at home while the larger boats are of steel, painted grey, with an almost naval appearance. A few are still junk rigged carrying a couple of sails.

Eventually we clear Taiwan Strait into the South China Sea, passing the present day haunts of all-too-many pirates (of which more later) to Singapore, where any vacant space is topped up with timber, steel, rubber and latex, for Colombo. But of our next cargo there is as yet no sign. In Colombo it is noticed that more and more of the Tuticorin Express are converting to power, appearing in pastel shades with wheelhouses, though it is also noticed that they still set sails at every available opportunity for these lads are at heart true sailormen. We watched one black beauty putting to sea. No engine chugged in *her* stout hull and through binoculars we admired her tall, red-saronged captain swinging easily on his tiller, guiding her through the shipping in the harbour, through the narrow gap between breakwater and mole, out to sea where a fresh breeze caused her to heel slightly and increase speed. More sail was set and we wondered if he wished he had an engine. Or was he thankful he had not? One Sunday morning, returning to the ship from a night with friends and early morning church, we were delighted to see two sailing vessels putting to sea. But the breeze inside the harbour was negligible, hardly stirring the water. The two craft had every sail set; topsails, bonnets, spritsails, watersails – plus a few more. . . The first one edged up to the exit where a light air filled her topsail, taking her out. The second seemed to hang motionless, her crew of ten clearly discussing what best to do. One lad put the end of a rope line between his teeth, gleaming white in his dark face, and dived overboard, swimming rapidly to the anchor chain of a moored vessel. Deftly he bent his line around the chain, signalling to his shipmates to heave on the line. Breaking into a shanty they eased their vessel ahead. Soon he unbent his line and swam to the next anchored ship, repeating the process. We realised we were watching an ancient scene – a sailing vessel taking herself to sea in a calm without the aid of a tug. And of course, we had left the cameras ashore!

As this second craft also caught the freshening sea breeze, she suddenly surged ahead, the boy on the buoy only just getting onboard in time, to the laughter and cheers of his shipmates.

The daily round brought me back to the present, not without realising that with our union-purchase derricks and non-containerised cargo we ourselves were almost as rare a bird as the sailing vessels. . . For the ship I currently had the honour to command was built in 1970 at Flensburg as part of the German Liberty Ship Replacement programme. Built in various yards with slight variations many were eventually bought by the Mainland Chinese and placed under their flag.

Similar in size, speed and carrying capacity to the far more numerous SD14 and with the same all-important 'tweendeck, the German hull is distinctive, with raised forecastle over bulbous bow and almost no sheer. Some of this class – my own ship included – have a small open-sided afterdeck under the poop, abaft the galley and crew messroom, which makes a useful crew recreation and fishing deck. The arms-akimbo bridge, funnel, engines and accommodation are right aft, leaving a clear working deck forward of the poop, with two masts and five cargo hatches. Launched and originally run as the *Martha Fisser* of Lubeck she spent much of her early life on the North Atlantic under charter to the Canadian firm of Saguenay as the *Sunbaden*. She subsequently became the Peruvian *Alpamayo*, when notices in Spanish were added to those in German around the ship. Sold again she was next the *Golden Amman* of the Jet Navigation Company of Panama, then the *Golden Land* of Singapore, and finally and now, the *Golden Bear* of Singapore. On a gross tonnage of 9,338, overall length of 139.73 metres with 21.1 metres beam, propulsion is by MAN K6 diesel of 5,820 kw power. Having been especially strengthened for ice navigation, the hull is very strong and, generally speaking, the accommodation better than in the SD14. Certainly this is so for the captain's suite, where – in the German fashion – a large 'saloon' is part of his dayroom, bedroom and bathroom – which actually boasts a window, rare in any modern ship. (Watch the world go by as you take a shower!)

But would we get a return cargo? In any liner service it is highly desirable for cargo to be carried in both directions if the ship is to fully pay her way. The term 'liner service' implies that a ship sails regularly over a given route, accepting cargo as offered by numerous shippers, the key word being 'regularly', whether cargo fills the ship or not.

Any merchant ship exists simply to make money for her owner – preferably as much as possible as quickly as possible, certainly sufficient to pay for her eventual replacement in a world of escalating costs, as well as enough to justify laying out the venture. For everything about a ship is expense;– fuel, registration, provisions, repairs, classification, port charges, wages – the list is endless – and the only return which defrays these costs is the freight payable on the cargo carried. One of the reasons why sailing ships so rapidly disappeared from liner shipping once steam became established was that they were so slow – over their voyages, and consequently earned less per year than a steamer. Despite well documented reports of fast sailing passages, the average speed of even a clipper ship in superb condition and properly commanded and manned was little over three knots a voyage, less if the distance she had to travel is compared with the much shorter, direct courses available to the powered vessel. Few nations today can afford to subsidise their merchant fleets – few even man them with their own seamen – so as never before the most efficiently run ships are the survivors, and cargo must be carried as often as possible, for the more cargo a ship can carry in a year the more she earns.

General cargo out of the Persian Gulf is virtually non-existent and dates have never been exported in vast quantities. Oil is the principal export – oil and its by products – one of which is urea, used as fertiliser. But production ceased during the Gulf War and was only now resuming. During that War vessels often had to return to China empty, or at best pick up a cargo of soya meal in India, as had the *Golden Wonder* when last I joined her.

From Colombo we rolled up through the early SW monsoon to Karachi, thence along a hazy Makran Coast to the Gulf, where calm seas and blue skies attended us for the next seventeen days. I was advised by radio we had been fixed to load bagged urea at Dammam, for China. But first Dubai, to unload the last of our westbound cargo, and where the Indonesian bosun and his merry men cleaned holds and tweendecks, sweeping and scrubbing, before – when all steelwork was thoroughly dry – spreading polythene sheeting as protection (for the urea from the steelwork which urea attacks mercilessly).

Kuwait had not yet returned to our itinerary and so far the furthest up the Gulf we had ventured was to Dammam, in Saudi Arabia, where I was ordered to load. A queue of waiting Chinese ships there however warned of long delays and I was diverted by radio to Jubail, further north, to load 10,500 tonnes. There is nothing glamourous about carrying fertiliser, but China needs it to help feed her rapidly expanding population (still increasing at the rate of twelve million souls per year, despite all restrictions).

There were, we found, few signs of the recent war, even less than 200 miles south of Kuwait city. An occasional whiff on the breeze reminiscent of old steam railway trains told of Kuwait's still-blazing oil wells – sabotaged by the fleeing Iraqis – but there was no more smoke in the air than the long streak of dark horizon cloud which has hung about here since oil production began decades ago. Fleets of Arab fishing dhows were obviously enjoying a bonanza season in a pellucid sea teeming with marine life. Of oil pollution there was no sign. Chief reminder of the recent war was the lack of merchant shipping; the occasional tanker or reefer going about her lawful business was outnumbered by the warships of many nations and in particular by grey-painted freighters wearing the Stars and Stripes, many obviously brought out of long lay-up to carry the men and materials for Desert Storm, now returning home via Bangladesh where ships, equipment and US troops rendered valuable life-saving service in the wake of the latest disastrous cyclone. Many of these elderly ships carried on their 'stacks' the red-white-and-blue or blue-and-yellow narrow stripes of the US Military Sealift Command. Meanwhile acres of sand-camouflaged tanks and trucks were parked around the port and as far as the eye could see out into the desert, together with rows of white-cocooned helicopters ready for re-embarkation; – some indication of the tremendous effort expended in ensuring the failure of Iraq's attempt to annex Kuwait.

In Jubail (Al Jubayl) our cargo was loaded by two huge mechanical contraptions shooting the 50 kilogramme bags on the last stage of their overhead journey by conveyor belt from the nearby production plant, down a helter-skelter to be stowed by no more than four blue overalled men per gang. Powerful stuff containing 6 per cent nitrogen, the ammonia fumes given off occasionally caused work to cease. But despite the occasional pause for breath, or to move along from one hatch to another, work proceeded steadily, averaging 2,000 tonnes per day into the ship. The almost complete absence of visible people, the lack of noise and bustle usually attending cargo work was deceptive: almost as though work had ceased. But after a week all was loaded, hatches battened down and on Sunday 28th July 1991 we sailed for Singapore. No shore leave is permitted in Saudi without a great deal of Special Permission so there had been no possibility of even a stroll along the quay, but the variegated bird life provided interest as "in mist or cloud on mast or shroud, it perched for vespers nine". . .

No Fishing was allowed by the authorities – we came to accept that in Saudi Arabia the answer is always an emphatic "NO!" – but the port's occasional comings and goings and the distant activities of the US military provided some entertainment. Our cargo's destination would be revealed later – so far it was simply for The People's Republic of China.

Hot, fine weather followed us down the Gulf as we avoided Iran's

Exclusion Zone (from the previous Gulf War between Iran and Iraq), 'swept' minefield and still-active oilfields to pass, 24 hours after departure through an eerily quiet Straits of Hormuz. Next day we renewed our acquaintance with the SW monsoon, now in full flight, driving rain, cloud, sea and swell before it in its annual four months onslaught on the west coast of India. With wind, sea and swell on the starboard beam we rolled steadily, up to 35 degrees off vertical in an eleven-second cycle. Meals were cooked and eaten as best we could, wedged in, all those little knick-knacks and personal belongings which transform a ship into a floating home safely stowed in drawer and locker as the Arabian Sea took us to her bosom, enfolding us in her warm embrace which cascaded across the decks at every roll, to roar and gurgle out through the scuppers. We are spoiled, weatherwise, on this trade, basking for most of the year in warm sunshine with lightly lapping blue sea. Only the occasional China Sea typhoon and the SW monsoon serve to remind us what real seafaring is like – and even so we are spared the cold.

On July 31st our Burmese radio officer, ("Sparks" in every tongue at sea) presented me with the news that our discharge port had been declared as Xiamen – pronounced "Shar-Men", which brought broad smiles from those of my shipmates who knew. "Best Port in China" was the general verdict. But for the present we continued to roll heavily and I and the others whose lot it is to type reports, store indents etc were glad when we ceased rolling for half a day under the lee of the Lakshadweep Islands, out of sight to the west. Low and dangerous, they are not places to approach too closely on a rough night when spray, rain and low cloud inhibit visibility.

The tiny fishing craft working near the SW Indian port of Trivandrum always provide interest, especially at night when dim oil lamps were often concealed among the ocean swells. Sometimes radar picked them out, sometimes not. A sharp lookout was, as always, essential. Driven by a single triangular sail set on a whispy mast the height and consequent power of which is controlled by the simple act of grabbing the head of the sail and raising or lowering it by hand – they could sail at up to ten knots in a good breeze. Far from the land we felt that they, like all ocean fishermen, certainly earned their living the hard way. Across the Gulf of Manaar in fine weather these human fishers were replaced by a school of dolphin, homing in on our bulbous bow to play around it as though we were one of their own.

I strolled forward to watch them, as the school was increasing, heading in on us from port and starboard. Only feet ahead of our submerged bulb the baby dolphins kept a steady straight course while all around them their elders criss-crossed in and out of the water in an amazing display of aquabatics. It was quite clear that they were enjoying themselves.

Rolling round Dondra Head I kept south of the main traffic lanes across the Bay of Bengal where the sun dried our decks into an assortment of autumn tints which the chief officer and bosun failed to appreciate – rust in every shade! Liquid rust remover however, vigorously applied via bucket and broom soon restored the situation. On arrival in Singapore the Company's ships must look immaculate!

We spent a few days at anchor in the Eastern Roads carrying out certain mechanical modifications and I was handed the National Shipping Association's latest bulletin on pirate attacks in these waters, of which 22 had been reported in 1991 already, while it was believed that many more incidents passed unreported. Singapore and Malacca Straits themselves were now reasonably safe thanks to the purposeful patrolling of the Singapore, Indonesian and Royal Malaysian navies and most attacks were now occurring south east of Singapore Strait. A particularly nasty attack occurred however on 23rd August, some 90 miles north of Singapore Strait's eastern end, near Tioman Island, where a 'Blue motorboat' approached the *Springstar*, a motor vessel bound from Singapore to Phnom Penh with a cargo of electrical goods. That this cargo's value exceeded US$ 3 million suggested inside information; the attack was determined and ruthlessly executed. Pirates, believed to be Thais, boarded the ship by the dawn's early light, immediately running to the bridge to shoot dead the philippino chief officer and throw his body overboard. Suitably cowed, the rest of the crew and the master were locked in a storeroom handcuffed, except for the chief engineer who was forced at knifepoint to run his engine to an appointed rendezvous where the cargo was transferred to another vessel, unseen but heard by the *Springstar's* crew. Having smashed all navigational equipment with axes, the pirates left her to find her way by guess and by God, dazed and frightened, back to Singapore. She arrived just as we were about to sail. . .

Four days out, well on our way toward Xiamen, I was taking my customary hour on the bridge between 0645 and 0745 to allow the chief officer to go down for a spell, when I spotted a low, black-hulled solitary fishing boat fine to starboard, three miles off. She appeared to be stopped and I felt her lone presence unusual as such craft usually work in pairs, if not in fleets in these waters. As she began to cross our bow I altered course to starboard to place her on our port bow.

In these waters a few years ago the Vietnam Boat People would wait, hoping to be picked up. But where the Boat People made a point of showing their women and holding up babes to melt the stony hearts of passing captains, this particular boat, I saw through binoculars, was full of hungry-looking men. They were flagging us down, signalling for the *Golden Bear* to stop. Mental bells shrilled in warning and I sent the watch AB to alert the chief officer and bosun to stand by to repel boarders (we still had our deck hoses ready). As the boat increased in speed to come alongside our quarter I did the only thing possible; went suddenly hard a 'starboard presenting our stern, causing the boat to rock violently in our wake. Floundering in apparent confusion as they fell about, they gradually dropped astern and I resumed my course across a leaden sea.

Whether or not they really were pirates we shall never know, and whether the sight of a (very) white faced figure in white naval uniform on our bridge caused them to have second thoughts I shall never know either. The remainder of our passage was uneventful – my wife asleep at the time was disappointed to have missed the fun! Soon after midnight on 11th September we anchored off Xiamen to proceed in at first light. The ship was suddenly covered in a swarm of bright salad-green beetles, pretty little things the size and shape of a thumb nail which entered the accommodation through every open window, nook and cranny. But by morning time all had died, or flown off elsewhere. . .

The entrance to Xiamen was particularly interesting as the large island of Qemoy, to starboard, was still defiantly under Taiwan rule, flying the Nationalist flag, bristling with guns, tank traps along the shoreline, and proclaiming in huge Chinese characters painted on rocks facing the mainland how much better life was under Capitalism than under communist Tyranny, etc. We also saw the telescopes set up by the said Communist tyrants to enable tourists to study Qemoy fortifications for ten cents a look.

Having been granted that all important pratique (permission to enter port) in the Quarantine Anchorage by Port Health, two pilots took us in while Customs and Immigration made light of the formalities. We moored to buoys off the town, and my wife and I were struck by the likeness of the place to our English Lake District. Green hills of similar height surrounded the blue 'lake' of the harbour. Great Gable must lie over there, Skiddaw yonder, and surely the Langdale Pikes were just beyond that range! Main difference was the absence of leisure craft – nobody in China has enough money to waste on such fripperies – but plenty of working craft thronged the harbour day and night.

A fleet of sand barges chugged past our moorings each morning from some distant shore, carrying their loads to a nearby beach where coolie-hatted men soon unloaded them by the simple process of suspending two sand-filled baskets from a bambo pole over their shoulders. Walking along a gangplank to the shore they tipped the sand into heaps from which it was shovelled by hand into lorries and taken to one of the numerous neighbouring construction sites. Then the 'sandies' chugged back for another load, dozens of them, working the tides to advantage. A ferry service was established from our ship to the Custom House Quay where it was necessary to scramble ashore over a trio of washing-festooned small ships of the Chinese Navy.

Xiamen has prospered thanks to many Overseas Chinese bringing their fortunes earned in Hong Kong, Singapore, Taiwan and the West home to invest, not only in sumptuous houses, but in good works. The resultant

Golden Bear at Xiamen waiting for barges.

Unloading our cargo into barges at Xiamen.

university, schools, pagodas, temples and numerous pavilions stand as testimony to their philanthropy. We learned with astonishment that even in the days of harshest Communism, the late, great Chairman Mao publicly welcomed his wealthy kinsmen, proclaiming them to be heroes of the revolution. Good Chinese logic!

But what about our cargo?

"Ah, yes", said the agent, a pleasant young man – "Barges here tomollow". Soon twenty-one of them were nestling alongside, the ship's winches and derricks swinging out the bags forty at a time, the barge ladies energetically helping their menfolk to stow the cargo while keeping an eye on the regulation one infant playing about his floating home's narrow decks. Two puppies were also playing from barge to barge, when suddenly to the anguished howl of a small child one puppy fell into the water between the barges, with a strong tide running. Immediately men busied themselves with poles, all giving orders. Other children on other barges joined in the chorus of howling. Calmly, Mother, a hefty lass in black trousers, long black plaited hair and pink jumper, strolled down aft – plunged her hand into the water and hauled out dripping puppy, which manifested its joy by shaking itself vigorously uttering yelps of glee. Order had been restored! Scenes like this on the barges made them fascinating companions. . . but as they filled with cargo they were towed away, until all had gone. "What now?" I asked. Next day another barge turned up, the following day two more – but this was not work to capacity by any stretch of the imagination and I realised we were being used as a floating urea warehouse, from which our cargo was taken in dribs and drabs as required. I pointed out to the agent that time for us was "of the essence" – a phrase he rather liked – that we were needed in Shanghai to help progress China's Five Year Export Plan. . . This, coupled with a terse "Hurry up!" from Singapore generated a few ripples and we were moved alongside the new Dongdu Wharf. This is planned to take a total of twenty deep sea ships in the near future and was already busy with four at a time. Here our cargo was swung out into little trucks hauled in trains by tiny tractors driven by women to the nearby 'warehouses', which turned out to be neat open-air 'haystacks' of bags covered by green tarpaulin, until being carted off by small lorries with completely open engines steered by the driver in his open cab wielding large wheelbarrow-like wooden shaft handles.

Even alongside, our discharge rate was unimpressive, though our sightseeing was simpler with no ferry to catch and no Chinese Navy to scramble over. We strolled all around the town, saw the university and many other lovely buildings and monuments, including some wonderfully executed sculpture murals of historical scenes, some for the recent past, many from long ago, for this part of China is rich in history. One day we made a long walk out to a large temple which is also a college for young monks. We felt the Chinese government is living up to its self-proclaimed 'religious tolerance' by supporting the Buddhists, whilst perhaps leaning on the Christians who – from their vigorously active participation in Eastern Europe's recent anti-Communist uprisings – pose more of a threat to the Chinese government than the more passive Buddhists. The temple was beautifully decorated, and vast – we walked wonderingly from courtyard to courtyard, glowered upon by enormous fearsome gods. . . The *Orient Venus* had brought a large party of Japanese tourists, mostly middle aged and older, who were wandering around chatting happily and camrecording everything. We wondered what these dear old folks were doing fifty years ago. . . but they smiled upon us, seemingly quite at ease with English Tourists.

The town map we had been given showed a 'short cut' over the wooded hill from this temple back to town, which we took. To our surprise that part of the track shown as dotted lines which we had taken to mean 'unsurfaced road' turned out to be a long winding tunnel – not much used by the look of it, but which we entered nonetheless. High enough for a double deck bus – but without any traffic at all except one car which came through when we were well inside – we felt the place was distinctly 'creepy'. Dimly lit, with dark narrow exits leading off at intervals to who knew where – we plodded on. Well ventilated but damp and dark, we were glad when we saw Light At The End of the Tunnel and came out into the sunshine. The tunnel had a haunted feel, and we were not unduly surprised when our agent expressed astonishment that we had dared enter it. He told us during the War the Japanese occupiers kept many prisoners there, in less than luxury. . .

A couple of typhoon warnings came to nothing apart from a temporary cessation of cargo work but as the National Day Public Holiday approached (it lasts at least two days at the beginning of October) we watched hundreds of trawlers coming in from the sea – for the holiday, we imagined. But this was a serious typhoon warning, they were coming in for shelter. A severe typhoon had not hit Xiamen for thirty years, the island of Taiwan seems to deflect them, but the only predictable about such phenomena is their total unpredictability and this time a steadily plunging barometer, rising NE wind and ugly, threatening sky seemed to indicate this typhoon meant business! All ships were ordered by the Harbour Master out to the anchorage and left, one by one, *Golden Bear* last as she was furthest up the quay. Just as well we left last – our Turkish chief engineer had been savouring shoreside delights and only came back as the gangway was being raised.

We still had 300 tonnes of cargo onboard. In the anchorage were at least thirty other ships, mostly coasters come in from the sea seeking shelter from the storm raging outside and we spent a worried night watching the weather and barometer. During the early hours, however, this began to rise, the wind veered steadily to the east, then became squally and fitful, indicating the

172

typhoon had passed to the north and curved back out to sea. Next day dawned bright and sunny and the agent promised barges – "Maybe this evening".

True to his word the largest barge we had so far seen was towed alongside, a ferryload of dockers followed and all cargo was out by seven next morning – by which time the typhoon's aftermath was, as it often is, a dense fog. By mid morning however this had cleared sufficiently to sail. We retraced our steps out to the sea.

Steep, partly mist-shrouded hills, glassy water dotted with junks whose sails hung limply, the glimpse of a pagoda through the trees at the water's edge – it all resembled a classical Chinese painting. In our next port, Shanghai, we would for the first time, load containers on deck – we were still in business!

Containers at last! At Shanghai.

16. THE PERFUMED SEAS

Nineteenth century fiction described the waters surrounding the vast archipelagos north and south of the Indonesian chain as 'The Perfumed Seas', a name which I found still suited when I passed that way in November 1992.

Downwind of the islands the fragrance of bougainvillea, frangipani, hibiscus and a thousand other tropical flowers, plants and vines hangs sweet and heavy in the air giving the illusion that their scent is indeed off the sea itself.

I was to relieve Captain Charles Read while he took some well-earned leave, at Singapore on 5th November. An almost identical sister to the *Golden Bear*, the *Golden Harvest* came from Rickmers of Bremerhaven as the *Irmgard Jacob*, a standard German Liberty Replacement. When I joined she lay anchored in the Eastern Roads with a cargo of animal feed in the shape of bagged rape-seed and groundnut-meal loaded in Bedi Bunder, NW India. There were, I found, thirty three of us onboard – Ghanaian chief officer, Philippino electrician, South Korean chief engineer; both cooks and the second engineer from Singapore (Chinese), ten Burmese including the radio officer and third officer, and sixteen Indonesians who included the second officer – the usual congenial mixture! Fortunately, the basic language is English. My orders were to proceed to Tanjong Priok (Jakarta) then, if the charterers so wished I was to retain some of my cargo onboard and take it to Tanjung Perak (Surabaya). Both of these ports are on the island of Java and it was up to me which route I took – normally the shortest and safest, of course. The shortest route lies down through Riau Strait and Banka Strait, the way we went in the *Malaysia* in 1969. Interesting to navigator and tourist alike, this way winds past a succession of vividly green islands – the perfumed seas indeed – dotted with quaint local sailing craft. But these waters are now considered unsafe for deep-draught vessels (such as we at 9.2 metres).

Not only are the channels becoming shallower than their charted depths due to coral formations and accompanying silting, but piracy is increasing. I would receive scant thanks for running my ship aground to provide easy meat for the pirate horde. How about Gaspar Strait? Well, the same conditions apply. . . "shallow patches, depths decreasing. . ." ominous words on any chart. So I decided to take the less exciting but probably safer long way round, through Karimata Strait, a passage of 692 miles pilot to pilot. All this, of course, I discussed with the second officer (the navigator) before sailing on the evening of 7th November after taking bunkers, fresh water and provisions.

Having disembarked our pilot, equatorial dusk deepened rapidly into night as we crossed Singapore Strait, joining the eastbound traffic lane which, that night, included several super-tankers carrying three red lights in a vertical line – "I am constrained by my deep draught, please keep out of my way as I am unable to keep out of yours". Bound from Gulf to Japan they kept us on our toes, avoiding them while at the same time seeking a safe chance to 'turn right off the motorway' past the guardian to Singapore's eastern approaches, the Horsburgh Light. Next morning, Sunday 8th, we Crossed The Line – without ceremony. Not only had we all been south of the equator before but King Neptune and his attendant jollifications are of the West: not, I think, part of Eastern culture. We didn't even feel the bump as we crossed. Next morning the chief officer and I found a few tiny bones and a pathetic handful of feathers on one of the forward mooring bitts – clearly the slaying ground of a hawk we had seen pursuing the swallows which were still darting around masts and rigging.

Most of the weather encountered on this passage was clear and sunny, but this *was* the rainy season and occasional torrential downpours blotted out everything, even occasionally the screen of our state-of-the-art radar. Such showers were usually of short duration however – an hour perhaps, two at most – and one just had to be patient and, of course, ever vigilant, slowing down if necessary to ensure the tricky parts were negotiated in clear weather, if not always in daylight.

Charts and pilot book warn navigators to proceed with extreme caution in the approaches to Javanese ports, keeping the sharpest lookout for the fish traps which lurk, singly and in clusters in the form of stakes protruding a few feet above the water. Some are brightly lit, others are not lit at all. But, after carefully picking our way through a rainwashed gloomy dawn we arrived off the port 10th November to be told on VHF by Port Control to anchor two miles off the entrance and await Port Officials. Port Health (to give me pratique), Customs (their leader armed with a stubby holstered pistol), Immigration, Coast Guard and of course the Agent, whose job it was to pave the way for me and see to my company's interests. They drank our coffee, smoked our cigarettes, scrutinised our passports and the ship's papers, cholera vaccination certificates, sealed our bond, and left:– a little piece of drama enacted aboard every ship arriving at every port in the world; the only differences being in the number of boarding officials and the extent of their 'requirements'. A pilot would board 'tomorrow'. Having radioed Owners of their ship's safe arrival and that we were in all respects ready to unload our cargo, we had time to admire the scenery. The coast was disappointingly low and unspectacular but the pilot book – always a mine of information – states that an advanced civilisation thrived here as long ago as the fourth century AD and probably earlier. Indonesia, we learned, consists of 12 main islands and over 3,000 smaller ones. Supporting a population of 13 main ethnic groups of which the predominant is Malaysian, mainly Muslim. In the eleventh century a great Javanese trade expansion began: the Portuguese came, in search of spices, to be ejected by the British. They in turn were ousted in 1595 by the Dutch who reigned more or less supreme until 1942 when the Japs arrived in force, to be themselves defeated by the Western Allies three years later. The Dutch relinquished colonial power soon afterwards and in 1950 this extensive and vastly interesting land became the Republic of Indonesia. And here we were, anchored off the capital, Jakarta, founded 1619, Batavia to the Dutch. Next afternoon the promised pilot came aboard immaculate in whites. I explained that our wheelmen were Indonesian sailors, thinking this might help with his steering orders, but not a bit of it. The Indonesian pilot gave our indonesian sailors – in Indonesian waters – orders in English! With tugs secured we made our way in, passing the smart dark-red-hulled white-superstructured Stulcken-derrick-rigged *Sunderland Endeavour*, wearing the Cypriot ensign. At our next port her twin sister *Sunderland Craftsman* (of Valetta, Maltese flag) was loading down to her marks with bagged rice for Italy, so her Greek captain told me when I met him in the agent's office. I also learned that the Greek owner of these vessels had studied happily in the north east coast of England, so named his ships with nostalgic affection after Geordie places. . . The tanker *Sunderland* in the same colours, with the same black topped white funnel bearing the company houseflag was lying at the nearby oil jetty. Made me feel quite homesick!

The picturesquely curvaceous ketches which abounded here in 1969 all now have motors, though most still carry a rag or two of canvas to set with a fair wind, helping the fuel bills.

Our own winches swung out the Jakarta cargo in fine style, on our union-purchase-rigged derricks* – the gunny sacking bags showering a fine dust overall. But, with our air-conditioning working well, by keeping doors and windows firmly closed the dust remained outside and not all over cabin furniture and carpets. Another reason for keeping our accommodation secure was the night-prowler, who, we found, helped himself wherever he could. *Our* sixteen stalwart Indonesians were deeply ashamed of their low countrymen's behaviour; but I found the Indonesians in the main are a delightful people, cheerful, lively and industrious. Sure, some of them (not seafarers) will steal your inflatable liferafts from under your very nose, but somehow it was difficult to sustain the anger even this aroused. Local newspapers reported an increasing epidemic of dengue fever, urging householders to do all they could to discourage the mosquitoes which spread it. Even a tiny puddle of water can become a fertile breeding ground, and despite all precautions we found ourselves well and truly bitten, fortunately without the dreaded dengue afflicting us.

It was confirmed by Singapore that I must on carry almost half my cargo 415 miles eastwards along Java's northern coast to Tanjung Perak – and made

---

* Union Purchase (A pair of derricks is set up with one plumbing the hold, the other overside. Their lifting wires are joined at the hook so that cargo can be lifted and swung in or out as required).

that port's offing at daybreak, 16th November, a glorious roseate dawn which we had ample time to appreciate as we waited, drifting, while the pilot chugged out to meet us. Lying on a low plain some 25 miles up a narrow inlet where mangrove swamps gradually gave way to rolling green hills in the distance, it came as a surprise when, rounding a bend, a wide landlocked harbour opened before us, full of ships. We counted over 20 at anchor, many more alongside. In the distance, at the Ujung naval dockyard, we espied the three masted training barquentine *Dewaruji* while nearer to hand, bright peacock among so many dowdy little freighters, lay the *Athira* of Ujong Pandang which close inspection through binoculars revealed under her white paint as the former *Nippon Maru* of Tokyo, an interisland ferry. Sail lingers on over here in Eastern Java and in this upper harbour were numerous blue-sailed craft whose diverse rigs included not only the lateen, gaff and bermudan but also that amazing South Sea Islands rig which seems to owe its suspension to neither yard, gaff nor even mast! Many of these little vessels were fishermen, elaborately carved and painted, while other, larger ones carried huge hardwood logs and sawn timber in from the outports. There were log barges, too, pushed or towed by tugs, showing that Indonesia is into the business in a big way, exporting to the ends of the earth timber for building, furniture – anything requiring beautiful wood.

But what about the rain forest depletion? Well, yes, say the locals, but this is our livelihood!

One evening we were required to warp ourselves a ship's length astern to make room for a ship which would come in during the night. Warping is an ancient evolution in which a ship moves without engines or tugs simply by leading mooring lines as far as possible along the quay and heaving on them with winch and windlass, interchanging the lines on the bollards as she goes. It is the essence of simplicity but one must be careful with an offshore wind blowing, or your ship will come off the quay very quickly and hauling her back alongside can prove difficult; especially if some idiot lets go all your lines at once. However I (directing operations from the bridge) perceived that my lads knew exactly what to do and were getting on with it – quite happy to suspend activity to assist ashore two ladies – Indonesian wives who had to catch the train back to Jakarta, having travelled round the coast onboard. Next morning I strolled forward and leaned over the bow to study the name of our new neighbour.

Moored only a couple of yards ahead of us, her name and port of registry took some figuring out as lettering was Cyrillic, but eventually I deciphered *Dekabrist* of Saint Petersburg;– first time I had seen the 'new' port of registry on a ship's transom. Feeling sociable I ambled round that evening to greet her captain. Speaking fluent English he received me with utmost cordiality and we soon had the world put to rights (as seamen, with their 'immense breadth of knowledge and wisdom' always can). Didn't I find it rather lonely with no fellow English to talk to? Well, yes, sometimes, but how was he faring? He pulled a wry face. Because of Recent Events he now finds that some of his crew – even some of his family! – are suddenly "foreigners" through living in 'Ukrania', Georgia etc. But they were doing their best, as seamen must, and we parted on the best of terms. Next morning at six it was time for us to sail, the last sweepings of cargo having been bagged and removed from our holds. Next port, Singapore had advised, would be Isabel, to load bagged phosphate for Shanghai.

Isabel, where is she? (I had not passed this way before).

On Leyte Island, in the Philippines. Only the *latest* supplement to our pilot book mentioned Isabel as a port, recently developed since the construction a decade ago of the phosphate factory and wharf. Moreover our chart outfit, Isabel-wise, was incomplete, the second officer scoured the Indonesian chart shops in vain. The agent assured me that only Indonesian charts are available in Indonesia – British Admiralty charts did not, for them, exist! But Indonesian charts only cover Indonesian waters. Ever resourceful, our second mate went aboard a Panama flag ship nearby. Her Hong Kong Chinese master kindly allowed his charts to be borrowed and taken ashore for photocopying, full size, and on these copies we made our way to Isabel. There had been no time for the usual DHL package of charts from Motion Smith in Singapore to reach us.

Heading north east across the Java Sea the good ship *Golden Harvest* made her way up Macassar Strait into the Celebes Sea. From here into the Sulu Sea there was a choice of channels, all narrow, but I chose the way which – I hoped – would take us through the narrowest parts in daylight. Thus we passed Jolo Island and went through the Pilas Channel. Green dappled hills and gleaming white reefs basked in the afternoon sunshine on either side, while further distant, mountains reared heads covered in sun drenched virgin jungle. As we swept by tiny villages of thatched houses on stilts it seemed the people were totally oblivious to this big ship passing, intent only on their canoes, nets and fish traps. We saw no ships for days up here, only stretches of blue water surrounded by green islands and could sense something of the feelings of those early Spaniards whose visits predated those of any other Europeans. As we entered Philippine waters the shores became studded here and there with the lovely old churches for which these islands are famous. The Spaniards, naming the islands after their King Philip, spread the Word effectively so that even today this is the only Christian nation in Asia.

Night had fallen by the time we cleared Pilas Channel, but daylight on 26th November showed us Mindanao's purple mountains, to the Bohul Sea, passing SE of Negros Island and west of tiny Siquijor. Across a flat Cebu

Sea, then, with night again falling fast as we approached the mile-wide Hilutangan Channel off Cebu City, the nation's second largest after Manila, glowing and flashing in neon splendour to port. Tidal streams were strong here but fortunately always followed the channel's axis; either slowing you down or sweeping you along but rarely trying to put you on the bank. Though naturally we checked our progress all the way, Camotes Sea next, forty miles, then a dog-leg to starboard round the Camotes Islands and, as midnight approached, there ahead was a low line of yellow lights. Isabel!

But had the Manila agent received my ETA message? And if the pilot was not there to meet us what should I do in these tide-wracked waters with – so the pilot book cheerfully told me – only poor anchorage in very deep water? Forty five fathoms with a foul bottom, the kind which is full of rocks and snags just waiting to rip your anchor off the end of its chain, so easily. . . Of course, these gloomy forebodings were simply my dread of the unknown;– worth considering nevertheless, as must now be all these will-o'the-wisp lit fishermen whose canoes we suddenly found around us. . .

But to my relief the pilot awaited in his little boat and by 0200 27th November we were safely tied up alongside the phosphate works. Next morning tall, belching chimneys, overhead conveyors, silver storage tanks and huge corrugated sheds depicted all the accoutrements of modern industry. There was also copper smelter, and "gold in them thar hills". But over the high wire boundary fence the silence of the forest reigned supreme. Loading 11,000 tonnes of bagged fertiliser using ship's gear would take about four days, weather permitting.

One day the agent took me across the harbour to the town by ferry, one of many, each around forty feet long, little more than four feet wide, stabilised by bamboo outriggers port and starboard to form a simple trimaran. Open apart from a flimsy canvas awning they were brightly painted in vivid colours, powerful inboard driving them at good speed across the glassy waters to Isabel City. Little more than a village like the ones we had passed, despite its grand title, city hall and most roads were of concrete but most houses and buildings, even the Nite Club, were tiny, wooden and thatched, perched on shoulder height stilts among the coco and banana palms. Principal transport was trishaw, some motorised, mostly bearing religious slogans on their tailboards. Children crawled and ran everywhere, everyone seemed happy. There was a rare innocent, almost dreamlike air about the place. Even the swallows darted undisturbed around out ship – the hawk having disembarked in Jakarta.

Apart from the most unusual town ferries, which could carry five passengers each at a pinch – and to have stood up would have risked capsizing – a couple of other ships seen here deserve mention. The huge bulk carrier *Nyon* of Bale, wearing the exceptionally rare flag of Switzerland,

A farmhouse near Isabel, in the Philippines.

came in with rock phosphate from West Africa for the fertiliser plant, and an interisland ro-ro ferry whose name must go a long way towards the record for the longest – *Our Lady of the Sacred Heart*.

Isabel proved delightful but on 1st December it was time to go. Cargo was all loaded, hatches battened down and our ship secured against any weather the China Seas now liked to throw at us. Heading north we emerged from the islands into the North Pacific Philippine Basin via San Bernadino Strait and as we put our nose outside on the Road to Shanghai the NE monsoon greeted us with all her usual vigour. As our bow dipped to the swell, dark water laced with white crashed aboard, the first of many to baptise us over the next few days. We had left the Perfumed Seas astern. . ..

17. SHANGHAI CHRISTMAS

When our present cargo of bagged phosphate fertiliser was unloaded we would be going to the Shanghai East Shipyard, across the Huangpo River from Shanghai city, for routine repairs and survey. This would involve dry-docking to inspect the ship's underwater parts and enable her bottom to be cleaned and painted. German surveyors from the ship's Classification Society, Germanischer Lloyd, together with their Chinese counterparts would inspect everything, recommend which work must be done now and which could perhaps be postponed. Now, more than ever before, the world's ship classification societies – (Lloyd's, G.L., American Bureau, Norske Veritas, and Co) were having to tread warily. Like any other business they existed to make money, in their case from shipowners whose vessels must by international law be registered with a reputable society before they could be insured. Make your classification surveys too demanding – too strict – and the ship's owner might take his custom elsewhere. Be too lax, and the ship may be lost through causes attributable to "improperly conducted survey". . . The toll of sunken ships was placing a heavy strain on the insurance companies' resources and the classification societies had come in for criticism for 'laxity' in Parliament. A sensible, realistic approach was the only acceptable attitude to adopt. Surveyors must concentrate on keeping the ship seaworthy without being too exacting about "non-essentials". Ah – but what were the "non-essentials?" That was often the rub!

Meanwhile, however, our good ship *Golden Harvest* rolled her way through a brisk north east monsoon, the seasonal wind which blows over these waters steadily and strongly from September to April. With decks constantly awash, ventilators all canvas-covered and secured against moisture entering the cargo, we were rolling ten degrees off the vertical each way in an eleven second cycle – not unpleasant – and which eased as we passed between the Ryuku Islands, Japan's southern rocky outposts which have been able, for some time, to bridge the ideological gap between the Two Chinas. The small port of Ishigaki, too shallow alongside for our ship, has become a Port of Entry and Departure if proceeding from Taiwan to Mainland China. You steam in to anchor in the harbour, Rising Sun courtesy ensign flying – to be boarded by the Japanese agent bowing and smiling and requiring six copies of your crew list, bonded store list, cargo manifest and all the paper paraphernalia needed at a "proper" port. After a cup of coffee and much signing, he hands you Clearance From Japan, and off you go on your way to Communist China. Doubtless this arrangement, profitable to the Japanese and ideologically acceptable in China, will continue as long as China and Taiwan remain cooly disposed to each other.

But bound from the Philippines this little charade was not necessary and we carried on across the East China Sea with the added interest of fog patches as the wind weakened – towards the Chiang Jiang Kou, literally – Chiang River Mouth – CJK to all.

Daybreak filtered weakly through a clammy opacity as we "proceeded at a safe speed" blowing a prolonged blast on our siren 'at intervals not exceeding two minutes'. Occasionally other ships were heard, when we tried to decide which whistles matched which echoes on our radar screens. Almost imperceptibly the fog became thick drizzle, which – we soon found – even our new state-of-the-art radar set was unable to penetrate perfectly. Five miles off the Chinese coast I nipped into the chartroom to plot our position, referring to both satellite navigator and radar, when the Burmese sailor on lookout suddenly cried out, pointing ahead. Burmese third mate yelled "Hard 'a starboard!" and Indonesian helmsman spun the wheel as I careered out onto the bridge. A sixty-foot wooden fishing boat was sliding down our port side, very close. "Hard a 'port' then, to avoid clouting him with our stern and I looked down upon half a dozen white-faced Chinamen frantically hauling their net. We were sure they shared our sentiments – that was a close shave! Ten minutes later the drizzle ceased and the sky cleared. Gazing astern we saw we had passed through a small fleet – eight of these craft – none of which had shown on our screens.

Anchoring in the appointed place along with a dozen or so other ships awaiting upriver passage, I was ordered on VHF to embark a pilot at No.5 Buoy, South Channel, next morning at 0730. This required weighing anchor at six, still in darkness. But at least it was clear, round the CJK "Roundabout" to the channel entrance. When he came aboard the pilot advised we should take the deeper north channel because of our deep draft and the state of the tide. This we did, in thickening fog again, at one point having to anchor for an hour when zero visibility closed the port completely. I have the greatest admiration for these Shanghai pilots. Smart in naval uniform, always cheerful, they work one of the world's most complex waterways in which charted depths are ever changing due to the Yangtze's unpredictable silt-carrying currents. Gales, fog, blinding rain and snow in winter are commonplace in a river always thronged with every kind of nautical traffic. Out pilot did the usual efficient job, urging the Inspection people who came aboard at Wusong anchorage to please be quick about their business as we had a tide to catch. These uniformed officials are a much pleasanter bunch than their predecessors of even a few years ago. In those days this visit was indeed an inspection, with every ship searched by suspicious officials from top to bottom, all hands interrogated. In today's greatly relaxed atmosphere however it is a normal formality, an inspection only of my ship's papers, our passports, cholera vaccination certificates, etc, all with high good humour. Not quite finished, our visitors remained undismayed when we weighed anchor with them still aboard. Their white, diesel-engined tender followed us and came alongside to take them off when we turned to port to enter the Huangpu River, on whose banks Shanghai has stood for more than 4,000 years. As we passed the power station's tall red and white chimney I noticed the pilot staring over the side into the café-au-lait ebb. "We are still moving", he announced with satisfaction, "still afloat! This is the shallowest part". Hard 'a starboard then to avoid a large green and white outward bound coastal ferry, its decks crowded with passengers; port ten degrees to avoid a huge barge full of sand being pushed by a stumpy black tug; a slowing of our speed as we passed the container wharf to avoid parting mooring lines of the many ships lying there. . . heart in mouth as an orange and white ferry full of waving school children disappeared under our port bow – breathing again as it reappeared to starboard having missed us by all of ten feet. . . and so on, up the river to Shanghai where we tied up to buoys fore and aft, off the city. It was dark by now and immediately a dozen barges jostled alongside and were only persuaded to leave with the greatest difficulty – eventually by casting off their lines on the pilot's advice. I suppose from a barge all ships look alike in the dark, but the vessel they awaited would arrive later. Our cargo was destined for Wujin, half a day's passage up the river, upon which we set out at first light next morning. Ships were everywhere, ships and strings of barges, and shipyards were busy all the way up the river on both banks. Most of the ships were Chinese but fewer now wear the COSCO* colours, the once familiar yellow funnel with red band studded with yellow star and waves. . . more and more appear in private disguise, while COSCO itself took on a new image when it changed the funnel to black top, yellow below, broad blue band carrying a white logo consisting of an anchor and COSCO in small white letters. From small beginnings with old, second-hand ships, the Chinese merchant navy has grown to become the world's largest, much of its tonnage brand new and able to carry every kind of cargo.

Dozens of barges which had been moored for the night were now greeting the day. Cooking fires smoked, dogs barked, cocks crowed, children skipped nimbly from barge to barge, an old man cleaned his teeth from a red plastic bucket on deck. We passed sawmills with their adjacent timber yards stacked with planks, ponds on which floated hundreds of logs, seasoning. Some of these were being lashed together into rafts by an agile gang of men working with long poles, while women from nearby barges daintily picked their way across the floating mass of timber, shopping baskets in hand, clearly bound for the day's purchases in the market. Passing a cement factory we saw a

---

* COSCO – China Overseas Shipping Corporation

183

gang of merry girls in bright blue overalls sweeping up a wharf with besom brooms, raising clouds of dust and not apparently achieving a great deal, though obviously enjoying their work. All the way were ships, large and small, including one very old coaster, painted black, her bar stem and heavy counter stern relics of bygone years but still in commission with a modern bridge, radar, and diesel propulsion.

After the week's rain everyone had their washing out to dry and a barge full of logs or clinker would have a brave string of brightly coloured garments hung rainbow fashion from forward to aft over the cargo. At one place a hill on the low bank turned out to be a mountain of domestic rubbish, brought by barge from the city and unloaded by crane onto a series of conveyor belts, each one carrying its spoil higher and higher up the mountain. As we drew closer we perceived that numerous persons were picking objects off the belts and scavenging, filling plastic bags with we knew not what, possibly cans and bottles for sale to reprocessors. At the far end of this dump, upstream, the ancient mouldering rubbish was being quarried out and loaded into more barges, presumably for further use as fertiliser. Little is wasted in China! There were steam locomotives hauling long goods trains, and in between these scenes of Dickensian heavy industry, fields of fresh spring green were lined by trees. Small fields, they were dotted with men and women wielding long-handled rakes while others were on their haunches planting, row by row.

Persons were using a couple of small tractors to build a path of bright red bricks through the fields while others with bags patrolled the shoreline beachcombing and attending the many fish traps along the bank. Occasionally we passed the entrance to a canal, guarded by its lock and lock house, the inevitable string of barges waiting to enter, while at landings all the way up the river crowds of people on foot or bicycle waited patiently for the next ferry. One man stood alongside his bicycle which binoculars revealed to be carrying a huge wire netting bag full of live ducks. He was assiduously feeding each inmate a sip of water from a baby's bottle – duck soup on wheels! Houses were mostly small, of brick, seeming old, but new blocks of flats occasionally rose over the horizon, beyond the flat fields.

At every turn we expected the river to narrow but instead it seemed to widen, until on one long reach the pilot announced we would be "berthing in ten minutes, please stand-by fore and aft". A couple of tugs appeared to make fast alongside and manoeuvre us to a fine, modern, wide concrete wharf where several ships unloaded their cargoes, including a Russian carrying the still-to-us-novel, new/old, white, blue and red on flag and funnel.

We had arrived, and at once our hatches were opened, unloading commenced, and our white bags of phosphate were trundled away on little trains of tractor-hauled trucks to be built into neat heaps of 1,500 bags each, then covered with green tarpaulins securely lashed down; – Chinese

Wujin Wharf. Our bagged urea cargo is being built into heaps covered with tarpaulin – Chinese warehouses.

Home sweet home for one man at Wujin.

UP THE CREEK which leads off the Huangpu at the Barge Station. Father comfortably seated at the tiller, Mother up forward fending off the bank where necessary. Their barge is a Brickie.

Barge station at Wujin.

warehouses; portable, convenient and cheap; adequately protecting the contents until needed elsewhere.

My wife and I went ashore for a stroll, and it was soon evident from the incredulous looks on bystanders' faces that such as we were rare birds. We passed a barrack yard where a dozen rookies of the People's Liberation Army, smart in their new green uniforms and peaked caps, were undergoing short arms drill. Each soldier held a pistol pointed at a man-sized picture across the yard. Spotting us strolling by – as one man they turned their heads towards us, open mouthed, pistols still wavering towards their target; – an incredibly funny sight had we dared use our camera!

Time seemed to have passed this part of China by – once we had walked beyond the port – and agricultural persons with wooden rakes over their shoulders were pictures straight out of the National Geographic. Amidst all this, a middle-aged white woman with auburn hair cycled sedately past, eyeing us and smiling faintly as she passed. How had she come to this spot, we wondered; and fell to pondering – as she rode on without speaking – if she had perhaps been an Eastern Europe student, or even an English girl, who had come here to find out for herself what life under communism was like; stayed, married perhaps, and come to accept these people as her own. . .

We came upon a barge station quite suddenly, as the canal was, of course, below road level. Covering a sizeable area, this concrete, glass-roofed platform-lined building at the convergence of a canal and the river looked exactly like a small rail metropolis where the steel railway lines were replaced with green water. Instead of trains alongside the platforms stood barges, some full of bricks, some working general cargo. Outside, a barge family were unloading 45-gallon steel drums of oil by the ancient practice of parbuckling, where a rope is passed round each end of the drum's cylindrical shape. One end is made fast on the shore, the other end is hove upon by enthusiastic workers to roll the drum up and ashore . . . It was fascinating, as was a new office building under construction whose scaffolding consisted entirely of bamboo poles lashed together with twine.

When our Wujin cargo was all out and our holds swept clean, we moved downstream a few miles to buoys 84/85 for a week, waiting to enter the shipyard. The river bank here was contained by brick and concrete walls, some twelve feet high, with heavy gates at intervals which would be closed when the river rose in spate to protect the low-lying countryside from unwanted flooding.

At one gate standing open, motor barges arrived daily full of bricks. The barge would be run up the beach at high water, its contents discharged by the simple process of the crew each carrying two baskets of bricks ashore along a plank, the baskets suspended from a long pole over the shoulder. On the bank the bricks were loaded into lorries – not a fork truck in sight! Nearer to hand came dull, unpainted muddy-looking barges whose purpose had us completely mystified. The barge would anchor near the shore, and a pair of women dressed in heavy grey rubber suits would lower themselves over the side until they sat waist deep on the overside stage plank they had rigged. Then the man of the barge would dredge the bottom with a net on a long pole, hoisting the net's contents towards the overside women who grubbed into the basket, removing some small items, rejecting others. It looked extremely cold, backbreaking work for all hands. Eventually, usually when the tide turned, they all climbed aboard and disappeared from our sight below the barge hold's coaming. But what were they doing? One day the agent came out and explained. They were dredging for mussels. Highly illegal, he pointed out hastily, in this polluted reach of the river; but the tourist hotels to which they sold them didn't know that!

Eventually a party from the shipyard came to discuss our forthcoming work. Foremen and managers were accompanied by the delightful Miss Li (pronounced Lee), our appointed translator/interpreter, who told us our ship's name in Chinese was *Jing Fung*, which translates literally as *Golden Plenty*. When, during our discussions, words failed even the eloquent Miss Li, we drew little diagrams: (as Confucius is said to have said, "One picture worth a thousand words"). Alongside the shipyard at last, we lay first at the foot of a slipway on which stood a half-built reefer ship. Reminiscent of the Tyne forty years ago, other vessels lay alongside three abreast – new ships fitting out, older vessels in for refit. Of these latter, the *Sea Architect* had suffered a serious fire across the Pacific in one of the US west coast ports, in which her captain and at least one crew member had died. Towed to Shanghai after purchase by the Chinese, her accommodation block was almost completely rebuilt and her name changed, even as we watched, to *Ocean Glory*. After burning off the old name the new was substituted in two-feet-high steel letters welded in place; likewise the name in Chinese characters, of course.

A small reefer ship built in this yard was in for her first dry-docking inspection. Painted overall a pleasant cream, the *Blue Sky* bore in blue the logo and name of her charterers, Cool Carriers, latest reincarnation of the seemingly indestructible Salen Group. Managed by Ahrenkeil Shipping of Hong Kong, her master was British, the chief engineer German and all other personnel Burmese, which matched her port of registry, Yangon (formerly Rangoon) Yangon was being burned off the stern. Was she flagging-out, we wondered, or changing ownership? No, the port of registry's letters were too small, her owner had decided, insufficiently prominent. So larger letters were cut and welded into place – to the merriment of our lads when the second 'N' was accidentally welded on the wrong way round – YANGOᴎ. Naturally our ten Burmese crew members and hers were soon coming and going between

In floating drydock, Shanghai, Christmas 1992.

ships, when we discovered her radio officer had been Sparks with me in the *Golden Harvest* four and a half years before.

Work began on our own ship, increasingly diverse as the days passed. Dry-docking was 20th December, when shipyard tugs and pilot moved us into the submerged bright blue floating dry-dock *Baiyunshan* – 'mountain with head in clouds'. The dock's tanks were pumped out and we rose steadily until settled firmly high and drying on the keel blocks. Before it dried out completely the hull was hosed down with freshwater jets while weed and barnacles were scraped off by workers wearing basketweave hard hats wielding long-handled slices. Both four and a half ton anchors were lowered to the dock floor, their chain cables ranged alongside them to be measured for wear. Freed of their chains both windlasses were overhauled and new brake linings fitted. Double bottom and peak tanks were drained, their brass screw-plugs labelled and placed where they would not be forgotten (which sounds basic but such bottom plugs have been overlooked in the hurry to refloat a ship with consequent capsizing as water flooded in). Our rudder was inspected in great detail. Found to have suffered slight wear and tear damage it was repaired in situ, but the four-bladed bronze propeller was unshipped, placed on a barge and taken across the river to the Prop Shop for refurbishment and rebalancing – a meticulously precise process which our superintendent and I watched closely – involving the use of tiny gramme weights to achieve perfect balance. The ship's bottom and part of her topsides were grit blasted to remove rust, raising clouds of black dust which got everywhere, while another ship upwind of us nearby was also gritblasting, adding to the grime spreading overall. Rain soon transformed this dust into mud. At first the weather was cold and clear, throwing into sharp relief the majestic old European buildings along the embankment known as the Bund – and their

189

modern skyscraper backing – while the river resembled an updated version of those splendid paintings of British rivers at the turn of the 20th century. Perched up in our drydock we enjoyed ringside seats. The large coastwise colliers bringing coal to Shanghai from the north were reminiscent of the old New Zealand Shipping Company in their black hulls, white superstructures and pale yellow funnels. At least one arrived daily, decks piled with snow. Tankers, coasters, container ships, tugs, ferries, enormous floating cranes, barges by the hundred and all kinds of freighters passed continually, day and night, regardless of the state of the tide. The SD14 was still a common sight and we recognised a few of our own class, the German Liberty Replacement, some of which did not have the bulbous bow. Most memorable perhaps was a new Japanese-built Chinese passenger liner, the gleaming white *Suzhouhao* which had been placed on the Shanghai-Japan route.

As Christmas approached the weather deteriorated into almost constant rain, blown horizontal by cold winds. Cabin windows were removed here and there – three in my own accommodation – for renewal "tomollow". Our engineers coped magnificently with their workload but inevitably boilers and pipework had to be inspected, so hot water, and occasionally all water, ceased to flow from the taps; usually of course when one needed a hot shower. The ship's accommodation grew damp and drear despite the installation of small electric heaters, but I was heartened how cheerful our lads remained. Born and brought up in the tropics – Burma, Indonesia, Ghana, the Philippines and Singapore, they must have felt the cold more than I, yet they willingly carried on working throughout the days, evenings too when occasionally required, snatches of their singing often heard. Of course, they were able to savour the delights of Shanghai by night, which doubtless helped morale.

Christmas is not a public holiday in China, though it is recognised, and many shops in the fashionable Nanjing Road were brightly lit with Christmas motifs, Santa and reindeers playing starring roles to piped carols, with cotton wool snow around the shop windows. Our Ghanaian chief officer, Abeku, knew of a Christian church not far off Nanjing Road but could not recall its exact location. When we learned there was to be a Christmas service there, I asked our translator.

"On Tibet Road, I will show you. Tomorrow night OK?"

And true to her word, there she was on the dockside, in pouring rain with an icy wind blowing our brollies inside out. But she and her boyfriend whisked us into a bus – and a Shanghai busride is an experience in itself – the bus is considered full when no more persons can squeeze aboard. But grey hairs are respected and I was touched when a young teenage girl stood and insisted I take her seat!

Moore Church, an inset wall stone declared, was built by British Methodists in 1879. Miraculously it has withstood the ravages of war and revolution ever since. The Imperial Japanese Army stabled their cavalry mounts here during the 'forties and twenty five years later the Cultural Revolution removed all signs of Christianity and used it as a school – a virtual temple of atheist ideology. But now it was beautifully restored and an elderly Chinese gentleman advised us to get there early on Christmas evening as the church would be full and the service would begin at 7pm. By way of thanking them for their trouble, we took our young friends to the famous Peace Hotel. Built pre 1930 as the Cathay Hotel at the foot of Nanjing Road, it reopened after the war years as the Peace Hotel in 1956, since when it has been handsomely renovated. Our two young guides had not before been here, and enjoyed a few drinks in highly civilised surroundings in the presence of the Old Jazz Band in the English style pub. The players are all in their sixties if not seventies, some having played in British trans-Pacific passenger liners prewar. Now they were belting out Christmas carols along with 'The Saints', 'China Nights', 'Twelfth Street Rag' and other old favourites in traditional jazz style, sans electronics, to a rapt audience of mainly tourists.

On Christmas Eve we were invited by The Small Potato – as our ship chandler insists I call him – to the Beijing Hotel for Special Christmas Dinner. His party of nine, all Chinese, included three well-behaved children, smart in their best clothes. The meal was Chinese, to be eaten with chopsticks of course, with the dramatically-introduced addition of a large, beautifully roasted turkey. Everyone eyed this curiously, wondering what it was. The Small Potato then rose to announce, "Captain Mister Kinghorn will now carve Special Christmas Turkey!" And if you've ever tried to carve a turkey with chopsticks. . . To much merriment our ship's cook, (who had brought the turkey from the ship) dived into his bag beneath the table and produced a large, broad bladed Chinese knife and a small fork. But nobody went short. Whisky was served neat in small china bowls.

Afterwards we were rushed by taxi to the International Seamen's club, now housed in what was, prewar, the British Club. Here already assembled and in excellent form were several hundred seamen from all nations, including most of my own crew who drew us to their large round table under festive lights and paper streamers. Entertainment was about to commence. First, a middle aged man tumbled amazingly, then imitated bird calls, first one – then two, until we seemed to be surrounded by birds all calling and singing, which he pretended – convincingly – to pluck out of the air and feed. This remarkable act was followed by a conjuror in full evening dress who matched Paul Daniels with his wizardry. All this, I might add, was 'On The House', as were the mini-buses which returned us to our ships. Our Burmese lads had expressed the wish to visit their compatriots aboard the *Blue Sky*, so thither our obliging driver took us. The British captain made us most welcome and introduced his chief engineer who, it transpired, was from the former East Germany, where he had done his national service as a Border Guard on the Berlin Wall. The four of us 'saw in' Christmas Morn to 'Silent Night', sung in German very touchingly by the chief, while our Burmese made merry below. We should, by Regulations, have been back onboard own ship by midnight. When we breezed up the gangway at 0130 our green uniformed People's Liberation Army Frontier Guard, instead of arresting us, wished us a beaming Merry Christmas.

It was business as usual for the shipyard and the day was spent quietly until Noon, when the *Blue Sky* sailed "Towards Long Beach, California", although her people knew that before she arrived she would most likely have been diverted to load elsewhere, for that is the nature of life in reefer ships. Meat in Australia perhaps, would become her next cargo, bananas from Ecuador, fish from the Falklands or fruit from Valparaiso. . . I learned later she had gone to New Plymouth, New Zealand, to load butter. She departed with a great blowing of whistles, waving of hats and much cheerful Burmese banter across the ever widening stretch of water.

In the evening we accompanied Abeku the Ghanaian mate and Armando the Philippine electrician by taxi to church in good time, arriving soon after six to find the pews filling rapidly. We were shown to excellent seats in the gallery, almost like a theatre box, where were already several Americans and a few Britons and Australians. But the predominant congregation, numbering well over a thousand, was Chinese. Old ladies the men in Mao suits and caps (!) well-dressed middle-aged citizens and many young folk, including children, all entered into the spirit of Christmas wholeheartedly. The choir, fifteen men and twenty five ladies, sat above the altar in spotless white surplices with cherry red wimples thrown back. The service was conducted by a lady in black cassock, also red wimpled. After 'O Come All Ye Faithful' which *we* sang in English to everyone else's Chinese (no one seemed to mind) there followed a service which could have packed the Albert Hall so superb was the quality of its contents and rendition. And there was not even a collection! (I was told later that collections of money are not allowed in Chinese religious houses). The choir sang sweetly, the grand piano and organ were beautifully played, often by quite young persons, and a girl led a young blind man down from the choir to play the Chinese Xylophone, never missing a beat to the piano accompaniment. Most of the musical pieces were recognisable sacred works with Christmas emphasis but a few were clearly Chinese hymns sung with great gusto by choir and congregation together.

The last part of this two hour service was the Nativity Play, performed by young adults in traditional costume, Chinese theatre-style, where the cast mime dramatically while the same voice for all parts came over a loudspeaker. All in Chinese, the Story is of course the same in any language. Herod and his soldiers were magnificently villainous and never have Three

Wise Men looked more like Wise Men from the East! (In the order-of-service sheet, translated for us next day by Miss Li, they came across as "Oriental Doctors"...)

Emerging from church it was difficult to accept that this was still Red China, amid the abundance of tree-strung lights, illuminated shop signs and flashing neons, well stocked department stores and elegantly dressed people.

Next evening, Boxing Day, our own ship's party was held in the crew messroom, attended by all hands with Mr Ang, our Singapore superintendent as guest. Once again my mixed crew showed they had not lost the art of Own Entertainment; with guitars, keyboard, tin whistle, singing – even dancing... and plenty to eat and drink, of course.

Yes, despite the rather chill comforts of a winter drydocking, this had indeed been a memorable and very Happy Christmas!

18. CARRY IT BULK!

Guan Guan's Golden Line ships carry mostly break-bulk general cargo (ie. cargo not in containers) on a monthly liner basis from China to Karachi and the Gulf with occasional calls at Colombo, "if sufficient inducement". They are one of only two non-Chinese companies to have been granted this privilege, the other being the German Rickmers Line, which runs to Europe. But Eastward cargoes are whatever can be obtained, usually urea or meal, and whereas at first these commodities were carried bagged, as bulk handling facilities became available at the ports visited it grew more and more the practice to carry it bulk. Quicker to load, at least as quick as bags to discharge, and of course the ship can carry more in bulk, as the cargo flows in, filling all the spaces between beams and frames which bagged cargo cannot. . . hence more freight.

Early in June 1993 the *Golden Harvest* loaded a cargo of chrome ore at Karachi, for the steel mills near Shanghai. On this Karachi visit I had been promised a trip to Gadani Beach to see the shipbreaking there. Old ships by the dozen are run up onto the beach at high water and broken up in situ, their steel being sent for 'recycling' and all potentially useful mechanical items stored for resale. As a ship such as mine passes her twentieth birthday, spares become increasingly hard to obtain: that particular model is "no longer made", the manufacturer often having gone out of business long ago. Armed with a list of useful second hand machinery parts, I intended using this as my reason to go. . . and there is also a sort of gruesome interest in seeing old ships in their final resting place. But the road from Karachi passed through a military zone; strict security was in force, Gadani's secrets remained unrevealed.

A grey, dusty, lumpy rock mined in Baluchistan, chrome ore now makes a substantial contribution to Pakistan's liquidity. Brought to the port in heavy lorries, the loads were tipped onto the concrete West Wharf, to be moved by giant yellow bulldozers into smaller heaps alongside each of the vessel's five cargo hatches. Loading was by the ship''s derricks and gear with stevedore's grabs attached, swung in and out at ten tons per hoist – the maximum safe working load of the derricks. One early morning around six, our Burmese second mate was digging amongst spare gear in the forward mast house with his sailors to find a cargo block.   The steel wheels and hook in their steel shell proved heavier than expected, getting it out awkward. But one more heave should do it, lads!! Suddenly his back was shot through with pain and he had to be carried up to his bunk. Work proceeded of course, but the company port doctor – highly skilled in ship's medical matters and very pleasant also – said he *should* go to hospital. But the prospect of a Pakistani hospital, however efficient, did not appeal to our Burmese second mate.

Although his English was good he spoke no Urdu, and had found (the hard way) that Pakistani food disagreed with his interior. For a couple of days we applied the lotions and potions prescribed and hoped he would recover without the need for hospitalisation. But by this time the doctor was growing firm, reminding us all that if treatment were not given soon our second mate may be permanently crippled. He was, therefore sent for X-Ray. No bones broken; but he should stay in for observation. . . I could not help feeling that the prospect of a handsome compensation for "industrial injury" was encouraging the hospital to believe there would be no cause for concern in their obtaining eventual payment. But the second mate only wanted to fly to Singapore

Loading chrome ore at Karachi..

where his wife could meet him and he would be among friends who could visit him there, if hospital still proved necessary. I realised that by keeping him out of hospital in Karachi I may be doing our lad a grave disservice longterm: and could not help recalling how, quite recently, the man I had helicoptered ashore from the *Limari* had tried to sue me for negligence when his leg did not completely heal. . . But our second mate cheerfully wrote me a note accepting full responsibility if I sent him to Singapore. So, after a morning at the hospital persuading the doctors, I signed him off and his shipmates accompanied him to the airport in a wheelchair as a travelling patient. The happy ending was – on our return to Singapore two weeks later he and his wife returned onboard to thank me. He had made a full recovery in Singapore without need of hospitalisation; – and, having been shipmates off-and-on ever since, we remain good friends.

A densely heavy cargo, our chrome ore would by no means fill the ship and Abeku and I decided that some 30% in the 'tweendecks and 70% in the lower holds would be satisfactory under the circumstances, provided the

The injured second mate landed at Karachi with Sparks (who took him to the airport)

'tweendeck cargo was 'winged-out' to prevent undue weight being placed on the 'tweendeck hatchcovers (the steel lids over the lower holds). This would be achieved, we were promised, by using small bulldozers, called bobcats, which would be hired from another firm. But as the 'tweendecks were loaded no bobcats appeared, and untrimmed chrome ore rose in heaps, far above the metre-high white line we had chalked around bulkhead and ship's side. I suspected no bobcats would appear because the stevedore was reluctant to hire them. It is a fact of sea life the world over that stevedores & Co are only interested in filling the ship with cargo as rapidly as possible, so they can send her off to sea and load the next one. . .. all as cheaply as possible, of course, for time is money.

I issued an ultimatum. "No bobcats by four pm and the ship's electrical power switches off" – rendering our cargo winches inoperable.

Four pm came and went with negative bobcats and at ten past, power was switched off. Bobcats appeared ten minutes later, with much mumbling about how their arrival – intended all along of course! – had been delayed "by the Port Authorities" . . . who always provide a convenient excuse as they can never be traced!

On the wharf our chrome ore resembled nothing so much as the colliery slagheaps once so common in Industrial Britain. The air was filled with grime and cleaning ship was futile until all was loaded and hatches battened down, when a thorough hosing by the crew would soon restore our pristine beauty.

Karachi's dockers are as dignified a band of mostly elderly gentlemen as one could meet anywhere. Their city is renowned, if not perhaps for sanitation and hygiene, then certainly for the stateliness of its inhabitants, and the dockers, grey-bearded and Muslim-capped, long flowing shirts worn outside baggy trousers, their faces carrying eternally lofty expressions are, in my experience, unique. Older parts of the city (which I had seen en route to hospital) resemble illustrations from a children's Bible, with small groups of such gentlemen standing in earnest conversation at street corners while their veiled womenfolk sway by gracefully, carrying on their heads bundles of shopping, or ewers of water. Ancient, pastel shaded buildings, dusty palm trees, lines of horsedrawn taxis, donkeycarts and camel wagons all enhance this atmosphere of timelessness. But back on West Wharf loading was in full swing. The Harbour Master sent me a note saying he wished me to move to another berth across the harbour as by his calculations we should soon be aground at low tide. Without wishing to appear 'clever' I 'sounded-round' with the third mate using the hand lead-line at lowest low water and decided we would remain at all times afloat even when our cargo was all loaded. The Harbour Master graciously accepted my argument – to have shifted us would have required pilot and tugs anyway – and these were always in short supply in this very busy port.

Upon completion of chrome ore loading, 499 empty containers were taken aboard, for carriage on deck to China, for containerisation demands that empty boxes are returned for reloading and as such comprise cargo in their own right, attracting good freight.

Amongst all the other persons working onboard we had noticed one chap in Muslim garments and cap, a trifle darker and more African-looking than the rest – but then, Karachi is such a melting pot of nations that no particular race stands out. I met him in the crew alleyway asking for a drink of water, and directed him to the galley. . .

The southwest monsoon was in its infancy as we sailed, heading south across The Swatch, that deep natural trench in the seabed off the mouth of the Indus which has for centuries given navigators a good idea of their position from soundings – taken nowadays with the echo sounder. In the long, grey swell our ship was pitching and rolling, beginning to ship water over the deck. At eight in the next morning our seventy-year old Indonesian Cassab* came to the bridge grinning from ear to ear, with an African chap in tow. I recognised him as the man who had asked for water, but now all he wore were grimy trousers – no shoes, no shirt. Whilst taking morning soundings Cassab had heard mysterious noises, as of someone shouting. Casting around the fore part he had eventually located Jimmy securely battened down in the

---

* Cassab:– Storekeeper, bosun's mate

197

forward hatch – No. 1 'tweendeck, amongst the dusty iron ore – a stowaway!

When presented to me on the bridge Jimmy immediately prostrated himself on the deck, then rolled over whimpering, like a dog expecting to be kicked. I ordered him to get up which he did and promptly asked for a cigarette. Realising he was exhausted – swaying on his feet – probably half starved and certainly dehydrated I sent him down for a hot meal and drink, allocating him our only spare cabin, where he slept soundly for two days and two nights. Abeku the Ghanaian chief officer was sympathetic to a fellow African and between us we got what we probably felt was close enough to the truth. Born, he told us, in Mozambique but taken as an infant by his parents to Tanzania to escape the horrors of Mozambique's civil war, he had lived the next 27 years or so in countryside near Dar Es Salaam. But being an illegal immigrant there he lacked formal education and was unable to find work when he grew up – though had acquired a good understanding of English. There was work, he heard, in Bombay, so borrowed money from a moneylender to buy his ticket. But at Bombay airport he was turned away by Immigration. On his return flight homewards he had to change planes at Karachi. Here he was interviewed by Pakistan Immigration, who, he says, took his passport and ticket, promising to return them "after making a few enquiries". Had he had with him the needful to grease palms the vital papers would probably have been returned to him. As it was, he hung around the airport for a month, receiving nothing but glib assurance. In penniless desperation he eventually walked to the coast where some fishermen befriended him and took him in their boat round to the commercial harbour. "Get a job as a seaman aboard any one of these big ships", they suggested. But of course, with no papers, no captain would employ him. His fishermen friends had disappeared and Jimmy conceived the notion of stowing away, to Canada. He had always fancied Canada, having read tales of the Yukon and fancied himself as a latter day gold digger. "That ship at the top of the harbour" was loading chrome ore for Canada, someone told him. But he had been misled. The ship was indeed loading chrome ore, but she was the *Golden Harvest,* for China.

Observed by our fifth engineer wandering round the engineroom he was chased ashore but returned, later to be chased out of the accommodation as a suspected thief – for thieves are not uncommon in Karachi Port. Although Jimmy's African features differed from the more usual Pakistani, wearing a Muslin cap and gown he passed unremarked in the throng which boarded us for their daily work. The cook gave him a drink of water in the galley and that was the last seen of Jimmy until the day after we sailed. . ... Had Cassab not heard him and let him out it is doubtful if Jimmy would have survived for long down in No. 1 'tweendeck among the dusty ore, without food and more importantly, without water. . . for three weeks.

But what was I to do with a stowaway who had a plausible tale but no passport or papers? At Singapore, instead of anchoring in our usual handy patch we had to go the Quarantine Anchorage with utmost formality, Jimmy under lock and key for the whole of our two days visit. At Shanghai he became such an object of interest to our People's Liberation Army Frontier Guards that they crowded in to see him daily. So much so that Jimmy suggested I sold them buns to feed him while he performed simple tricks. A full-blown African is still a rare sight in China! As we were to be there several weeks I prevailed upon Authority to allow me to escort Jimmy for walks up and down the foredeck each evening, for exercise, and during these hour-long strolls he told me his life story. Unfailingly cheerful, his favourite expression was – "No problem!" Unfortunately, he was; the shipowner is liable for stowaways the world over, responsible for any cost involved in their recapture if they escape, fines if they get away with it – running into fantastic sums! I went to see H.M. Consul in Shanghai – after all, Jimmy was a Commonwealth citizen. Proof of this Captain? Well, er no. H.M. Consul made helpful noises but eventually decided I was no concern of his, as my ship was registered and owned in Singapore.

The Singapore Consul was equally pleasant but could not give me five minutes as he had "an urgent appointment". . .

Ships are sailing the seas with stowaways they cannot get rid of, doomed forever to sail on with attendant complications at every port. And what, we wondered, would be Jimmy's fate when the ship was eventually broken up? I have known ship's captains whose stowaways have been downright mutinous, a danger to all on board; but Jimmy was the perfect gentleman, working hard for his daily bread at any given task. Thanks to the traditional generosity of Jolly Jack he was also, now, one of the best dressed men onboard. "No problem".

There have been cases of stowaways being cast adrift close to land, to make their way ashore on makeshift rafts and many have perished in the process. In one notorious case not so long ago the captain cast his stowaways adrift – wearing lifejackets he stoutly maintained at his trial – but the sharks got them and he was convicted of murder. . .

We often wonder where our Jimmy is now; and if he ever did reach Canada to strike it rich on the Yukon. NO PROBLEM!

Having sailed from Singapore for China (Jimmy was still with us) radio forecasts began to come through of Typhoon Koryn boiling up east of Luzon, in the Philippines. Koryn was reported to be heading WNW at 12 knots. Surely, I felt, with our 14 knots we would easily cross her path, well away from the 107 knot winds howling around her centre. Typhoon means, in Chinese, Great Wind – no misnomer. Sunset on 25th June was luridly spectacular. Pinks, vivid orange, yellows and gold shaded to deep purple on the horizon with overhead, long pink outriders reaching out into a weirdly greenish sky. A glassy sea reflected this remarkable display perfectly. But was this the Calm Before the Storm? It was! Next day sea and sky became an unhealthy grey, racked with scud while the barometer plunged and the NNE'ly which began as a light breeze soon developed into a gale, Force 8. More importantly, its direction remained constant, sure indication that we were right in the storm's path. But still we could pass ahead of it – until a rising sea and swell inevitably slowed us down. Seas soon began crashing over the bow as we dipped. . . Weather reports from Tokyo and Hong Kong gave ominous if not always identical forecasts of the storm's track and anticipated progress and, as requested, *Golden Harvest* sent three-hourly coded weather-at-ship reports to Hong Kong Radio. From these and other ships' reports a more accurate picture could be assessed and more reliable forecasts issued. And there was no doubt now – we were right in Koryn's path, headed for the storm's "eye" – no place for a self respecting ship deep laden with chrome ore to be! So I turned back, at 2pm.

I put the wind on our starboard quarter, according to the Law of Storms devised many years ago in the age of sail. Our ship's progress became less laboured at once, she rode again like a gull on the waves and seas no longer crashed aboard. All that day we kept the wind on the starboard quarter and when in the evening it began to back, we followed it round – a game of blind man's buff – with an eye always towards the proximity of Stewart Bank, 85 miles west of Luzon, over which the sea under present conditions would be dangerous, heavy and tumbling. During the night the wind backed rapidly as the barometer first steadied, then crept upward, sure sign that the eye of the typhoon had passed north of us. Course was resumed for Shanghai and we carried on, more fortunate than other ships on the opposite (western) side of the South China Sea where at least three were overwhelmed and sank with great loss of life. Others got into collision in Hong Kong harbour. Anchoring in the CJK designated holding anchorage in pouring rain, we watched the weather carefully, checking our position constantly, until called in to berth at Khang Hua Bang Wharf, near the mouth of Shanghai's Huangpu River on American Independence Day, 4th July. To my surprise I slept the clock round that night.

Discharge completed satisfactorily we spent a few days at Hudong Shipyard, alongside a bridge-amidships Chinese tanker, *Daqing 51* – reminiscent with her streamlined bridge and elegant lines of those beautiful Onassis tankers of 35 years ago. She herself lay alongside the Russian freighter *Kapitan Bakanov* which was having a major refit. Here we underwent routine "Small Lepair" which included modifications to the ballast system pipework. To enable this work to be done the ship had to be trimmed down by the head and the simplest way to do this was to flood No. 1 hold with river water. The resultant private "swimming pool" was greatly enjoyed by the crew who delighted in diving in from the upper deck coaming, high above. By 14th July work was completed, the crew's prodigious efforts had ensured that all holds and 'tweendecks were again clean and dry, to the satisfaction of the Chinese surveyors, when we moved across the river to one of our usual loading berths, Gaoyanglu Wharf, and commenced loading general cargo for Karachi and the Gulf.

With a full load of break-bulk general cargo below, containers full of pilferables on deck, two 41-ton bulldozers for Dammam and two mobile cranes for Dubai all lashed secure and tarpaulined against the SW monsoon, we sailed from Shanghai on 22nd July.

Next eastbound cargo was bulk urea from Umm Said in Quatar, to where we proceeded from our final unloading port of Dammam, with crew again cleaning hatches. From the sea Umm Said resembled a huge factory with flame-belching chimneys, gleaming silver oil tanks in profusion and huge corrugated buildings clustered together against a backdrop of shimmering desert sand under a bright blue sky. We were to load exactly 12,100 metric tons but before giving the go-ahead to proceed, surveyors examined our holds and 'tweendecks minutely before passing them free of all moisture, rust and dirt – fit to load.

Loading at Umm Said was impressively fast. A single mechanical spout delivered the white granules – fine, white, soft and silent as snow, in less than three days. This urea was prilled, that is, each granule is plastic coated to enable it to do its fertilising work slowly when scattered over the ground. When all was in, paperwork completed, we battened down and took our departure for Ilo Ilo, in the Philippines, via Singapore, on 2nd September. For the first few days, crossing the Gulf and the Gulf of Oman, the weather was, as expected, fine and calm, enabling the crew to make all secure around the decks, store rooms and engine room against what we know would soon be quite heavy rolling when we crossed the long swell of the SW monsoon, now in full swing. Normal for this time of year, the swell caused our deeply laden ship to take water aboard at every roll, roaring across the open deck, lapping greedily round the hatch coamings, to cascade overboard through the scuppers as she rolled the other way. But all this eased as we approached India's southern tip, Cape Cormorin and, as usual, we spotted large schools of dolphins in the Gulf of Manaar. But at 14 knots we were just a little too fast for them to come and play around our bow – 12 knots seems the maximum they can cope with. I crossed the Bay of Bengal well south of the main 'motorway traffic', firmly believing that the more room we give to other ships the safer our passage will be.

Entering Malacca Strait between Rondo and Wé islands (a deep channel 11 miles wide), taking particular care of the powerful currents which can set here in any direction, we were in fine, calm weather some seven miles off the

Sumatra coast basking green in morning sunshine, when the chief engineer had to stop the engines to effect repairs which would take about one hour. From nowhere, it seemed, two large wooden fishing boats crowded with men appeared, almost alongside, one to port and the other to starboard. Fishing here is a laborious process, the nets cast and hauled by hand, hence the large crews. Their dialect was one which even our own Indonesians could not understand, but there was no doubt what they were after from their unambiguous gestures – beer and cigarettes. Thanks to our heavy cargo our freeboard* was low, our deck only a few feet above theirs. Despite the anti-pirate hoses we had rigged ready, it would have been simple for them to have boarded us had they been determined. But we all made "Go-Away!" faces at them, I strode from side to side of the bridge in white uniform trying to look intimidating, until at last, with disappointed grins, they went away and resumed their fishing. But had we broken down at night, a visitation would have been inevitable – and undesirable even if the natives had turned out to be friendly!

Singapore was from late on the 14th to first light on the 16th, with everyone getting the chance to run ashore on 15th, from our usual Eastern Roads anchorage. Our Indian Ocean/Persian Gulf charts were landed here for correction and updating by the famous firm of Motion Smith, who returned the China Seas charts handed to them westbound on our previous visit. During the voyage the second and third mates make any other necessary corrections to charts and light lists etc from Notices to Mariners sent from Singapore by DHL, so that we are always in possession of the latest information.

To Ilo Ilo would take four days, across the southern end of the South China Sea to a point off the Borneo coast and I intended entering the Sula Sea of the Philippines via Balabac Strait, which we would reach around 0300 on 18th September. But pirates had been active here recently, at night – the machine gunners who come up in a fast motorboat, guns blazing, to scramble aboard, take over the ship at gunpoint, before turning the ship's crew (including any injured) adrift in the ship's lifeboats. After looting anything considered sufficiently interesting or valuable, they set the ship on fire – Nice People! so to avoid any such unpleasant nocturnal disturbance I turned the ship round for a couple of hours while still in the open sea, thus making the Balabac in glorious weather just after breakfast, with not a pirate in sight. Through Nasubata Channel then, across a smiling Sulu Sea to the southern entrance of Ilo Ilo Strait where we anchored to await high water and the pilot. This splendid gentleman – "seventy next month" – recommended I should lighten our draft if possible as the channel was silting up, not as deep as charted. After we had pumped out the after peak tank he brought us into the inner anchorage, off the town, in the one-and-a-half-mile-wide strait which

---

*Freeboard:– height of a ship's main deck above the sea.

Filling the bags under the hoppers.

Unloading at Ilo Ilo.

separates Panay from the much small Guimaras Island, jungle covered and topped at its highest point by a handsome old church and a huge cross, illuminated at night. Narrow, swift, blue-sailed craft with stabilising wide outriggers port and starboard dotted the harbour, white interisland ferries and small landing-craft type ro-ro ships passed continually. We found the wheat ship occupying "our" berth had not yet completed her discharge, so waited while a launchful of Customs, Port Health, Immigration and Coastguard officers paid us the usual visit to "Clear us Inwards". In their case, "clear" was just the word! We berthed next day, 21st September, alongside a wide, modern concrete quay, long enough to take two deep-sea ships as well as several coasters and barges. Ferries berth down strait, nearer the city, which lies on a wide alluvial plain and consists of more permanent buildings than the primitive thatched dwellings lining the river bank. Busy streets were thronged with the colourful small buses called Jeepneys – elongated jeeps – with a narrow rear entrance. The jeepney ride is interesting, in that even a person of my modest height must duck to enter – your fare is passed along to the driver by the other passengers, and the bus stops when some one knocks on the underside of the metal roof – at any requested spot.

Ilo Ilo has a colourful history. The fifteenth century Spaniards found the natives to be of Malayan-Indonesian descent, a race which had almost but not quite replaced what are thought to have been the original inhabitants, some of whose descendants are said to remain to this day. It is recorded that Magellan fought one of his fiercest engagements near here, establishing Spanish supremacy; and when the Patriots finally overthrew the Spaniards in 1898 and proclaimed an Independent Republic, it was no time before the USS *Petrel*, a white-painted ram-bowed gunboat, came to bombard the inhabitants into accepting American Protection. This annexation lasted until 1935 when the Republic of the Philippines was established. The Japanese did little to enhance their reputation for humanity during their WW2 occupation, but were ousted by the local resistance fighters with US help in 1945.

Unloading our cargo here was spectacular and colourful, employing dozens of men, women and children – some not yet in their teens, three generations of a whole family, all neatly dressed in colourful clothes. A large steel hopper was wheeled into position abreast of each hatch and around twelve men down below shovelled the urea – looking more like snow than ever – into rope-strengthened canvas slings which were then hoisted by the ship's derricks up, out and over the hoppers, to be emptied by two men to each, who then danced on the urea to ensure its free flow down through a grid to three spouts below, where girls bagged it. Five seconds on average to fill a bag. Young persons then trotted the filled bags on barrows to where ladies in wide-brimmed hats standing under large umbrellas to protect them from the hot sun, weighed each bag while children with scoops adjusted the contents from the reserve bin until the required 50kg was achieved exactly. More children carrying bundles of brightly coloured tyers then moved along the rows of bags tying the inner plastic bag's neck, when others barrowed them along to where the Stitching Ladies sewed the outer bags' edges using hand-held electric sewing machines. The stitched bags were then carried on the heads of vigorous young men and women to be loaded on big red lorries waiting nearby. When a lorry was full it roared off with a black snort of exhaust, often to cheers from the children.

This scene was continuous, except for meal breaks, day and night. Everyone seemed full of fun and I never heard a cross word. Indeed, a holiday mood prevailed and off duty, at meal times, youngsters would swing out arm over arm along the ship's mooring lines, dropping off into the warm green water with yells of delight, to swim to the quay ladder for another 'go'. Little boys raced each other elaborate races with the handbarrows, girls played schoolyard games. It seemed a way of life too good to last – full employment with everyone enjoying themselves must, eventually, be overtaken by mechanisation. And then, unloading a cargo of 12,100 tons of bulk urea will take less than twelve days, but will not be half so interesting, or fun to watch.

Playtime at Ilo Ilo!

19. SUGAR FROM SIAM

This ancient mariner considers himself singularly fortunate in that, even after forty-three years at sea, he is still kindly being found fresh ports to visit. This voyage included a consecutive five – Bangkok, Koh-Si-Chang, Hakata, Uno Ko and Qingdao – all in what we in the West rather comically call the Far East. But first let us return to Kuwait City where our good ship *Golden Harvest* completed unloading her general cargo from China back in March 1994.

While the port was never actually idle, and most of the war scars have gone, no longer do ships crowd the anchorage awaiting berths as we did in the past. Post Desert Storm, Kuwait's population is greatly diminished. The large number of Palestinians, who tended to favour Iraq in the conflict, have left, as have the wives and families of most of the expatriates from India's sub-continent who form by far the greater part of the nation's workforce. A depleted population means less trade and our cargo of domestic, medical and industrial goods was unloaded in a mere two days. Shore leave is still forbidden but my wife and I were allowed to stroll up and down the quay for an hour in the shadow of the ship during the cool of the evening, which made a pleasant break. The Bangladeshi dockers stared at this quaint old couple walking hand in hand. In *their* world it is the men who walk hand in hand, womenfolk follow at a respectful distance!

Our next cargo was to be bagged urea from Dammam, in Saudi Arabia, for Colombo (bagged as Colombo has no facilities for bulk handling). The 'Big Hurry Up' was on as this urea was needed – urgently they said – to spread over paddy field and plantation before the monsoon rains broke. . . so we made haste. Before loading urea the ship's 'tweendecks and holds are meticulously inspected for cleanliness and must be perfectly dry as urea is highly hydroscopic. So our lads pitched in – scraping, sweeping and scrubbing away the detritus left by crates, drums, boxes, bales and – most tenacious of all – stains left on the steelwork by the residue from bagged graphites, oxides and dyes.

Before we would reach Dammam however we found we had a few hours in hand so steamed eastwards with hatches wide open, enabling them to dry out thoroughly in the rays of the morning sun. During the previous Gulf War between Iran and Iraq, the former nation staked out an extensive exclusion zone which has never been formally revoked and which is still pencilled-in on our charts. But we noticed a procession of tankers cutting across it on their way between Ras Tannurah and the Straits of Hormuz, so felt brave enough to enter the zone ourselves, albeit north of the tanker traffic. . . But sure enough, there ahead moving threateningly out of the sun's glare was an Iranian frigate. Our holds were nicely dry now anyway so I prudently turned

Anchored off Colombo, in the Panadura.

back, to berth at Dammam that afternoon. Surveyors "passed" us at their first inspection and loading, using the large orange-painted dockside cranes, from low rail trucks full of bagged urea, began at once.

No shore leave at all is allowed in Saudi, nevertheless our time passed pleasantly over the next nine days. Whereas most of you shore-abiding citizens spend much of your lives travelling to and from your places of work, we at sea live on the job, so to speak, and so have these otherwise 'travelling hours' to ourselves. Work does indeed take much of one's time, often at erratic and unsocial hours, but in between times we can afford to relax a little. Scrabble, Othello, Mastermind, gin rummy, reading books and writing letters rushed the days along as we watched the world go by, and when our 12,300 tonnes were loaded, away we went hot foot for Colombo off which we arrived in the evening of 6th April.

"Are we berthing tonight?" – I addressed Colombo on VHF.

"Well, no. Please go and anchor 15 miles south of the city in the Panadura, and await orders. . ." so said our agent (an old friend) apologetically, who explained that our charterers had yet to decide How Much went to Whom. (And perhaps, it occurred to us, as the monsoon season neared and the farmers grew desperate for fertiliser, prices would improve?) Panadura, SW of the fishing village of that name, is a long-term anchorage some four miles offshore. Although nothing but ocean lay between us and Antarctica to the south, South Africa to the southwest, and (round the corner of Dondra Head) Australia to the southeast, the sea was calm with only a low swell at this time of the year. A few months hence with the SW monsoon in full swing it would be a different story with great grey rollers pounding the coast. But now, all was tranquil and as the anchor rattled down to disappear in the dim, greeny-blue depths our bulbous bow, nine metres underwater, was clearly visible. Eight shackles of chain (120 fathoms – 720 feet) soon took the strain and we settled down to admire the scenery.

To the north shimmered Colombo's tall white buildings from which ran southward in an unbroken line a shining white sand beach, backed by coco palms. Behind, dense green jungle rose to the hills, cloud streaked, with the dark cone of Adam's Peak (7,352 feet) towering overall forty miles away. Nightfall provided spectacular electric storms over the land, rolling up the coast but usually avoiding the anchorage, in which at this time we were the only ship.

The day after we arrived, the motor lifeboat was lowered into the water, for the second mate and others to take away for a couple of spins around the ship, taking photographs, quite making a picnic of it, before the now well-tested boat was hoisted back in its davits. Next day, peering over the bows, we saw myriad shoals of tiny fish glinting gold in the sunshine, with larger fish below. Then we noticed, deep down under the bulb of the bow, twitching tails keeping them head on to the two-knot tidal current, the sharks. Dozens of them. An occasional flash of white showed one flicking over. They seemed disinterested in the other fish but when we dropped a couple of slices of raw bacon amongst them they became truly sharklike; and we wondered if we would have been so keen on lifeboating the day before had we known of their presence! At night they would come to the surface, often performing a sort of cartwheel over the water with great splashes of bioluminescence. As far as we could see they were not feeding:– could sharks be playing, gambolling like lambs?

With lights hung over the stern the fishing was good, the catch tasty. But were these boats around us all fishermen? Panadura even only a few years ago, was an anchorage often visited by pirates. . . One morning, before breakfast when I was doing my customary hour on the bridge while the mate went down for a shave and breakfast, a small motorboat edged towards us, six lean and hungry faces tensed for action. With our low freeboard they would have little difficulty boarding and I wondered, as they came alongside aft, what they were up to. If they were armed we had little chance. But we *did* have an old Schermuly rocket-firing pistol in a wheelhouse locker. No cartridges, but it looked suitably impressive, I hoped, as I cocked it and regarded the party in the boat, from my point of vantage on the bridge. They looked increasingly wary, and as I pointed it at them they suddenly panicked and departed, their engine roaring into life. Smugly satisfied, I felt – "That's the way to deal with pirates". Until the cook came up after breakfast and pointed out that, as we had been unable to purchase provisions since Dubai, a month ago, he was running short of fresh fruit and veg. True, he grew delicious bean shoots in his storeroom, fresh each day; – but he was now out of tomatoes, lettuce and melons. He had, he told me, made arrangements with a local fisherman yesterday to buy some here at the anchorage, and they had come out before breakfast – but for some reason had suddenly taken off before any sales were made. . .

Some of the local fishing craft still operate under sail only, an interesting rig made more so by – from one village – the great red crosses of Portugal on their sails. The Portuguese colonised this part of Sri Lanka in 1505, to be driven out by the Dutch a century later. But Portuguese tradition dies hard! Later I was able to inspect some of these boats drawn up on the beach and marvelled that while the upper edge of the narrow hull was of unpainted wood, supporting the antique rig, the lower hull – almost cylindrical in cross section – was of fibreglass! They carried an outrigger to port but no centreboard.

After thirteen days at this fascinating anchorage we were called in and our cargo discharged into lorries at Queen Elizabeth Quay, seemingly still soon enough to beat the rains. Each urea bag was clearly stencilled USE NO HOOKS, an admonition blatantly ignored by the Sri Lankan dockers who used a bright metal hook in each hand (by union decree, I was told when I protested). So by the time all was unloaded there was so much leakage that it may as well have been a bulk cargo! But nobody seemed perturbed.

Before she flew home Brenda and I spent a day being driven in an airconditioned taxi some fifty miles down the coast to Hikkaduwa – a fascinating ride in itself – on which we realised that what looked like deserted coastline from seaward actually teemed with life behind the palm trees fringing the coast. Little villages basked in the sunshine, each with its Town Hall, General Post Office, red letterboxes and other homely touches dating from British colonial days, still lovingly tended if rather quaintly situated among the Buddhist Temples and un-British houses. Main attractions at Hikkaduwa are the glass-bottomed boats in which one is taken out to the reef to peer down at the coral gardens, which we sampled with delight.

The *Fremantle Star* came in, one of my old commands from her *California Star* days on the UK – West Coast of North America service – immaculate still despite her years. (She was built in1971). Registered now in Singapore she was named *Mulbera* for a while when chartered to P & O before her transfer to Blue Star Line's Middle East Container Service from New Zealand and Australia.

Whilst we were alongside in Colombo our future employment was discussed at the highest level in Head Office, Singapore. Cargoes for efficient, 'handy-sized' vessels abound in this part of the world and the first idea was iron ore from an Indian east coast port to China. Such charters have to fit in with the Company's westbound-from-China general cargo liner service of one ship per month, so of course the cargo which will, hopefully, put us in the right place at the right time is the one eventually selected. Next under consideration was cargo from another Indian Bengal port to Indonesia. Then, and this one nearly happened, urea from Chittagong to the Philippines. As poor old Chittagong was at the time suffering its annual devastation from cyclone and flood, we were not sorry when this idea too was dropped and I was ordered back to Singapore, whence we would proceed to Bangkok for raw sugar; – 12,000 tonnes for 'South Japan'.

The fishermen in the northern end of the Gulf of Thailand earned a pretty reputation a few years ago by shooting at any ship careless enough to cut across their nets. Using high velocity rifles. With the sea liberally sprinkled with fishing craft whose nets stretched for miles, marked only at the far end by a dimly lit dan buoy, it was difficult to determine which net belonged to whom. We soon found that night however, that a boat spotting us approaching her nets too closely would direct blinding white light upon us, a searchlight beam. However disconcerting, this was, we felt, preferable to the contents of a Kalachnikov!

We had sailed from Shanghai on Friday 13th (May) – a particularly LUCKY DAY for the Chinese (I was assured). And our luck had certainly held

Loading bulk sugar from barges, Bangkok.

with the Thai fishermen. Off Bangkok (Krung Thep to the Thais) I was instructed (surprise, surprise!) to anchor and await a berth. Eventually we embarked our pilot and went in – over the rivermouth bar – twenty five miles up a stream which meandered through flat countryside between light and heavy industry all beset with green jungle. Ornate palaces and splendid temples rubbed shoulders with modern blocks of high-rise flats and, eventually, we moored alongside a concrete quay (with on-site Buddhist temple).

After the usual hatch inspection we began loading raw brown sugar from large barges towed alongside. Our workforce of dockers moved onboard and took up residence under a large canvas awning they brought and rigged over the poop. Their ladies came too, with their own Calor Gas in large steel bottles, great shiny aluminium cooking vessels – every utensil right down to the chopsticks. Perhaps they begged a few bags of rice from our kindhearted cook. Their black cotton hammocks soon festooned the ship's accommodation alleyways and the women set up shop in the crew messroom, selling garments and curios mostly but also video and cassette tapes. Occasionally one or more ventured up to my curtained doorway and, knocking, offered fruit for sale, or fresh fish. Or maybe I would "Like Massage?" Mostly very young, they would reach out to touch me, to see if I was real – as I don't suppose they get many Olde English Mariners up this way these days – and they looked quite relieved when I opted for the fruit only, thanks – no massage! Their highpitched conversational clamour on the poopdeck was incessant, but our lads did not seem to mind. One enterprising lady carried a long-distance cordless telephone on which she sold overseas calls, a facility I *did* use a couple of times, much appreciated.

Maximum depth of water on Bangkok River Bar, at this state of the moon, was 26 feet (yes, it's still good old feet in Thailand!) so we had to calculate how much sugar we could load to bring us down to a permissible draught of fresh water. It worked out at 8,500 tonnes, the final few hundred of which came in right speedily at an efficient loading spout down-river. The evening of the 27th May saw us heading for sea once more – passing a small naval yard where, among other warships lay what looked to me like a single-funnelled British WW2 destroyer – possibly early 'Battle' Class. But no! "Jane's" advises that the *Maeklong* was built at Uraga, Japan, in 1937! Still with her original triple expansion reciprocating engines and service as a training ship with the Royal Thai Navy, she looked quite 'modern'.

Safely over the bar our Thai pilot disembarked into his launch at a circular red and white chequered tower reminiscent of the Martello Towers which once studded the south coast of England. "Shallow water" – as when crossing the bar – means less water under the keel than the vessel is drawing, in which case steering is often adversely affected and has to be watched even more carefully than usual. Heading off for 17 miles in a roughly ESE'ly direction, carefully avoiding the fishing fleet, we came to Koh-Si-Chang – a large sheltered anchorage where lay many ships. By now it was dark, so I anchored off for the night, proceeding in next morning at first light (no pilot here). Surrounded by pleasant green islands on which occasional yellow-painted statues of various Buddhas towered above the trees, vessels loaded from barges and floating silos. One ship was surely on fire, scarcely visible through a pall of thick white smoke! But she was not on fire, merely loading bulk tapioca. Conditions onboard can hardly have been pleasant. By contrast our sugar made no mess at all, only giving off a faintly sweet savour. This was the rainy season and any sugar spilled on deck became instant toffee when wet. We loaded the final 3,500 tonnes here using ship's union-purchase gear shackled on to shore-owned grabs, from more large barges.

The ladies were still with us, having donned their best party frocks for our departure from Bangkok – for all the world like first class passengers, pretty as you please! They remained onboard until our loading completed three days later. The night before we left they threw a party for all hands on the pool deck, under their awning – to flashing fairy lights and disco music. The ship seemed very quiet after they had gone.

Evading the fishing vessels on our way south out of the Thai Gulf, we headed through rain and murky weather towards our first discharge port (disport) of Hakata, in Japan. The charterers had revealed this at the last minute, enabling me to fax Singapore for the required British Admiralty charts, supplied by Motion Smith. They arrived per DHL just as we were about to weigh anchor. Even these were only for our first disport as the second had not yet been declared.

Two thousand, seven hundred and twenty six miles – 8$\frac{1}{2}$ days – through

Trimming in the sugar, at Koh-Si-Chang.

the gloom, brought us to the approaches off Hakata on the evening of 8th June. So, not knowing the port and unwilling to risk venturing inside the narrow entrance by night, I stood 'off and on' at reduced speed, to arrive early next morning. By this time I knew our second disport was to be Uno Ko, and as there are several of these in Japan, clarification was given with a latitude and longitude, in which I should anchor on arrival. One hundred miles inside the Inland Sea, it lies between the busy ports of Hiroshima and Kobe, on the large island of Honshu.

At Hakata, bulldozers were lowered into our holds and pushed the sugar into large heaps, to be grabbed by the grabs – all into hopper-fed lorries Here (as in Uno, I found later) formalities were conducted for me by one man – the agent – quietly and efficiently, which made a refreshing change from the clamouring horde of grasping uniformed officials who swarm aboard in *some* places I could mention.

The dockers here were almost clone-like – all wearing identical yellow hard hats and light blue denims with 'NIPPON EXPRESS' in yellow letters across their backs. The men of yesterday's Japan have grown – thanks to an improved diet which includes meat – into hefty, even burly figures: and indeed, I was finding today's Japan very different from the one I visited regularly in 1971 in the *Caledonia Star* from New Zealand. The intervening generation has brought the benefits of national prosperity. High living standards are matched by high wages – and high prices. On my previous crossing of the Inland Sea, 23 years ago, a pilot was automatically provided. Now, when I mentioned 'Pilot?' to the agent, polite eyebrows were raised and I was told rather sternly that these days only BIG ships (over 10,000 tons grt/200 metres long) are required to take pilots by law; that if I insisted, the cost would come to over a million yen as two pilots must accompany each other (so as not to get too tired!). In other words, the Inland Sea Pilots are steadily pricing themselves out of work.

As a concession I would be provided with a pilot through the 12-mile Kanmon Strait, the Inland Sea's western entrance, between the islands of Honshu and Kyushu. Thereafter, about 90 miles, it would be D.I.Y. This would be interesting and I studied charts (sent by Motion Smith per DHL to Hakata), likewise current tide tables and the Admiralty Pilot Book which speaks gloomily of the numerous frequent strandings and collisions which occur in these waters. Traffic is heavy, always, currents a fierce nine knots at times, and in this rainy season good visibility could not be expected. Cheering words indeed!

With our 3,000 tonnes of Hakata sugar unloaded, we moved in evening sunshine off the berth to an anchorage just outside port limits until midnight, when I weighed anchor and proceeded the fifty miles round the coast to Kanmon Strait pilotage station, near Shimoneseki, arriving at 0400, by previous arrangement. By then, I was told, the worst of that night's Kanmon Strait's tides would have slackened.

Arriving at the appointed place at the appointed time, out of the clutter of assorted lights from shore, ship and fishing fleet, a pilot launch zoomed alongside out of the predawn darkness. Twenty three years ago I had observed Japanese pilots to be elderly, dignified gentlemen – and this at least had not changed. In his smart grey suit, deerstalker hat and polished brown shoes, our man could have been a prosperous lawyer on holiday. The strait, winding between steep banks, was busy with shipping of all kinds. Ferries dashed hither and yon – some at over 40 knots! Huge, hoarding-like signs on the banks at occasional Tidal Stations – shown on the charts – indicated the present state of the tidal stream in flashing yellow lights. For instance, an 'N' followed by a '7' followed by an arrow pointing upwards, meant that the current was running northwards at seven knots, increasing in strength.

When nearly through, the pilot disembarked with glad handshakes, and off we went. With grey dawn came a light mist shrouding the little islands, reducing visibility to less than half a mile. Under such conditions it becomes curiously easy to feel safely cocooned – but this, of course, is a most dangerous illusion! A sharp eye must be kept at all times on the steering, the radar, the ships one can actually see with the eyes, the set of the current, and the wind. Thanks to Hasan, the Indonesian chief officer's assiduous training, we now had five ABs who were good helmsmen and I made them relieve each other after one hour's trick at the wheel, for steering under these conditions demands unremitting concentration. One 'wheel to port' instead of 'to starboard' (eg) could spell disaster. The officers did their normal four hours on, eight hours off, while down below the engines were on stand-by, ready to slow down, stop, or go astern as may be required. I remained on the bridge throughout, of course, conning the ship with the second mate (the navigator) to assist me at the trickier parts by constantly checking the ship's position.

The first few hours were straight forward and fairly quiet. Small, white fibreglass fishing boats carrying a rather incongruous little gaff-mizen as steadying sail, would race past us at twenty knots and stop immediately ahead to tend nets. Hydrofoil ferries hurtled past in the gloom, shipping of all kinds came and went, many of them 'floating bomb' gas tankers. Our charts indicated recommended courses in dotted lines and with so many routes criss-crossing these busy waters, 'crossroads' abound, where alertness is even more important.

As we approached the narrows of Tsurushima Suida – a mile wide but very busy – the water became broken with overfalls and tiderips swirling into mini-whirlpools and this commotion increased as we carried on towards the Kurushima Strait. This divides into two channels between islands, both roughly parallel 'S' curves. The 'western' channel must be taken against the current, the 'eastern' when going with. Tidal Station flashing lights told me the Westside Story with the tide running seven knots and increasing; not equably, I soon noticed, but in great surges. Two permanently stationed salvage tugs wait here, like vultures (it seemed) ready to pounce on any unfortunate who gets into trouble.

At the narrowest part a particularly vicious swirl of white water threw us off course to starboard, taking us straight towards the beckoning rocks. To reduce speed would have been fatal as the current would have swept us broadside on, so 'hard a'port' and a few silent prayers at Full Ahead were all we could do. Slowly – ever so slowly – she began to turn to port and – with yards to spare – we were through!

The mist, which had dogged us all day, was growing patchy now and in the early evening sunlight suddenly cleared away to show us the whole glorious vista of Bisan Strait ahead, dotted with green islands, flanked by hills, crowded with shipping and spanned by a graceful bridge carrying road above and railway below, striding for miles from island to island and under which we passed, to wrestle once more with tiderips in its shadow. A one-way system obtains here.

Eastbound ships, like us, keep to the south side, the right. West-bounders keep to the north channel, under a different set of arches spanning different islands. Here and there along the banks of this amazing water (Seto Naikai to the locals) tall red and white cranes proclaimed shipyards, often in the most unlikely places. All seemed busy and prosperous.

215

As the sun lowered astern of us it became time to think about crossing "the motorway" into Uno Ko's approaches, to the north. We had left the one-way reaches astern, but since the bridge, oncoming traffic had been quite light. Now, however, as we approached the appointed turn-off point, we perceived a vast armada coming from ahead. Current strength against us here was clearly indicated by No.2 buoy, red and white striped, leaning far over with the tide. Gas tankers and coasters stretched as far as the eye could see, dozens of them. To have awaited this lot's passing would have plunged us into darkness and I was determined to get an anchor down at Uno Ko before sunset. (No, I don't like entering strange ports in the dark!)

After allowing a bright orange LPG tanker to pass there was a slight lull; so it was two deafening blasts on our siren and 'hard a 'port'. Almost in formation the oncoming vessels also turned to port responding to my repeated double siren blasts, allowing us to pass into the quiet waters on the other side. The final few tricky miles were negotiated with a sense of relief, especially when our anchor went down at the appointed spot off the town just as the sun's red orb dipped behind the hills in fiery splendour, bringing instant night.

This anchorage, we found, was tiny – less than half a mile across – and the bottom was sand and stones – *not* the best holding ground for an anchor. So, despite having plenty of chain out, we waltzed up and down that tiny dance floor for the next 36 hours, as next day was Sunday and it seemed *nobody* worked on Sunday, not in the shipping industry anyway. We were so close to the shore we could see if the barman in the waterfront pub was giving correct change to his customers (so the chief engineer said). A Mitsui shipyard clung to the foot of a hill with two large bulkers fitting out and at least five other ships on the stocks. An assortment of brightly painted ferries came and went every five or ten minutes.

On Monday morning a light fog descended but our pilot came aboard at 0600 to take us in, – away off my British chart and onto a Japanese one the agent had thoughtfully provided. As we approached our berth, a concrete quay, I noticed strange tidal upwellings in the harbour around us. With so many entrances and exits for the powerful tides to course through, the Inland Sea produces some interesting tidal phenomena. Our course took us straight towards the quay, then hard to starboard round a buoy marking a sandbank, to come alongside. A dredger was parked alongside at the berth before ours. The pilot gave the correct helm order as we passed the buoy – "Hard a'starboard" – at which time I saw, from my coin of vantage in the starboard bridge wing, a surge of water upwelling around us, which carried us head on to the quay. We had tugs fast by this time but they too were affected and to have let go an anchor would have dropped it straight into the tug. To have gone full astern would have swamped the after tug and probably put us into the dredger. The impact almost threw us off our feet, but our bulbous bow was strengthened for ice and took only a dint, as we backed off, to berth without further ado. The concrete quay however, received the imprint of our bulb some metres below the waterline. It took all my persuasive powers, assisted by my little model ships, to convince the ensuing Enquiry that the fault was neither mine nor the pilot's.

In this delightful little spot, surrounded by National Parkland, we unloaded our remaining 9,000 tonnes of sugar. The lads invested in second hand bicycles – very cheap here – and I studied charts, tidal tables and pilot book once more, planning the way we would leave. Here, too, our cargo was bulldozed and grabbed into barges which took it to a nearby refinery, all for local consumption.

Working hours were civilised – 8am until 5pm. No grinding cargo winches disturbed our night slumbers, no work on Sunday: so on Sunday afternoon I borrowed the third mate's bike – a handsome yellow bow-framed lady's model – and set off for three hours respite in the National Park. Sparkling in the sunshine; hills, lakes, tumbling streams, the gloriously fresh scent of trees and flowers, birdsong and butterflies, all worked wonders and I returned onboard greatly refreshed.

After eight days here every teaspoonful of sugar was out and at five next morning (my request) we sailed. I had hoped this early departure would give us the benefit of the tides all the way through the Inland Sea and to my delight it did. At last, we had glorious summer weather in which the scenery was a succession of breathtakingly beautiful pictures. We reminded ourselves that tourists pay vast sums just to see all this. After negotiating Kurushima East Side channel with the help of an immaculate Panamanian-with-pilot-onboard who courteously advised me to wait a few minutes until the tide turned, then follow him, I decided to take the easy way out. Much less tortuous than Kanmon Strait is this south western exit, Hayasui Strait, with the rugged headlands of Sada Misaki to port and Taka Shima to starboard flinging us a last cheerful *Sayonara* with flurried tiderips, busily crossing ferries and the obligatory fishing fleet. So we passed through Bungo Strait out into the North Pacific Ocean, on our way to Qingdao, China.

The Sugar Trip was over.

20. GOLDEN HARVEST HOME

"Grandad, there's an owl on the anchor!"

We were twenty miles off Xingang, North China, awaiting a berth, starboard anchor well embedded ten fathoms down in the mud while our port anchor protruded from its hawsepipe ready to let go if required. According to our 'World Bird Book' this owl perched upon it was one of the world's largest, a Eurasian Eagle Owl, glaring balefully up at us through enormous orange eyes under fierce, long-tufted "ears". Launching into the air on brown rounded wings, it flew purposefully round the ship where pathetic little scraps of bones and feathers showed why it had taken the trouble to fly out so far from land. We had spotted seven species of small landbirds hopping and fluttering around the decks – Chinese versions of our finches, nightingales, wrens, rails, goldcrests and wagtails, themselves feeding on the myriad flies, tiny insects and seeds blown aboard on an offshore wind.

We were now seeing our nautical world through the eight-year-old eyes of our grand-daughter Sarah, who had accompanied my wife out from home to Singapore to join the *Golden Harvest* for a ten week trip to Bangkok and China. Since taking Sarah's father and his young sister on a round-the-world voyage in the *Tasmania Star* twenty years ago, my wife and I have realised the value of a voyage in the education of the young, and this had been too good a chance to miss. Originally planned to coincide with school summer holidays, the inevitable delays in a cargo ship's schedule had pushed this proposed trip over to September. Sarah's headmaster, however, said he wished he could come too and kindly gave her leave of absence, allowing Sarah and Grandma to join the ship anchored in Singapore's Eastern Roads on the 19th September 1994.

The *Golden Harvest* had never before carried passengers, but a pleasant two-berth forward-facing cabin with own bathroom and toilet was available, situated two decks down from the bridge. The 'bedroom' area was painted light blue and white, while the 'dayroom' was tastefully panelled in light oak. Four large windows opened onto the foredeck. The Company, seemingly quite charmed at the prospect of signing on a little girl, had refurbished this cabin in such a way that my ladies were delighted. To simplify the paperwork they were signed on a supernumeraries. Whereas children at sea are now by no means uncommon, grandchildren are rare rare birds still! Sarah insisted on taking over the 'housework', vacuuming and polishing the brass. After another day taking bunkers, fresh water and stores while Sarah settled into her 'Golden Harvest Home' and I completed my work at the office ashore, we weighed anchor late afternoon 21st September and took a turn around the anchorage, checking our magnetic compass. This stood in its binnacle on the monkey island, above the wheelhouse, clear of all obstructions for taking celestial and terrestrial bearings, with a periscope down to the wheelhouse to enable the helmsman to steer by it if the gyro failed. By law, the magnetic compass must be checked for accuracy every two years, and if found to be 'way out' its magnetic field must be corrected by placing magnets or soft iron in the binnacle. Sarah learned that the monkey island is so named because it is the highest deck in the ship, and in the days of the old sailing navy the cannon's crews were tended by little boys carrying shot and powder as required. To make them visible to the guncrew these lads, called "powder monkeys", stood perched on a platform built above the deck, the monkey island.

Finding that our compass needed no correction, the adjuster signed and gave me the vital certificate and left in his launch. Crossing Singapore Strait in the gathering dusk we turned east towards the Horsborough Lighthouse, where we would alter course to port, heading up the Gulf of Thailand towards Bangkok. These waters were, until quite recently, infested with pirates, but it was now reassuring to see the navies of Indonesia, Malaysia and Singapore working in co-ordination on anti-pirate exercises, maintaining a regular patrol.

Sarah at boat drill.

Indonesia had received a bad press recently for apparent indifference to the pirates operating in her waters. But when one considers that Indonesia is a vast archipelago – 12 large islands and 3,000 smaller ones – extending from the northern end of Sumatra to the western end of New Guinea, some of their policing problems may be appreciated. Perhaps to counter world criticism, Indonesian military forces recently leaned heavily on the police chiefs of islands suspected of harbouring pirates, with the result that over forty known sea-robbers were thereafter seen hobbling on broken legs. This reduced Indonesian pirate activity dramatically and if thought harsh, remember, it is not so long since our own Royal

Navy hanged pirates from the yard arm!

Next day we held fire and boat drill. Sarah appeared on the bridge wearing her orange lifejacket accompanied by my wife, who is "Auntie" to our Burmese and Indonesian crew members. Emergency fire pump was used to direct powerful jets of water through the hoses, portable extinguishers were tested and new crew members were shown how to launch the inflatable life rafts before both boats were swung out and lowered to boat deck level, the motor lifeboat's engine tested. Sarah took to shipboard life like a duck to water, vastly interested in everything and everybody, writing it all down in her diary and, under Grandma's supervision, keeping up with her schoolwork – when nothing more interesting was to hand!

The 12,000 tons of bulk urea we had loaded in Jubail, Saudi Arabia, had us too deeply laden to cross the Bangkok river bar, so we went first to the large sheltered anchorage of Koh-Si-Chang to lighten into barges. The dockers, of course, brought their wives, rigged their large canvas awning over the poop deck, slung their cotton hammocks from every available hook, set up red plastic chairs and tables under the awning, cooked their food in their own large utensils and generally made themselves at home. The Thai ladies made much of Sarah but she was none too keen on having her cheeks pinched, an expression of endearment in the East. Soon we were surrounded by barges from which their crews fished at night, the ship's lights illuminating the clear, green water. This fishing, and the continuous unloading of the cargo by large grabs slung from the ship's derricks became absorbingly interesting to Sarah, increasingly so as bedtime approached, of course!

After two and a half days steady work we had unloaded sufficient to raise our draft to the required permissible maximum – 26 feet – but had to remain at the anchorage overnight awaiting official clearance and the morrow's morning high tide. Dockers and their wives left, as did the barges – and the four Thai watchmen I had employed to dissuade thieves. That night, when the ship was quiet, persons unknown came aboard forward, probably by shinning up the anchor chain from a boat, into which they carefully and silently loaded drums of paint, tools, coils of rope and, more seriously, our six-man inflatable liferaft in its canister from its rack on the forecastle head. Only next morning did we realise we had been robbed. I notified the agent giving a description of the missing goods, with little hope of ever seeing them again. Never before had I seen stolen articles returned, so was indeed pleasurably surprised when, a few days later, two young Thai police detectives brought everything down in their pickup truck, having not only recovered the goods but apprehended six thieves, caught in possession – a gang they had been trying to catch for some time.

The 6th October dawned bright and clear as we took our departure, holds empty, down the sunlit river past the naval base where the two training ships

Sarah with Grandma and Indonesian shipmate.

Maeklong and the *Phosampton* (ex-RN 'Algerine' Class HMS *Minstrel*) were laid up awaiting sale, canvas covers over their funnel tops to keep out the rains.

We anchored off Xingang on 15th October after a good passage up the China Seas and were called in five days later towards a sunset lurid through atmospheric layers of coal dust, for this is a major coal exporting centre. As we weighed anchor, the birds disappeared – whether to another ship or back to the land we would never know.

We berthed near the coaling wharf from where the locally-owned colliers shipped this power station fuel down to Shanghai. Mined far inland, the coal was brought by long trains hauled by steam locomotives to nearby Tianjin, thence to the docks in lorries which tipped it onto the quay. Here it was moved by bulldozer and much use of hand shovels into long heaps alongside the ships, to be loaded by big dockside cranes with grabs. Compared with the elaborate but efficient drops, hoists, and spouts employed in our own British coaling ports for well over a hundred years, this system seemed laborious, not to be compared with the highly mechanised loading systems now in use in the USA and elsewhere. But this was China, where cheap labour abounded.

We commenced loading general cargo here, for Karachi and the Gulf, and were fortunate in that the agent laid on a car with driver, and took us for a day out. The new toll motorway to Beijing carried little traffic that day and we made good time, across the coastal plain where rice and cotton grew, also sunflowers in profusion, tended by peasant farmers using age-old methods and equipment, horses and bullock carts being much in evidence. Skirting Beijing we headed for the mountains and were soon on the Great Wall in perfect, clear weather. The Wall – on what we were told was a comparatively quiet day though it seemed busy to us – lived up to all our expectations, and it was good to see how well it is being maintained, with old ruined parts being rebuilt into the as-was condition of hundreds of years ago. One of the very few man-made items visible from outer space, this remarkable construction is now a major tourist attraction, originally built to protect the Emperor and his people from the marauding Mongolian hordes. Tourist liners arrive in the port to disgorge their passengers frequently – two during our short stay there. The passengers are then bussed for a couple of days up to the Great Wall, on then to see the Terracotta Warriors and other attractions, during which time the liner moves out to anchor while her crew use the time to clean ship.

From the Wall, our own little tourist party of three was then taken back to the capital – a fine city, much cleaner than many we have visited – to stroll in Tiananmen Square and gorge ourselves on Pekin Duck in the city's Number One Roast Pekin Duck House.

On 24th October we sailed for Qingdao, arriving to anchor there next day. Here were two Maltese flag ships laid idle for years as their real ownership was Yugoslav and UN Sanctions had, for the time being, made them unemployable. These sanctions had brought severe privations upon the ordinary people of Yugoslavia, many of whom have been forced to seek work elsewhere. Thus, our chief and second engineers were from Kotor, in Montenegro – Yugoslavia – and were able to extend some hospitality and solace to their comrades, virtually marooned aboard their ships on barely subsistence wages until sanctions are lifted. One of these vessels was the *Budva*, the other, the Sunderland-built *Orjen* (named after a mountain in Yugoslavia). This latter ship had been sailed in a few years ago by our chief engineer, who spoke enthusiastically of the high quality of her Sunderland construction. "Real steel, and real workmanship went into those vessels", was his comment, making less complimentary remarks about several ships he had sailed in since, under the old Yugoslav flag, built in the Far East. . . (Sad, I feel, that by insisting on building quality, our own shipyards were forced out of business. With the Common Market applying the political pressure the British shipbuilding industry stood no chance – to my mind, one of our government's most shameful legacies).

The eastern sea side of Qingdao is called the Front Sea and the large, enclosed harbour west of the town is the Back Sea, where we were taken by a pilot to the inner anchorage on 28th October. Formerly the German colony of Tsingtao, Qingdao's architecture carries an unmistakably Germanic stamp, including the twin-spired cathedral. A large, rambling building now called

The Guest House was built by the German Governor in 1914 as his Residence regardless of expense, it was said, which earned the said governor the wrath of his Berlin masters. He did not enjoy the fruits of his extravagance long, however, as the end of World War One removed German control. Now a state-run tourist attraction, the house carries brass plates outside the bedroom where Our Great And Beloved Leader Mao Tse Tung slept, etc. The top floor now houses students. Kaiser Bill's Far Eastern Fleet was based here and it was from Tsingtao that the cruiser *Emden* set off on her final cruise in 1914, enjoying remarkable successes including the bombarding of Britain's oil installation at Madras before being pounded to pieces by the guns of HMAS *Sydney* at the Cocos Keeling Islands. The Chinese continue running a large naval base here; many submarines were in evidence and not a few frigates, destroyers and corvettes. Sarah enjoys history as a subject, and took it all in... One foggy morning as we lay at anchor, she and I were gazing through the mists when slowly and silently a dim shape appeared, coming towards us. A very elderly warship, she passed us by and disappeared into the gloom. Could this have been, we wondered, the ghost of the *Emden* eighty years since sailing on her last voyage. . . We looked up Jane's and decided rather sadly, that she wasn't!

Stepping ashore here in bright sunshine we found a delightful seaside resort with fine bathing beaches (each one numbered, in the Chinese manner) and pretty public gardens. Even the docks were set about with large pots of growing flowers, changed as these died off by night gangs working from a lorry. A port health officer and an English lady working in Qingdao kindly showed us round, up a hill where stands, over-looking the sea, a younger-than-it-looks pagoda, used as a popular backdrop for wedding party photographs, many of which were being taken that afternoon. Our charming guides then took us to an excellent little Chinese restaurant we would never have found on our own, where Sarah managed her chopsticks as to the manner born.

From Qingdao we headed south to Shanghai where we spent nine days, partly at anchor, partly at buoys, but mainly alongside our regular loading berth at Gaoyanglu Wharf, handy for the city, which Sarah saw by day and by night and where she did much of her Christmas shopping. We took afternoon tea in the elegant surroundings of the Peace Hotel and at night took her to see and hear the Old Jazz Band there. Somewhat apprehensive as to how our very modern miss would accept such archaic entertainment, we were delighted when she enthused. She even shook hands with the Leader of the Band, an old friend of mine. . .

Our ship loaded more general cargo here, a vast assortment of break-bulk plus containers of pilferables on deck. With the largest general cargo she had ever carried – over 11,000 tonnes weight – the *Golden Harvest* anchored at Wusong awaiting the tide – her nine-metre draft maximum even for the deep

The old man, off 'those cliffs' on his sixtieth birthday.

North Channel out of the Yangtze – and took her departure from China on 11th November.

The Road to Singapore took us past the east coast of Taiwan where we saw the world's tallest sea cliffs – Ch'ing Shui Shan, 2,422 metres high with a sheer drop of 1,220 metres into the Pacific Ocean some thirty miles north of the port of Huan-Lien. As we came upon them just on sunrise, in fine clear weather with calm sea and no other shipping about, I went within five miles of the coast where sunshine creeping down the cloudstreaked peaks presented an unforgettable sight. The South China Sea provided Sarah with a few whales and dolphins, and good weather to Singapore where, on 22nd November, she and Brenda left to fly home. I was told the ship was to be sold.

At twenty-five years our *Golden Harvest* was in good condition both structurally and mechanically, but all her special surveys were falling due within the next few months – the nautical equivalent of the MOT test. To put her through these surveys – especially rigorous as she reached her quarter century – would require drydocking and be expensive, against which costs must be balanced her possible future earnings, bearing in mind the loss of trading time involved in such a big refit. Although she had this voyage loaded her largest-ever general cargo, it *had* taken three ports to get it, and the simple facts were that her derricks in 5-ton union purchase were unsuitable for the larger, heavier containers and other lifts now being loaded in China. Next question was – would she go for scrap?

Cargo on the quay at Dubai, ours in the foreground.

My mate at Dubai.

The Iraqi Ghost' tankers off Kuwait, since the Gulf War.

Today's main shipbreaking centres are Port Alang in North-West India, Gadani Beach in Pakistan near Karachi, and Chittagong, in Bangladesh – none of which appealed – certainly not to those of us who had experienced the tiresome regulations of sub-continental bureaucracy. We did not want our little ship to go for scrap – anywhere! So we kept her clean, washing holds and 'tweendecks after unloading at Karachi, kept her painted, and lived in hope!

In next port Dubai it was confirmed our ship would be sold as a going concern to an Arab gentleman who came aboard in flowing white robes. For generations his family had run dhows from Dubai down to East Africa and across to India in a centuries-old trade which continues to this day: and on which he had sailed as a young man, eventually commanding his own ship. Now he was building up a fleet of handy-sized cargo ships to trade further afield, to the Far East. He and his Goanese captain (who joined for the trip up to Kuwait and back for familiarisation) enthused about the *Golden Harvest* and so liked the name that they decided only *Golden* would be painted out, while port of registry Dubai would replace Singapore on the stern. Terms of the sale agreement required change also from her Guan Guan colours, so the funnel was painted white instead of blue.

Glad that she was not going to scrap after all (for even today's sailors are sentimental souls who hate to see their ship destroyed), cleaning continued after Kuwait, where our last cargo was discharged. On Christmas Eve we sailed from Port Shuwaikh, Kuwait City, at 6pm. Our second officer had left us at Dubai and flown to Singapore to join the *Golden Grace,* so for the short trip to Kuwait and back to Dubai I kept his twelve-to-four-watches on the bridge. Thus it was that after negotiating our passage through the swept channels between minefields, past the three large unlit, unmanned Iraqi tankers which have been anchored off Kuwait since the Gulf War, and a buoyed channel in between oilfields, I was on the bridge at 3am alone with the 12-4 watchkeeping Indonesian sailor. The weather, cool in Kuwait, was warming up again as we headed south early on Christmas morning, in bright moonlight. Suddenly, in the eastern sky appeared an amazingly bright white light. This had to be an aeroplane, coming in low, but binoculars soon revealed this was not the case – no navigation lights.

I turned to the young AB, himself a Christian. "That, Jishari, is the Christmas Star in the East!" and we marvelled, quite expecting angels to appear in heavenly chorus. Instead, Venus slid behind the clouds and disappeared – but a Venus much brighter than I had ever seen before.

On Christmas evening we had a modest party in the crew messroom, only a small party as by now stocks of everything were low. But, as sailors will, we made the best of it, recalling previous parties here – my own sixtieth birthday, Christmas in Shanghai two years ago and many others. Arriving

back in Dubai on Boxing Day, we returned alongside our former berth to hand over.

This was eventually achieved on 30th when I received the word from Singapore by telephone to go ahead and sign my ship away. At four that afternoon the bus collected us and – with many a mixed feeling – we left our old "Golden Harvest Home" for the last time.

Painting the bridge front, *Golden Harvest.*

21. CAPTAIN AND SON

We had last sailed together in 1976, around the land from Liverpool to Avonmouth in the S.S. *Auckland Star,* a cargo liner loading for the Fiji Isles, Australia and New Zealand.   Before that he and his younger sister accompanied their mother and me on a six month round-the-world trip in the sistership S.S. *Tasmania Star*, a marvellous voyage which could have ended – for us – in tragedy when Michael developed an acute appendicitis. Fortunately we were in Bluff, New Zealand at the time and between them, Doctor Judy Driscoll and the staff of Kew Hospital, Invercargill, undoubtedly saved our son's life as the operation was by no means a simple one.   But thanks to the expert care there, for which we shall always be deeply grateful, his health has never looked back.   Although at that time he wanted to follow in father's footsteps it soon became apparent to us both that the seafaring of the future was not going to be as I had known it.   I had been one of that fortunate generation who came to sea soon after the War. . .   But last year his little daughter Sarah so enjoyed her voyage with her grandparents in the *Golden Harvest* that Michael wondered if perhaps he could spend the two months leave he had accrued by accompanying me for a short trip.   Guan Guan were, as usual, most kindly accommodating and agreed for him to sign on as a supernumerary.

Flying out to Singapore by picturesquely efficient Bangladesh Airlines, he joined the *Golden Bear* at her Eastern Road anchorage, 19 July 1995, having had three days since his arrival to explore the city – his first visit.   After a superb dinner at Raffles Hotel (preceded by several Singapore slings in the Long Bar, where we scattered our peanut shells across the tiled floor in time-honoured fashion then the Writer's Bar – we repaired aboard our ship by the last boat, ten thirty pm.   Next day we sailed for Zhangjiagang in China with 13,000 tons of bulk urea loaded in Shuwaybah, Kuwait.

A smooth passage up the South China Sea soon refreshed Michael's shipboard memories; the sounds, the smells, the sights and the evocative atmosphere of a cargo ship at sea.   A ship very different from his last, on a different trade with a different crew, but he settled in as to the manner born. The spare cabin became his home and of course he had the run of the ship and my accommodation, where our very palatable meals were served by Myint, the Burmese steward.

'Those Cliffs', the world's highest – on Taiwan's east coast – had their heads in the clouds but were spectacular notwithstanding and we watched two intrepid paragliders floating down, having leaped into space from a sheer drop of 1,200 metres.   The weather remained fine as we embarked our pilot from his cutter near No.5 buoy in the Yangtze estuary (the CJK) and made our way up the North Channel. The river was its usual busy self with a large ferry overtaking us seemingly bent on collision – until hotly admonished by our pilot as he took us neatly to anchor off Liuhe Kou, six miles above the Baoshan Steelworks, themselves occupying a river frontage of over five miles. Here we changed pilots. I have learned that the most senior pilots, those nearing retirement, work the ships moving around Shanghai from berth to berth – not so rigorous as joining or leaving a ship down at the CJK where the weather is often boisterous, the sea rough. The middle men, experienced pilots all, work the lower reaches from the sea up to Shanghai, while the younger fellows are employed in pairs working "up river" above the Huangpu.

Thus two cheerful youngsters came aboard to take us up to Zhangjiagang. But in the evening we anchored three miles below Nantong for the night as navigation in these upper reaches becomes tricky and is consequently restricted to daylight hours. The river ran strongly and we had not been at anchor long when our alert Burmese third officer, keeping the evening 8-12 bridge watch, noticed we were dragging, slowly but surely. The bottom is sand here – not the best holding ground for an anchor's flukes – and inexorably we were dragging down towards an anchored tanker. If we missed her we stood to go ashore on a backbreaking sandbank as the tide fell. . .

With self and both pilots on the bridge on a wet and windy night, the chief officer and bosun went forward to weigh anchor and we moved to a safe spot. The Indonesian bosun had been at his Muslim prayers when the call came to go forward and we felt certain his Words helped to keep us out of serious trouble. When it came up after our dragging, the anchor flukes were polished like silver!

Next morning dawned bright and clear and the last thirty miles took us between low, green pastureland interspersed with canals, to Zhangjiagang where we tied up alongside the quay at 1130am. The agent here was a pleasant, bespectacled gentleman approaching retirement, dressed in shirt and shorts against the hot weather. After the conclusion of formalities he took us ashore, to a restaurant where, he said we would not be overcharged.

The town was pleasant, the natives friendly, standing and sitting in groups on the wide pavements chatting in the warm evening air, drinking beer and playing cards at little tables; – a tranquil scene. The restaurant turned out excellent Chinese cuisine remarkably inexpensively, after which the Seamen's Club across the road provided diversion in the shapely forms of Linda and Susan. These were the 'English names' – adopted to save occidental tongues being unable to get around their real Chinese names – of two charming 19 year old students working in the club's bar in the evenings to improve their English. This is still the international seamen's language despite the fact that we, as English seamen, were rare birds indeed in these parts. Light conversation was followed by readings from the girls' schoolbooks, a session which ended in much mirth – they laughing at our pronunciation and we at theirs; but all good natured. We were able to phone home from the club.

There are no taxis here as such, only pedacabs and motorbikes offering pillion lifts, both of which we declined with thanks, preferring to stroll back to the ship – only twenty minutes walk on a fine night along the clean dockside road. Onboard unloading proceeded apace – if not quite so fast as our stevedore had forecast. But then, he was accustomed to bulk carriers and found our 'tweendecks something of a drawback to the discharge of bulk cargo. But of course, 'tweendecks are necessary for the carriage of our westbound general cargo. The urea was slung out in grabs here, into hoppers, under which we were quite delighted to see small bagging machines "Made in England" by Simon, of Nottingham, which did the work in seconds – for the bags to be stored in a permanent large warehouse nearby. Where we would load our next cargo became a matter of conjecture.

A visit to the city of Zhangjiagang in the agent's new minibus, a ride of twelve miles from the port, gave an insight into modern China. Mostly built as a New Town over the last twenty years, houses were spacious and well designed. Our agent told us he and his wife moved here from a similar job in Shanghai fifteen years ago, apprehensive, naturally, of what the new port would provide. But to their delight it provided, after Shanghai's desperate overcrowding – a house with "own bathroom, own kitchen, garden for children to play in" – he has never regretted the move. Shops were well stocked, most of the goods amazingly inexpensive to us, though with Chinese salaries still at a very low level, not so cheap for the locals. Calculating prices, even in modern shops selling computers was, we noticed, still done on the abacus. The food markets were fascinating, stallholders quite happy to be photographed as they weighed their produce on hand-held scale balances. Meat in variegated joints lay on marble slabs, fish was alive-alive-oh! in tanks and tubs. There were many kinds of fish, also mussels, crabs, eels, lobsters, shrimps, prawns and turtles (small ones, very expensive!). All were freshwater-caught, from the lakes, ponds and canals round about the town, taken home alive after purchase in wet plastic bags, as refrigeration is still uncommon. There were even two hedgehogs. Our drive into the city had been along the new highway but our return, at our request, was a fascinating glimpse of rural China, a narrow lane winding between fields of sunflowers, cotton, vegetables and of course rice, which is a three-times-a-year crop here, with paddy fields in every stage of growth. Hedgerows were bright with wild flowers dapple-shaded here and there by broad leaved trees not unlike those at home – oaks, maples, planes and sycamores. The well surfaced road led through old villages of brick, wood and stone cottages where domestic animals roamed freely – back to the ship.

Our regular liner-loading was not due to commence at Xingang for several weeks, so rather than have us swing round an anchor for that time, our Singapore Head Office imaginatively decided to fit in an intermediate cargo. At first this looked like a load of coiled steel wire from Baoshan to Korea: but finally fixed as copra pellets from the Philippines to Inchon, to take the place of our sister *Golden Grace*, delayed by torrential rain in Hainan, South China.

Clearing the CJK at 1500 on August 5th, we arrived at Iligan, Mindanao – most southerly of the Philippine Islands – four and a half days later. Despite the typhoon season the China Seas had been kind to us and after a good passage we entered San Bernadino Strait with green, jungle-covered islands presenting white sand beaches under the palm trees on either side.

Away to the west the still-smoking volcano of Mount Mayon – on Luzon Island – stood above the lesser hills, a perfect cone almost 8,000 feet high. Having a history of eruption every ten years or so, its last was 1985. . .. Iligan, on the shores of Quinalang Cove, is unashamedly industrial. Copra mills, oil installations, a huge quarry slashing the hillside and a cement works fill the coastal air with fine dust, against a background of tropical mountain greenery. Away from the port, however, the countryside became instantly rural, small thatch houses lining the road slowly giving way to more permanent buildings on the edge of the city. (All Philippine towns are cities, no matter how small!) A small stadium advertised (in English, surprisingly, for most signs were in the local language) that here were held "Boxing Tournaments and Cockfighting". We had noticed several fierce-looking long-spurred cockerels tethered outside roadside cottages and guessed these would be among the contestants. The Philippinos told us that they, as a people, are great dog-eaters and recommended the flavour of a plump pup as being out of this world! We were prepared to take their word for it.

The local copra mills were established here en masse some twenty years ago when it was realised that, whereas the Philippines had EX ported copra (coconut shell) for centuries, they were now having to IMport the manufactured coco-products. DIY would not only come cheaper but would provide employment and many mills were established, often using second hand equipment to get started, some of which survives still in use. It is now a major industry. The coconuts, clustered high under the branches of picturesque palm trees, are harvested by the farmers who remove the husks for fuel or to make into coco matting. The kernels are then split and either sun or smoke dried (the latter process kills off insects) and sent to the nearest mill either by lorry or by sea. The lorries often bear religious slogans as "In God We Trust" while locally owned motor vessels carry out the seaborn traffic around the islands.

At the mill the copra goes through many processes which are closely guarded secrets. Michael and I were taken around "our" mill and had each stage explained very carefully and interestingly, but were asked not to take photographs or reveal the secrets. It is seldom we get the chance to watch our cargo manufactured from its raw state! Most valuable product is refined oil, exported in small tankers – to the United States mainly – for human consumption. Less refined oil goes into a wide range of products, from toothpaste to detergents, while the final product is the copra pellet, a light brown mealy substance. Full of protein and with a small fat content it is ideal for making cattle cake and other animal feeds, thousands of tons being exported annually. Our cargo was to be as much as we could load in the time available – around 12,000 tons it was hoped (eventually we loaded 12,080 tonnes).

Our Singapore chief cook was a lively lad of fifty eight, quite tall and quite distinguished – not a bad cook either. It was discovered that he got his kicks ashore by visiting the local "discos" and introducing himself as the Captain of the *Golden Bear*. This earned him gratifying esteem though naturally he was charged more. Known, however, as The Man With The Roll Of Notes, this only burnished his image even further. It was only when another captain and his son became well known figures in the little town that Captain Cook's alias was blown. . .

My next and final copra loading port was given as Roxas (pronounced as Ro-Ass) – not one of the several shown dotted round the Islands but a place so small it was not even on my British Admiralty large scale chart of Mindanao (or any other). I was told to head for Latitude 8 degrees 31 minutes North, Longitude 125 degrees 15 minutes East and embark a pilot half a mile off the beach. He would come out to the ship in a "blue-painted dugout canoe with outboard motor". Only seventy four miles westward around the coast from Iligan, we approached across a blue and sunlit sea with the distant hills slowly taking shape in the clear morning air. Six miles off we made out a large shed with S.I.O.M. in big red letters standing at the water's edge. No belching chimneys here we perceived – South Islands Oil Mills pride themselves on cleanliness and "No Pollution!"

Like the Iligan loader (only newer and cleaner) the cargo hoist stood half a cable offshore on a concrete pedestal, equipped with four concrete mooring dolphins alongside which we would moor. The hoist connects to the mill by an enclosed conveyor belt alongside which runs an iron walkway gallery – providing the usual means of getting ashore, once one had negotiated the copra-dust covered iron ladders and platforms of the hoist. As at Iligan, the ship must place her hatches under the loading spout, in turn. There are no tugs but sure enough, the pilot, Captain Taqaloquin, came out in his "blue-painted outboard canoe".

We had no sooner tied up than the ship was surrounded by tiny outrigger

Michael visiting friends at Roxas.

canoes, their wide-eyed owners offering fruit for sale, local bottled beer and coconut wine. Some were children, just taking a look at the big ship which had arrived, literally, upon their doorstep.

On either side of the small mill stretched the beach – grey volcanic sand here – backed by tall rustling palms under which were the most beautiful little thatched and raffia houses grouped into a village, with pigs, ducks, chickens, dogs and children all playing happily together. Less than a hundred yards from the ship one had strolled back to the dawn of time. Women, many of them expectant mothers, with their grandmothers accompanied by children, waded hip deep in the clear warm water off the beach, pushing large, triangular floating fish traps. The men and boys fished from canoes, many of them rigged with a simple spritsail. Huge water buffaloes (called caribou) wallowed in mud pools up to their shoulders. Cattle and goats munched the sweet grass under the trees. Everyone was friendly in such an innocent, kindly way that we were, as one man, captivated. The wicked world outside seemed far, far away! After a couple of days we were greeted with "Halloa Captain!" wherever we went (the cook too, no doubt!) and humorists introduced Michael as my father. . .. One star-spangled night under the palm trees he was invited by a group of young people to accompany them on an outing to a waterfall about twenty miles up country. There was a swimming pool there, among the rocks. We were not sailing until Saturday and tomorrow was only Friday, so after breakfast off he went – five young persons on one motorbike! An extra pillion had been welded onto the stern of this little machine. Nevertheless, he reports, it was a comfortably tight squeeze for the two lads and three lasses!

And of course, soon after the motorbike had chugged off into the jungle, I was advised that the tanker due "next day" had improved her speed and would now arrive at 1600 hours *this* day, August 18th. From our conducted tour round the mill we knew that when the storage tanks were full, as they now were, production must stop until the next tanker called to collect. Thus, quite rightly, tankers had priority, and as we were nearly full the letter written to me explaining the situation by the Resident Manager himself apologetically said he would have to "shut out" our last 300 tons of pellets to allow me to vacate the berth on time. . .

But where was Michael? Last seen heading for the hills with four others on a small motorbike! I had no idea of the location of his destination and no means of contacting him. The water off the berth was far too deep for me to anchor-off and wait for him. . . But I need not have worried – though did, naturally. The jungle tom-toms were beaten and he returned with over an hour to spare, laden with fruit and having spent a truly wonderful day in the simple surroundings of a pool under a waterfall, the tropical vegetation bright with flowers. Developed as a local resort, it seemed he was the first Englishman to set foot here and had been made much of. We were well off the tourist trail out here!

"Marvellous, – Dad!"

Our send-off was fantastic! The whole population turned out to see us depart, climbing onto every level of the loading hoist and waving from beach and canoe. Our lads had been exemplary guests of these charming, unspoiled people and I had been officially complimented on my crew's behaviour.

And so to Inchon as the tanker *Thor Stream* edged into our berth. Where we had been alongside for three full days, she would depart before breakfast time. August is the height of the typhoon season and as we headed north we were fortunate in that a rather boisterous Janis passed a couple of days astern of us. As she roared in over Shanghai, gathering force and doing her worst on an already flood-ravaged coast, Kent and Lois (as they were officially named) came along to join forces over the South China Sea behind us in what must have been a welter of white water, best avoided. While we sailed serenely on, Janis herself curved back over the Yellow Sea, blowing herself out right over the *Golden Bear* as we came to anchor off Inchon. Very low barometer, blinding rain in a constant deluge, but by this time only a fitful, failing wind, confirmed the reports of Janis' whereabouts. We had been lucky; the Roxas girls must have given us their blessing!

Ceaseless rain had caused cargo work to come to a halt days ago in this exceptionally busy port, with flooding causing chaos all the way up and down

Korea's west coast. Local television showed dreadful scenes of bridges, railways, roads and homes completely destroyed while a whole cemetery was wasted over a cliff! Ninety vessels waited to go alongside. As the rain eased off work resumed, at first aboard the container ships, log carriers and tankers, eventually on the likes of us, for copra must not get wet.

Port Quarantine officials came to inspect samples of our cargo for copra beetle infestation. A hatch was opened, the cargo revealed clean and dry. Not a beetle in sight. However, by diligently and determinedly sieving with circular hand-held sieves, like old-time gold prospectors, our taciturn officials eventually found six small black beetles. Triumphantly they announced – and did I detect a note of relief in their voices? – "You are infested, will have to be fumigated!"

"Where?" I asked.

"Out here at anchor of course. Everyone must leave ship while fumigation!"

I looked around at the swirling six knot tide. With twice-daily rise and fall of 28 feet, tidal currents run fast. I cast my eyes around the numerous unwieldy large barges being pushed, deep-laden with sand, across the harbour, passing close by. We were only one mile off the town dock entrance and ships passed close continually.

"No," I said.

Full of indignation they persisted. "*Must* fumigate. It's the Law!" Doubtless a highly profitable law for some fumigation company, too, I suspected. "OK," I said. "Suppose one of these barges hits the ship – after we have all left for you to fumigate – and parts our anchor cable, causing us to drift down onto another ship. Collision. Fire. Injury, perhaps death. Will you undertake – in writing – to pay for this?"

"Oh no!" they said, shocked at my suggestion.

Reluctantly they agreed then to the ship going alongside to unload the 4,000 tons of 'tweendeck cargo, which (they said – I had my doubts) would be fumigated ashore. We must then move out to a *safe* anchorage (I insisted on this *safe* clause) for fumigation of our lower hold cargo – some 8,080 tons). But still, of course, with enough persons on board, including myself, to man the ship safely and cope with any emergency. Also, I felt, to keep my eye on the fumigators. Thirteen of us remained, the other eighteen went into an hotel which, they soon found, was crawling with cockroaches!

But it was while we were in Inchon that Michael's leave expired and he had to fly home from Seoul. It had been an unforgettable voyage – how often do father and son have such opportunity!

Michael had got on very well with his shipmates, who included Yugoslavs from Montenegro, Burmese, Indonesians, a Singapore Cook and a Welder from the Philippines. He soon discovered that these lads, mostly in their

235

twenties and thirties, came away for long voyages – our Burmese Radio Officer had been in the ship five years with never a break – and tended to consider the ship their true home. They were professional in outlook – many were educated to university level with degrees in their homeland – Considerate of others, splendid shipmates, with whom it has been a privilege to sail. From the two Brits on board – that goes for both of us!

Golden Bear's crew (including Michael) at Inchon Anchorage.

22. CHINA CLIPPER

The words conjure up visions of *Cutty Sark* and her graceful sisters driving down the South China Sea under a press of canvas. Every stitch is set – skysails, stu'nsails, jimmy greens and watersails, tended by enormous crews.

Their holds were crammed with burlap-covered chests of tea for the London Market and the term "clipper" was applied to these fine-lined vessels – the fastest the world had ever seen – because they "clipped" time off all previous passages. For even in those gracious, spacious days, Time Was Money in the shipping world and the cargo which reached London first commanded the best price.

So, if a China Clipper is a ship whose Captain has been instructed by his Owners to clip his round voyage as short as possible on his way to and from China – this evocative style could perhaps even be applied to the good ship *Golden Bear* under the command of yours truly, for in November 1995 I was ordered to proceed with maximum despatch to China and load our next cargo "Before the End of the Year", another cargo of urea.

These orders came while we were in Dubai unloading the last of the previous west-bound general cargo. My wife joined here for the fine-weather passage to Singapore. Holders of British passports do not need a visa to enter the United Arab Emirates – but it was still pleasant for her to be met at midnight after the flight from Newcastle via Amsterdam by the amazing Mr Hanif of our Dubai agents Rais Hassa Saadi. While other passengers stood in long lines at the immigration desks this conjuror wafted her past smiling officials with no pause at all, to meet me in the arrival hall. A swift twenty minute drive in the agent's beautiful new white Japanese car brought us through the warm night to our air-conditioned ship, lying at her regular berth, No.21 shed, Port Rashid.

We were now literally down to the nuts and bolts – cases and cases of them – having already discharged the hinges, doorlocks and every kind of household requirement as well as industrial and medical equipment carried in case, crate, drum, bag, bale, barrel and carton; – we must be one of the last companies in the world to carry general cargo break-bulk on a regular cargo-liner basis.

Whilst a visit to the current Dubai Air Show would have proved fascinating, the intense heat of the day combined with the hustling crowds made us feel we perhaps had the best view of it from the ship, watching the French answer to our Red Arrows perform aerobatics leaving tricolour trails of smoke while the latest commercial aircraft showed off their paces. Instead, we took our Burmese Second mate and Yugoslavian Chief Officer and Chief Engineer out to dinner at Thatchers, which *they* maintain is the nearest one can get in the Gulf to a pleasant English pub.

With our holds and tweendecks empty we left Dubai on 16 November and anchored outside the port to complete cleaning, for Inchcape's surveyors at our loading port Ruwais require Cleanliness with a capital "C" before passing us to load urea. Most southerly port in the Gulf, Ruwais, in the Emirate of Abu Dhabi, began as an oil terminal and still huge tankers arrive at the end of long jetties, load their several hundred thousand tons of crude for Japan and sail away with no loss of time. A revealing comment on life in tankers today was made by the British pilot who took us in. His previous ship had been a VLCC whose American Captain told him this was the first time since he was promoted to command three years ago that he had actually berthed alongside a jetty. His previous life had been from one Single Mooring Buoy to another – miles out at sea – and he had only seen land at close quarters when he went on leave at the end of his tour of duty.

Carried in either bags or bulk, urea comes prilled, that is to say, each white granule is coated in a plastic which dissolves only slowly in water, thus retarding the release of fertiliser into the ground. This voyage we would load some 12,000 tonnes in bags for Shanghai where it would be offloaded into barges which would carry it hundreds of miles, then, up China's inland waterways to the far counties.

With hatches spotless we arrived at the outer anchorage on 19th November but had to await the completion and departure of a Greek before going alongside on the 20th. The urea terminal is now approaching twenty years old and the two lofty loading machines which transfer the bags from an overhead conveyor to the ship's holds were showing their age. Urea has a highly corrosive effect on machinery and the cool weather was not helping their hydraulic systems. The repair of daily breakdowns kept us alongside until 28th November. During this time no shore leave off the wharf was permitted, which gave us plenty of time to wonder if at this slow rate of loading we would be able to meet our deadline in China by the end of the year. Our destination was up the mighty River Yangtze which despite its immense length is quite shallow in the entrance. Our fresh water draft had not to exceed 8.5 metres (in winter, as this was) and this was achieved by careful distribution of cargo, judicious use of fuel oil and fresh water throughout the sea passage, with transfer of water ballast as necessary.

On previous visits to Ruwais my wife and I had, each evening, strolled along the quay as far as the gate where was a little beach of coral sand surrounded by pretty green thorn bushes with bright yellow flowers – a pleasant exercise – up and down for an hour or so's "walk in the park". On this occasion however we were stopped by a very dark-skinned Arab in gleaming white shirt and black trousers – Port Authority uniform – who told us apologetically that we may only walk as far as the bollards holding the ship's mooring ropes. When I explained that we had been here many times before and walked this way without let or hindrance he apologised again and said "the rules have changed". So we had to walk half the distance twice as many times. . . watching the glorious Arab sunsets surmounted, at that time, by Venus and Jupiter close together, after which the new moon in the old moon's arms appeared while oil jetty lights twinkled in the distance.

Out at sea with no interference from shore lighting we saw the "new" Orion Nebula in all its fiery clarity – a new "star factory" so the newspapers told us, beautiful to behold, just below Orion's belt. Clear of the Straits of Hormuz numerous dolphins disported themselves near us and in glorious weather with hot sunshine tempered by cooling breeze, a school of whales cruised past on the surface heading north west. On 4th December we passed the Lakshadweep Islands. Passing these from point to point gives a good check on the vessel's speed and with deep water all around them it is safe to approach to within a few miles in clear weather. Set like jewels in the Arabian Sea these palm-girt atolls lie right on the ship's course from the Gulf to Cape Cormorin – India's southern tip. Nodding palms in the sunshine, white coral sand beaches, bungalows set beneath the trees – they look like perfect island paradises – though at least one is marked on the chart as a leper colony. We passed Cherbaniani at 4am in predawn darkness, Chetlat at breakfast time, Kiltan at noon and cleared away from Androth just after 5pm. Next day we passed Trivandrum on the Indian mainland and stood in to see the sailing fishermen there. Most interesting little craft, still to be counted in their hundreds, they are little more than dugout canoes, sans outriggers, each manned by usually two or three men and setting a tanned calico triangular sail on a whispy mast stepped right forward in the eyes. To apologise for our nosey intrusion into their waters we cast small, knotted plastic bags each containing a packet of cigarettes in their direction; when it was a case of "Down sail, lads, out paddles" with a cheery wave of thanks as they contentedly lit up. Shameful, you will say in these no-smoking days, but the fact remains that in places like India, enjoying a cigarette is one of life's very few little luxuries. But these true sailormen are now having to compete with the ubiquitous fibreglass outboard motorboats and soon half a dozen of these were following us like angry bees, hoping (vainly) for a share of the smokes. . .

Rounding Dondra Head, Sri Lanka's southern point, a strong adverse current was running at four knots, setting us back somewhat until we reached the clear waters of the Bay of Bengal, crossing to pass south of the Island of Wé, through Bengal and Malakka Passages into the wide Malacca Strait. Down past One Fathom Bank then where Amazon Maru Shoal always reminds me of the handsome cream and green passenger cargo liner of that name which I used to see in the Amazon during the middle 'fifties, carrying Japanese emigrants to Brazil where they seemed to fit into the landscape

239

Trivandrum fisherman.

quite naturally. Whether it was this ship which left her mark in history on the chart of Malacca Strait I do not know, but feel it likely.

As soon as we arrived in Singapore's Eastern Working Anchorage at 0800, 12th December, a small tanker edged alongside with our bunkers, soon to be followed by the waterboat and a powered clinker-built wooden barge of considerable antiquity bearing stores. Such barges used to crowd the waterfront before the box boats took most of Singapore's cargo, and a few are now converted into tourist "junks" taking sightseers on trips round the harbour.

My wife left the ship here. Not only was Christmas at Home with the family important but China in the depths of winter is no place for a lady who likes the sunshine. There are many luxurious modern hotels in this soaring city but to us there is still nothing to compare with the elegance and comfort of the newly-refurbished Raffles, where she spent the night before flying home and where we had dinner, basking in the reflected glories of Kipling, Conrad, Maugham, Stevenson, Novello and Mitchener whose portraits smile down from the walls of the Writers' Bar. The ship sailed next morning at first light for Shanghai.

Not to be confused with a *typhoon*, that tropical revolving storm closely related to the hurricane and cyclone, the *monsoon* is a seasonal wind, one which blows from the NE in the South China Sea steadily from September to

April. It was now in full flight against us, but the Chief Engineer and his merry men had recently overhauled our main turbo-blowers resulting in improved speed. In the north-sweeping Kuro Siwo current we were making a steady 13 knots – not bad for a deep-laden twenty five year old twelve-knot ship. A China clipper indeed!

Approaching the entrance to the Yangtze Kiang River – called the CJK – through the back door, so to speak, between the Luhuashan Islands, we came to anchor at 0700, 22nd December, to weigh four hours later, embark our pilot at No.1 Buoy and go up the deeper North Channel on the tide, slowly slowly, anchoring for an hour at Wusong where Shanghai's Huangpu River enters the main stream, awaiting higher water. All night we crept up this busy, heavily industrialised waterway, under the graceful new bridge, to tie up at Gongpinglu Wharf at 0630. Immediately downstream from our more regular Gaoyanglu Wharf (Lu is Chinese for Street) the latter is not equipped with shore cranes while the former wharf is. After all night on the bridge the old man was ready for his bunk now but it was not to be. The agent had to be met and given all the papers required to clear the ship in, and cargo discharge had to commence. Only a few years ago, upon arrival, a group of smartly uniformed officers would come aboard on what was called The Inspection. Now this is all streamlined – as at most developed ports – into being handled by one man, the agent. But the Captain still has to greet him, of course. Plenty of time to catch up on the sleep tonight!

As soon as we arrived dozens of barges swarmed alongside – thirty at first count – and our cargo was swung out by derrick and shore crane in fine style. In the first twenty four hours we unloaded 5,000 tons – splendid – but then of course the stream of barges dried up and gangs of dockers hung around waiting, twiddling their Chinese thumbs. It was only by thumping tables and making a fuss that I persuaded the stevedores and others to land our remaining cargo onto the quay, to await collection when barges returned. This idea was unpopular with the shore people as the prospect of "double-handling" cargo always is, even in this land of low wages. I had to keep reminding them that it was the charterer's responsibility to unload our urea as quickly as possible as we were required up north. To load China's export cargo! So, our Christmas was spent in this rather unfestive fashion – even the ship's party organised in the crew messroom in the evening was not quite the event we had hoped for, despite the turkey and plum duff. Our Burmese Electrical Officer was ashore marrying a lovely Chinese lady whom he had been courting for years, and she was to have been the belle of our little ball, of course. But the nineteen year old green-uniformed conscript Frontier Guard of the People's Liberation Army stationed at our gangway refused to let the bridal party onboard. So that was that. We sailed next morning, 0400 on 26th December, a much faster trip down the river than had been our arrival as our draft was of course now much less and the tide was favourable, enabling us to go out through the South Channel (which is cheaper, as it does not have to be kept dredged). At 10am we disembarked our pilot and headed north towards Xingang-Tianjin, the port for Peking, which the Chinese usually call, nowadays, Beijing. (Our three Yugoslav senior officers are Eastern Orthodox Christians, celebrating Christmas on 6/7 January, when we *were* able to relax a little – so we were not without Christmas after all!)

The north east wind still blew, all the way up to the Bohai Sea, but we continued to make good speed and anchored off the port soon after noon, Thursday 28th December. A Chinese COSCO ship was on "our" berth so we had to wait until next day to go alongside. This was the anchorage where, last year in the *Golden Harvest*, our granddaughter Sarah spotted an owl on the anchor. But now a bitter wind blew down from Siberia, covering the harbour with frazil ice and making it too cold, even for owls. Never a good holding ground, the Admiralty Pilot Book warns that ships should not anchor closer together than half a mile as dragging is common and happens quickly. Sure enough, at three in the morning the Second Mate called me from my bunk to report we were dragging, slowly yet inexorably, down towards an oil rig. This despite the fact we had carefully laid out eight shackles of chain (120 fathoms – 720 feet). Still a mile off the red lights of the rig and with engines on Stand By in case needed, we watched, checking our position constantly. As we'd hoped, when the tide turned the gale eased and we stopped dragging – to be called in next day, 29th, by which time the sands of 1995 were fast running out. Would we get our cargo loaded in time to beat the deadline? Would our China Clipper win her race against time – or lose it?

Guan Guan's Mr Lee Khen Jiam, the Xingang representative was, as always, wondrously helpful. Not only does he know the people here and speak the language but he also knows the loading procedures, which do differ slightly from port to port. Part of our Karachi cargo was a consignment of 920 tons of black steel pipes, each one foot in diameter and thirty feet long – for Pakistani Oilfields Ltd. Even Mr Lee was unfamiliar with the likes of these and no one else onboard had previous experience. They made a formidable pile of pipes on the quay! When I just happened to mention that back in 1951 I had loaded almost identical pipes in the *Columbia Star* at Newport (then in Monmouthshire, now in Gwent) for the Alberta oil fields via Vancouver, I became the "instant expert". Even though I had only been a lowly cadet then it's amazing how much you remember from those far off days, and we loaded these Chinese pipes the same way. Those along the ship's side were laid fore and aft, filling the middle with pipes athwartships, making a good block stow which would be easily unloaded in Karachi yet would withstand the heaviest gyrations bad weather could throw at us. A busy coal-loading port, Xingang's dock area is covered with a thick layer of black dust and soon we were too, but sent back a consignment of wood dunnage (to lay under and around our cargo as protection) as it was just *too* dirty. The chandler changed it cheerfully, acknowledging that he had been just "trying it on" with us. Had we not refused it he would have pocketed his pelf satisfied that he had profitably got some rubbish off his hands. . . Loading had commenced on 29th December and continued without a break until 0700, 2nd January, by which time we had loaded over 8,000 tons of general cargo, 500 tons of it being drums of acids and oils stowed on the upper deck to avoid the risk of the occasional but inevitable leaker damaging other cargo. Sailing a mere half hour after loading completed, I anchored off the port, well clear of oil rigs and other vessels to enable our bosun and his six sailors secure this cargo with wire rope and bottle screw against any heavy weather we may meet outside. While at anchor here a glorious dawn was complimented by the sun rising with a bright green flash on the eastern horizon. This green flash – caused by the slitting of light – is quite common in the tropics in clear weather at sun *set* – but this was the first time I had ever seen it at sun *rise*. As the sky had grown steadily brighter I had watched for it, hoping. . .

On Saturday 6th January we came to our old anchorage in the CJK surrounded by many other ships but with no orders to proceed up the river to embark a pilot. Another gale sprang up bringing snow flurries – oddly enough with a very high, steady barometer – and although *we* remained securely at anchor a couple of small Chinese tankers began dragging towards us as the gale freshened "– in such manner as to involve risk of collision". Only safe thing to do then was to weigh anchor and head out to sea, which sounds simple enough but which took over an hour in the deteriorating weather, using helm and engines to ease the strain on the chain. Cosy and snug for me, the Third Officer and the Wheelman on the bridge but bitterly cold for the Chief Officer and Bosun on the exposed forecastle head. When eventually the anchor was home and secured I headed out to sea intending to "ride out the storm" in the classic manner, standing off and on until either the gale abated or we were called in, whichever came first. The sea in the wide estuary mouth was the colour of heaving café au lait, laced and curdled with dirty white foam. As the gale strengthened from the north the waves grew higher and steeper and soon our motion became uncomfortable with the occasional sea crashing aboard. I decided to seek shelter in the lee of the Luhuashan Islands. Rising to a height of 470 feet these resemble smooth light brown buns dropped by some giant baker from his cart: more than thirty other ships had also found shelter here. It was quite Biblical. At five o'clock we were pitching and rolling into the teeth of the gale, beginning to take solid water aboard. By half past we were snugly at anchor on sea as smooth as a millpond from where we watched the raging storm outside. Only twenty miles from the cruising white pilot cutter, we were called in 10th January and once again made a painfully slow all-night progress up the river, to berth at Gaoyanglu just on breakfast time. The pilot was happy to tuck into his omelette.

Loading at great speed resumed here but the Social Event of the voyage was at hand – the Wedding Celebration of our Chinese Electrician to his Chinese Musician. He had met Ye Si Long at the Shanghai Seamen's club years before, when she played piano and organ at musical evenings. At other times she plays in dance bands around the city. But her main work is to lecture in Italian Music at Shanghai University, no less! Mother China guards her daughters carefully and any foreigner wishing to take a Chinese bride must fulfill many strict requirements. We had gone through this lengthy procedure in the *Golden Harvest* the previous year when I wrote a glowing testimonial of his character and aptitude after he had taken all the necessary medical and other examinations. But, at the last minute the ship's sailing was brought forward and nuptials had to be postponed for another thirteen months. On our northbound call over Christmas they had managed the official wedding ceremony in the civic hall, but our quick departure early on Boxing Day precluded any festivities. Now, however, we were all invited to a reception in a pleasant restaurant quite close to the dock gate at which I would, in effect, have to give away the bride and pronounce them truly Man and Wife.

Until then I had believed it was only in Hollywood movies that a Captain may marry anyone other than his own wife. It is certainly not permitted on a British ship under British law. But we were not on a British ship were we?– And I was required to do the honours. Her own parents had died long ago in one of the yellow fever epidemics but her lovely family – sisters, aunts, cousins et al turned up in force – including her brother who acted as what we would call the Best Man – and several well behaved lively children. We were all sat round three large circular tables laid with white cloths, with lazy susans to circulate the dishes. And chopsticks, of course. Course after delicious course kept on coming, well washed down with gallons of beer and whisky. At the appropriate moment, before the soup (which is the final course in a true Chinese meal) I was passed a tiny red heart-shaped velvet box containing two gold rings. Summoning the happy couple I opened the box and placed the smaller ring on the bride's left hand fourth finger, then her husband's on his. I then had to say, "With these rings I thee wed", pronounced them Man and Wife and hoped they would be very happy – to cheering and clapter and the clicking of cameras. I had to leave soon after this auspicious occasion to meet the agent who came aboard with my clearance and cargo papers, but the party carried on till midnight. The poor dears did not have long together though, as we sailed at two am for Singapore. However, the people of the east have immense patience and Tin Hla is promised a good electrical job ashore in Singapore next year while Ye Si Long will have no difficulty in being accepted there. So, we hope they live Happily Ever After.

Some of our Shanghai cargo came as green tea in burlap-covered chests and yes, I was told in Singapore, by getting at least *some* of our cargo loaded before the turn of the year, our China Clipper had indeed won her race against time.

Golden Harvest in the Eastern Roads, Singapore.

23.   I SAILED WITH A MAN

I sailed with a man who had been in the *Titanic*. . .

When first I met him it was nineteen-year-old Cadet Kinghorn's job at the beginning of each voyage to collect from the master every crew member's discharge book and enter into it signing-on details, then make a Crew List, in my spare time, of course. Thus, equipped with the ship's rubber stamps, pad and one of those new-fangled ball-point pens I applied myself to the task. Each page was ruled into columns. Name of the ship with her official number, tonnage and horsepower came first, followed by date and place of "engagement" – as signing-on was called. The seaman's rank and description of voyage came next. HT was Home Trade, anywhere between the limits of Brest and the Elbe, while FGN was beyond those limits – Foreign. RUN was a special agreement from one HT port to another. Spaces were provided for the master, at the end of the voyage, to enter remarks on the man's Ability and General Conduct – his Character. "VG" was very good (ie, normal). "Good" was Not Very Good, while "DR" was reserved for such an exceptionally bad character that he was beneath description – Decline to Report. Finally came columns for end-of-voyages signatures of master and (to make it all legal) the Proper Officer at the Shipping Office, which was the Board of Trade or Ministry of Transport.

In those early 1950s one still occasionally came across the old, pre-war dark blue-backed discharge books. They were always full of interest (I had not realised until then that when a ship was sunk through enemy action, the seaman's wages stopped that day!) I used to read them avidly, right back to their owner's first voyage. And there before me, tingling my spine, first trip engagement in the book of our radio officer was "RMS *Titanic*" ! When I mentioned it he smiled acknowledgement and said, yes, that often called for comment. A spritely 59-year-old, he had, I noticed from his book, missed a year at sea recently, whereupon he told me he had become almost crippled with arthritis, to be medically advised he would probably never work, nor even walk again. Refusing to accept this grim diagnosis, our Sparks had taken the Walking Cure, forcing himself. . . and yes, he would tell me about the *Titanic* sometime. With this tantalising promise he commenced the stroll which took him every fine evening around the decks of our old Empire ship *Saxon Star*. A few weeks later, when we had all got to know each other better, he told me. As a fresh-faced nineteen-year-old himself, resplendent in brand new doeskin uniform with brass buttons and single fine gold stripe on each cuff, he had been sent on the Belfast night boat to join the new White Star liner as she commissioned, as a junior radio operator. But when she put in to Southampton to embark passengers he was told he must relinquish his position to a more senior man. So, with great reluctance, he signed-off – leaving the *Titanic* to sail into immortality.

Not many of the dark blue discharge books are around now; not many of the later light blues ones either, come to that! And the columns for VG, GOOD and the dreaded DR were done away with twenty years ago. Unethical, they said. So it occurs to me that it may interest some readers if extant ancient mariners set down in print some of the histories they learned in their younger years, before we are all gone and they are lost in the mists of time. . .

My father's cousin served his apprenticeship in the famous Loch Line of sailing ships during the earliest years of this century, his favourite being the fine four-masted barque *Loch Broom* which had the distinctive rig of single top gallant sail on the foremast but double t'gallants on the main and mizen. Although I never actually sailed with Sandy Gray I spent long, enthralling days with him on the Firth of Forth when I was a boy. He was one of the last pilots there to hold a square rigged master's certificate, which enabled him to pilot the full rigged Norwegian sail training ship *Sorlandet* on her visits to Leith, for at that time she did not have an engine auxiliary. In the *Loch Broom* Sandy had voyaged from London's Royal Docks to Australia, carrying general cargoes outward, wool, hides and other non-refrigerated primary produce home.

When Britain disposed of most of her sailing merchant fleet around 1912 he went 'into steam' and served with the RNR throughout World War 1, mostly on the Northern Patrol. One day the sloop of which he was first lieutenant captured a surfaced German submarine. The U-boat was towing a wooden lifeboat which her commander said had belonged to a Norwegian four-masted barque he had sunk a few days earlier. I was shown snapshots of the U-boat, her captain, and the ship's lifeboat. "Unusual rig", the German had commented, "she had single t'gallant on the foremast but doubles on main and mizen". And sure enough, climbing aboard the partly waterlogged boat, Sandy discovered carved, years before by an apprentice with nothing better to do, there on the centre thwart, his own initials – 'AG': – Alexander Gray.

I sailed with a man who had been second mate of a Blue Star ship early in World War II, loading frozen meat and butter in South Dock, Buenos Aires. Bound for London, sailing unescorted as she was a fast ship, the *Sultan Star's* people heard the German radio propagandist William Joyce, alias Lord Haw Haw, announce to the world that ". . . the British refrigerated line *Sultan Star* has left Argentina with a cargo of food for England's starving millions. But", continued the affected nasal drawl, "she will fail to arrive. One of our submarines will intercept her, and sink her. . .". Which was precisely what happened a few days later. The survivors, in lifeboats, were passed next day by a squadron of British warships including the cruiser *Exeter* which, they later learned, had been engaged in what became known as The Battle of the River Plate which ended when the *Graf Spee* "blew herself up". Soon afterwards the *Sultan Star* survivors were rescued to recount how they, unlike most who had their ships sunk under them, had had it prophesied by that old Nazi rogue Lord Haw Haw!

I sailed with a man who was a Steward in the *Arandora Star* , ex-cruise liner, carrying 1,673 passengers from the UK bound for St John, Newfoundland, in 1940. Many of them were German and Italian internees and had they arrived they would doubtless have spent the remainder of the war in reasonable comfort and safety, in Canada. But on 2nd July a German submarine torpedoed her in the North Atlantic and soon our Leslie found himself alone in a boat full of Italians. Realising the boot was, so to speak, now on the other foot, they began to give him a hard time, until they were rescued and landed at Greenock. Leslie was a spiritualist when we sailed together in the *Sydney Star* (I was second mate). He would hold seances and fascinate us with tales from 'Beyond the Veil. . ..'

Most of these are wartime accounts, for in the early 'fifties most of my older shipmates had sailed through the war. For some, those wartime voyages were surprisingly uneventful, only differing from peacetime with the enforced blackout, convoy work, grey paint overall and cabin doors 'on the hook' instead of closed to prevent an explosion jamming them shut with the occupant trapped inside. Even so, knowledge that one may at any time be blown sky high must have been trying to live with, especially for the older men who had known senior ranks in peacetime seafaring, and particularly for the engineroom staff. For the men working below had least chance of escaping a hideous death if the ship was mined or torpedoed, as every company Roll of Honour shows.

I sailed with a man who told me of his time as third engineer of a ship bound from the River Plate with corned beef ("for England's starving millions").

Torpedoed off the west coast of Africa late one fine, sunny afternoon, the ship obligingly remained upright as she slowly sank, enabling them to take to the boats in quite orderly fashion. "Like a boat drill". Darkness fell as the ship went down, with which the boats set sail "for home". The young master had a wife and children back in England while the chief engineer, in the same boat, was a rather crusty old bachelor. Throughout the voyage the two had not always seen eye to eye, to put it mildly. Now they discussed what to do if the submarine surfaced, for by that time in the war it was known that sometimes a U-boat commander would take a ship's master prisoner, as proof of his kill. The chief suggested that if this happened, he would pretend to be the captain, so that he would be taken prisoner, leaving the real captain to sail home. It was a kindly offer, but the captain bridled. "*I* am the master of this ship, mister, and don't you forget it!. . .." (Even though their ship was sunk).

This discussion only terminated when the surfaced submarine loomed through the darkness and turned her searchlight beam upon them. An Oxford-accented German voice from the conning tower politely invited the captain aboard. Silence reigned in the boat. "Come, gentlemen, do not be shy! I know your ship sailed from Buenos Aires on the 7th of this month. Delighted to meet you, Captain Smith and I must apologise for inconvenience caused. But this is war, and as you know, it may be my turn next. Now Captain Smith, kindly step aboard!" Captain Smith was immediately sat upon by a large and very fat second engineer who muffled his protests long enough for the chief engineer to step across to the U-boat's deck where he was helped down into the conning tower. The submarine departed after her commander had ascertained the lifeboat people had food and water and given them a course to steer to "where you will find a British convoy". That U-boat was sunk with all hands before reaching her base while Captain Smith and his men were rescued next day.

I sailed with a man – he was a lamptrimmer with us in the *Saxon Star* – who had served as an AB with the Royal Navy, which he referred to as The Andrew. Geordie had married a London girl and was thus a "Cockney by Contamination", as he put it. He was serving in a Portsmouth-based destroyer when the Luftwaffe began its heavy night raids on London. With the uncanny prescience of the Lower Deck Geordie suspected that his ship was about to sail away on a long voyage, and naturally he wished to see his wife and family first. But the usually generous RN leave was cancelled at the last moment, so he decided to go home unofficially, in uniform of course, and hang the consequences! Reaching London from Pompey in those hectic times took longer than it does today and it was early next morning when he arrived in the East End. Smoke and dust hung heavy in the air, fire brigade hoses snaked everywhere over rubble piled high along the street where he lived. Ignoring an air raid warden's weary attempt to prevent him entering the street – "Danger from falling masonry, mate" – Geordie found great difficulty in deciding which heap of smouldering bricks had been his own neat little house. Then he saw them, both at once – his wife climbing unharmed from an underground air-raid shelter and his own kitchen mantelpiece standing proud among the ruins. After the ecstatic reunion to which wardens and fire brigade turned a politely blind eye, Geordie and Mrs Geordie looked at the mantelpiece. The black marble clock was still keeping perfect time (he said) and there beside it stood the purple vase – from time immemorial repository for the housekeeping money. Realising that a slide could occur any moment, Geordie picked his way gingerly over the debris, to find all money intact.

Just then a cheer went up along the street and, lo and behold, there stood the King and Queen, come to see how things were. Handing the vase to his wife Geordie snapped a smart salute while his wife dipped a curtsy. "Your house?" asked His Majesty, sadly indicating the ruins. "Yes Sir", replied Geordie with a growing dread of having to explain how he came to be here. "Is there anything I can do to help?" asked the King kindly. "Well Sir, if you could make this leave I'm on sort of – er – official, I'd deem it a great honour". "Done!" said the King. Geordie showed me the following morning's newspaper cutting, faded and yellow now but still recognisably the two Georges deep in discussion. It bore the caption – "He got the Royal OK".

One man I sailed with round the coast had the unfortunate distinction of being ordered by the Royal Navy to scuttle his first command. When I knew him, Alec was a member of Blue Star Line's permanent relieving staff. At that time (early 1960s) there could be up to a dozen company's vessels in port or at sea around the home coast and to enable their deep-sea people take leave in between voyages they would be replaced on first arrival from overseas by members of the relieving staff. Mostly semi-retired men in all departments, the Suitcase Gang were thus able to retain their lifelong interest in ships while usefully supplementing pensions – and keep out from under their wives' vacuum cleaners! Without exception they had interesting stories to tell, in port when no cargo was working (and with no TV to watch). I was chief officer when Alec was acting third aboard a ship undergoing long refit at Smith's Docks, North Shields, when first we met. In those palmy days ships lay three abreast at the quays and any move into or out of drydock was preceded by a complicated game of nautical musical chairs. As many ships as lay across the drydock entrance would be towed out into the stream by tugs, as others reshuffled their positions. Rarely had the ships any power available and only two black balls hung vertically by day, two red oil lights at night, warned the steady stream of passing colliers that here were ships Not Under command, unable to keep out of the way. A lot of waiting was involved. Over the inevitable pot of tea and cigarettes, we had time to talk, and listen. . .

Alec had, prewar, been an officer in a British company which operated a large fleet of handsome, smallish cargo-passenger ships around the East, and particularly round the China Coast. It was an exciting life as not only were the Japanese intent on overrunning China at the time, but various freedom-fighters (or rebels, depending on one's point of view) were active throughout much of the territory administered by the colonial British, Dutch and French. But the outbreak of war in Europe in September 1939 seemed far away (It would all be over by Christmas). Alec was promoted to his first command just as the conflict (not over by Christmas after all) spread worldwide when the Japanese attacked Pearl Harbour. Alec's command, of which he was

251

justifiably proud, was a little beauty, all gleaming paint and varnish, polished brass everywhere; – a coal burner, as were many ships at that time. He arrived in Hong Kong a few days before Christmas 1941, shortly ahead of the invading Japanese. No sooner was the anchor down than a Royal Navy lieutenant came aboard, immaculate in whites but clearly very tired, dark smudges under his eyes. Alec was told he must leave at once, taking as many refugees as possible, for Hong Kong was doomed. "I'll leave as soon as they're onboard and I've taken bunkers", he replied, eager to comply. But of course no coal was available. His bunkers were empty and port chaos was mounting as air raids on the Crown colony intensified. The lieutenant told him the only alternative was to scuttle his ship in deep water to prevent her falling into enemy hands. With this most painful instruction, Alec had no option but to comply, of course.

But scuttling is not easy. The "Sea Cocks" so convenient to writers of nautical fiction who have them opened at the drop of a hat in just such emergency, do not exist in British ships, which are built to remain afloat. And it was only with considerable difficulty that his engineers managed to remove a cooling water inlet valve, allowing Victoria Harbour to gush in.

Next morning, looking out from his hotel, he saw the ship had not totally sunk – her bow remained above water. Probably a large air pocket had become trapped in the forecastle. The RN were not amused and Alec was taken out in the launch. By smashing a couple of porthole glasses and ramming several times a sudden hissing of air and loud gurgle was followed by the protruding bow sliding below the oily surface of the harbour. Alec, close to tears, felt there should have been "some sort of funeral service for the old girl" but there was no time. He spent the following four years as a prisoner of the Japanese. . .

I sailed with a man whose parents did not want him to go away to sea. He was 17 in the early years of the war and, with merchant losses mounting daily, his parents' concern was understandable. But young Mac was determined. With the connivance of an uncle who had survived the First World War at sea he was smuggled away to Glasgow for an interview and subsequently joined one of the well-known Scottish tramp companies, many of which then flourished. He was soon torpedoed in the North Atlantic, graveyard of so many ships, and found himself in a wooden lifeboat under the master's command with the second mate in charge. The remaining survivors included several Lascars (as Indian seamen were then called).

The master decided they would sail downwind to Trinidad which was also probably along the path of any prevailing current. They were short of rations, particularly water and several died, to be committed to the deep as best they could. One climbed back onboard after being committed. Sorry, wrong man – he had been only asleep! They were all feeling the strain. A period of weeks in an open boat with diminishing rations does little for the mind and it was apparent that their good captain was slowly but steadily losing his as he became ever more dictatorial. Eventually land was sighted ahead and as the boat stood in under faded lugsail and jib the second mate recognised it as being the approaches to Georgetown, in what was, then, British Guiana. Hopes peaked, but the captain would have none of it. "I'm taking this boat to Trinidad, mister, and to Trinidad we will steer. Hard a 'starboard!" "Yes Sir,", answered the second mate dutifully, "But don't you think perhaps we should put in here to land the sick and injured. Then *we* can carry on to Trinidad". The captain hummed and hawed and looked around at his crew, many of whom were without doubt in need of medical attention. "Right", said he at last. "But only to land these sickies mister, you understand me?" But of course the British authorities put them all in hospital, captain included, to which even he by then did not demur.

I sailed with a man whose ship was rocked by the explosions of her tyres bursting. Tyres, on a ship? They were, of course, part of the cargo. Loaded at Le Havre, three multiwheeled trailers – huge things – for the Alaska Oilfields, had been placed fore-and-aft, side by side secured with wire rope lashings on the *Columbia Star's* after hatch to obtain as much protection from the North Atlantic as her high superstructure afforded. The ship then proceeded to Liverpool and Greenock to complete loading containers. Previous trailer shipments had been across the North Atlantic to Montreal whence they had gone overland to Alaska – the cold weather route – but the *Columbia Star* was taking these via the Panama Canal to San Francisco. A fast ship, the passage to the Canal would take only nine days. For the first six all went well. Then, in the middle of the night, the master was awakened by a loud explosion. Leaping from his bunk he went to the bridge where the second mate keeping the middle watch reported that one of the trailer tyres had burst. Next morning a second tyre blew with the noise of a small bomb blast, rocking the trailer on recoil and of course slackening the lashing wires as the tyre deflated. With the ship rolling in the Atlantic swell it was imperative that the lashings be restored and it said much for her British crew that they carried out this work determinedly, if warily – for an exploding tyre was enough to take one's head off. No apparent reason could be found for these explosions and the telex sent to Head Office arrived – as such messages often do – on a Bank Holiday weekend.

By the time the Canal was reached, ten tyres had exploded, all on the port side vehicle and the master explained to the canal pilot what was liable to happen, to alleviate any concern. He also explained to the bosun of the canal crew who came aboard to handle the towing wires as the ship moved through the three sets of locks – the tyres were not dangerous provided they were not approached closely. The Panamanian linesmen seemed to look forward to

253

this possible diversion from routine and they were not disappointed. Twice the equatorial darkness was shattered by the now familiar bangs. By this time head Office had been alerted and had told the Shippers. At Balboa, the Pacific end of the Canal, three Frenchmen joined. Displaying the kind of bravery usually associated with bomb disposal experts, they first measured the tyre pressures, then carefully reduced them to normal. Their leader came to the master and calmly explained; – the pressures were over three times what they should have been, and they were not pneumatic tyres so much as hydraulic ones. Back in France the Shippers had remembered to omit anti-freeze from the hydraulic mixture in the two trailers to starboard and centre – but the port side vehicle-which had borne the full glare of the tropic sun – contained anti-freeze, which of course had expanded in the hot weather.

Sighs of relief were heaved when the trailers were finally unloaded by floating crane at San Francisco. I still see the master of that ship – each morning when I look in the mirror to shave!

GRATITUDES

I am grateful for having been born at a time and place which enabled me to go away to sea when the British Merchant Navy was at its peak, carrying the Red Duster to every port in the world. I am especially glad that my parents encouraged me, despite misgivings engendered through the numerous ships still disappearing in the years immediately after the war, through minings and natural causes. Their sending me to the *Conway* set my parents back at least two annual holidays, I know, but they realised that that old Wooden Wall, anchored to swing to the tides in the Menai Strait, provided some of the finest training available to a lad with nautical ambitions.

I am grateful to my employers past and present. In Blue Star Line I saw British Shipping at its best; – fine, well found, well maintained ships with top notch crews, excellent and abundant food, on voyages to some of the world's pleasantest places. In Guan Guan's Golden Line I have learned that the Men and Women of the East can also run ships in the classic manner. To have sailed with shipmates from Bangladesh and Burma, China, Ghana and India, Malaysia, Nigeria, The Philippines, Singapore, Turkey and Yugoslavia – to have frequently been the only Englishman amongst them – has proved a wonderful experience I would not have missed for anything. I am grateful to them all, for their loyalty and occasional forbearance, and also to the magazine *Ships Monthly* in which much of this, material has appeared.

I am grateful to my family who have borne well the disadvantages of having a mostly-absent father; and most of all I am grateful to my Wife, for Everything.

I suppose most of my generation mourn the passing of our once-great Merchant Navy. That it should and could rise again depends upon our politicians and business persons – and not least on those who may still wish to go AWAY TO SEA.